Learning R for Geospatial Analysis

Leverage the power of R to elegantly manage crucial geospatial analysis tasks

Michael Dorman

[PACKT]
PUBLISHING

BIRMINGHAM - MUMBAI

Learning R for Geospatial Analysis

First published: December 2014

Production reference: 1191214

Published by Packt Publishing Ltd.
Livery Place
35 Livery Street
Birmingham B3 2PB, UK.

ISBN 978-1-78398-436-7

www.packtpub.com

Credits

Author
Michael Dorman

Reviewers
Dr. Amrinder Arora
Dan Hammer
Baburao Kamble
Dr. Robin Lovelace
Dipanjan Sarkar
Dr. Makhan Virdi

Commissioning Editor
Akram Hussain

Acquisition Editor
Greg Wild

Content Development Editor
Mohammed Fahad

Technical Editor
Ankita Thakur

Copy Editors
Pranjali Chury
Adithi Shetty

Project Coordinator
Rashi Khivansara

Proofreaders
Simran Bhogal
Stephen Copestake
Maria Gould
Ameesha Green

Indexer
Rekha Nair

Graphics
Abhinash Sahu

Production Coordinator
Alwin Roy

Cover Work
Alwin Roy

About the Author

Michael Dorman is currently a PhD candidate at the Department of Geography and Environmental Development, Ben-Gurion University of the Negev. His research explores the response of planted pine forests to changing climate through remote sensing and dendrochronology. He uses R extensively for time series and spatial statistical analyses and visualization. In spring 2013, he prepared and taught a course named *Introduction to Programming for Spatial Data Analysis* at the Ben-Gurion University of the Negev, introducing R as an environment for spatial data analysis to undergraduate Geography students. The course material served as a foundation for this book.

Michael holds a Master's degree in Life Sciences from the Ben-Gurion University of the Negev and a Bachelor's degree in Plant Sciences in Agriculture from The Hebrew University of Jerusalem. He has authored or coauthored eight papers in scientific literature and actively participated in 18 scientific conferences.

I would like to express my gratitude to all the people from whom I have learned more about R and to those who have created this wonderful programming language. A special thanks goes to the excellent team at Packt Publishing for making this book possible.

This book is dedicated to my wife, Hila, who unconditionally supported me every step of the way.

About the Reviewers

Dr. Amrinder Arora is an adjunct faculty member in the Department of Computer Science at the George Washington University. He teaches graduate and undergraduate courses in Computer Science, mostly related to the design and analysis of computer algorithms and the design of data structures. He is also the author of the book *Analysis and Design of Algorithms*, *Cognella Academic Publishing*. He has been conferred the Instructor of the Year Award by the Department of Computer Science at the George Washington University and has received a VIP Grants Award by the Bowie State University. You can read more about his research at http://www.standardwisdom.com.

As part of his industry experience, he has served in the management teams of leading technology companies, including BizMerlin, Edifecs, and NTELX. As part of the Affordable Care Act, Dr. Arora designed a health exchange connector, a leading product in the $200 million market to connect insurance companies (payers) to the health insurance exchanges. As a leading expert in risk targeting, Dr. Arora led the technical design for US FDA's PREDICT system, which currently screens more than 16 million imports a year. His efforts in supporting FDA's PREDICT program were recognized by the FDA commissioner, Dr. Margaret Hamburg. The transportation management system designed by Dr. Arora for the port of Aqaba in Jordan won the award for the most innovative product by the Intelligent Transportation Society of America.

Dr. Arora earned an undergraduate degree in Computer Science from the Indian Institute of Technology, Delhi, and a Master's degree and doctorate, both in Computer Science, from the George Washington University. He served as a reviewer for numerous journals and conferences and many of his reviews have also been published in ACM Computing Reviews.

Dan Hammer is a data scientist and environmental economist who served as a Presidential Innovation Fellow at NASA as part of the White House program. He is a PhD student at University of California, Berkeley, and was formerly the Chief Data Scientist at the World Resources Institute, where he led the technical team behind Global Forest Watch. Dan writes code in Python, R, and Clojure on subjects ranging from spatial econometrics to information theory. He is currently reviewing *Clojure for Data Science, Packt Publishing*.

Baburao Kamble is an assistant research professor of Remote Sensing and Geospatial Data Analytics at the University of Nebraska-Lincoln (UNL). Currently, he works at UNL on developing machine learning and data mining algorithms using Big Data tools and techniques for climate and weather data. He has been involved in teaching Geospatial Information Sciences, Data Analysis using R, Python for Geospatial Data Analytics, and MATLAB courses at the graduate level. He is also the author of the upcoming book *Practical Data Analysis Cookbook, Packt Publishing*. He likes to spend his free time with new and interesting data science developments.

Dr. Robin Lovelace is an environmental geographer with 5 years of experience using R for spatial analysis, map making, and statistics. He has coauthored the popular free and open source online tutorial *Introduction to visualising spatial data in R* (2014), and teaches R to a range of professional and academic audiences.

Robin's latest book *Spatial microsimulation with R, CRC Press* (which will be published in 2015) demonstrates methods to generate and analyze multilevel data. By combining individual and geographical-level data, the technique can provide new insights into complex behaviors, for example, as an input into agent-based models.

Robin believes passionately in using open source technology to empower people to create a sustainable, post-carbon world—one in which we no longer depend on burning fossil fuels for a high quality of life.

Dipanjan Sarkar is a data engineer at DataWeave, one of India's top Big Data analytics start-ups, where he works on data semantics, information extraction, natural language processing, and machine learning. Prior to joining DataWeave, he worked as a graduate technical intern at Intel and received a Master's degree in Information Technology from the International Institute of Information Technology, Bangalore. Dipanjan is a technology enthusiast and loves Python and the start-up culture.

Dr. Makhan Virdi is a researcher at the Oak Ridge National Laboratory. He received his PhD from the University of South Florida in 2013. His current research interests include management and visualization of geospatial and time series data from satellite imagery for biogeochemical dynamics.

Dr. Virdi is also an independent researcher with a passion for using embedded electronics, robotics, and knowledge discovery to create machine augmented intelligence systems. In his spare time, he works on robots, ambient intelligence, and smart homes. You can read more about his research at TheXLabs.com.

www.PacktPub.com

Support files, eBooks, discount offers, and more

For support files and downloads related to your book, please visit www.PacktPub.com.

Did you know that Packt offers eBook versions of every book published, with PDF and ePub files available? You can upgrade to the eBook version at www.PacktPub.com and as a print book customer, you are entitled to a discount on the eBook copy. Get in touch with us at service@packtpub.com for more details.

At www.PacktPub.com, you can also read a collection of free technical articles, sign up for a range of free newsletters and receive exclusive discounts and offers on Packt books and eBooks.

https://www2.packtpub.com/books/subscription/packtlib

Do you need instant solutions to your IT questions? PacktLib is Packt's online digital book library. Here, you can search, access, and read Packt's entire library of books.

Why subscribe?

- Fully searchable across every book published by Packt
- Copy and paste, print, and bookmark content
- On demand and accessible via a web browser

Free access for Packt account holders

If you have an account with Packt at www.PacktPub.com, you can use this to access PacktLib today and view 9 entirely free books. Simply use your login credentials for immediate access.

Table of Contents

Preface

The defining feature of spatial data analysis is the reference within the data being analyzed to locations on the surface of the earth. This is a very broad subject encompassing distinct areas of expertise such as spatial statistics, geometric computation, and image processing.

In practice, spatial data is commonly stored, viewed, and analyzed in Geographic Information System (GIS) software, of which the most well-known example is ArcGIS. However, most often, menu-based interfaces of GIS software are too narrow in scope to meet specialized demands or too inflexible to feasibly accomplish customized repetitive tasks. Writing scripts rather than using menus or working in combination with external software are two commonly used paths to solve such problems. However, what if we can use a single environment, combining the advantages of programming and spatial data analysis capabilities with a comprehensive ecosystem of computational tools that are readily implementable in customized procedures?

This book will demonstrate that the R programming language is indeed such an environment and teach you how to use it in order to perform various spatial data analysis tasks.

Most currently available books on this subject are focused on advanced applications such as spatial statistics, assuming you have prior knowledge of R and the respective scientific domains. Yet, introductory material on R from the point of view of a spatial data analyst, which is focused on introductory topics such as spatial data handling, computation, and visualization, is scarce. This book aims to fill that gap.

What this book covers

Chapter 1, The R Environment, introduces the R environment, shows how to install R, and how to use it. Some of the basic concepts related to writing R code are introduced.

Chapter 2, Working with Vectors and Time Series, covers the basic data structure in R, which is vector. The main types of vectors (numeric, character, and logical) as well as basic operations on vectors (such as subsetting and summarizing vector properties) are reviewed. Working with dates and displaying a graphical output, two highly relevant abilities commonly applied later in the book, are also introduced in this chapter.

Chapter 3, Working with Tables, focuses on tables and automated calculations in R. This chapter teaches you how tabular data can be handled and how calculations of a repetitive nature based on tabular data can be carried out using loops and conditional statements. Reshaping and joining tables (vital skills for any data analysis) are also covered.

Chapter 4, Working with Rasters, brings the reader into the realm of spatial data analysis in R, starting with the raster data structure. Basic operations such as import and export, visualization and summary, and subsetting and extraction of raster values are covered here. Simple manipulations of raster values, including assignment, raster algebra, and reclassification are also presented.

Chapter 5, Working with Points, Lines, and Polygons, covers the second type of spatial data structures — vector layers. The basic methodology of working with point, line, and polygon layers is reviewed, followed by the coverage of more advanced operations, including reprojection, geometric calculations, spatial querying, and joining new data to existing layers.

Chapter 6, Modifying Rasters and Analyzing Raster Time Series, covers several advanced themes associated with raster data analysis in R. Geometric modifications of raster data, such as cropping, mosaicking, and aggregating are reviewed. Operations related to cell neighborhoods, including focal filtering, clumping, and topography-related calculations are covered next. Additional themes include resampling, reprojection, and handling of spatio-temporal raster data.

Chapter 7, Combining Vector and Raster Datasets, integrates the material presented in *Chapter 5, Working with Points, Lines, and Polygons*, and *Chapter 6, Modifying Rasters and Analyzing Raster Time Series*, by demonstrating how rasters and vector layers can be combined in a single analysis. Transformation between raster and vector data structures as well as data extraction from a raster based on vector layers are covered in this chapter.

Chapter 8, Spatial Interpolation of Point Data, presents the subject of spatial interpolation in R from a practical point of view. Using a real-world case study, several common interpolation methods are applied and evaluated. An automated interpolation procedure is then constructed in order to create a series of interpolated maps from point data.

Chapter 9, Advanced Visualization of Spatial Data, shows readers how to produce publication-quality maps mainly using the popular ggplot2 R package.

Appendix A, External Datasets Used in Examples, provides a summary of the datasets used in the examples.

Appendix B, Cited References, lists the cited resources.

What you need for this book

To follow through the examples in this book, all you need to do is install R (which is available for free) and download the example datasets from the book's website. Some of the examples also require you to have an Internet connection to download additional datasets and R packages from the R environment.

Who this book is for

This book is intended for anyone who wants to learn how to efficiently analyze geospatial data with R. This book primarily targets GIS analysts, researchers, educators, and students who are working with spatial data and are interested in expanding their capabilities through programming. The book assumes familiarity with basic geographic information concepts (such as spatial coordinates) and no prior experience with R and/or programming.

Conventions

In this book, you will find a number of styles of text that distinguish between different kinds of information. Here are some examples of these styles and an explanation of their meaning.

Code words in text, folder names, filenames, file extensions, and pathnames are shown as follows: "Here, we created a `data.frame` object named `df` by combining the vectors `num`, `lower`, and `upper`."

A block of code is set as follows:

```
> num = 1:4
> lower = c("a","b","c","d")
> upper = c("A","B","C","D")
> df = data.frame(num, lower, upper)
> df
  num lower upper
1   1     a     A
2   2     b     B
3   3     c     C
4   4     d     D
```

New terms and **important words** are shown in bold. Words that you see on the screen, in menus or dialog boxes for example, appear in the text like this: "Under the **Getting Started** section, select the **download R** link."

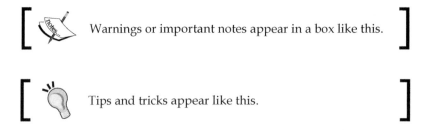

> Warnings or important notes appear in a box like this.

> Tips and tricks appear like this.

Reader feedback

Feedback from our readers is always welcome. Let us know what you think about this book—what you liked or may have disliked. Reader feedback is important for us to develop titles that you really get the most out of.

To send us general feedback, simply send an e-mail to feedback@packtpub.com, and mention the book title via the subject of your message.

If there is a topic that you have expertise in and you are interested in either writing or contributing to a book, see our author guide on www.packtpub.com/authors.

Customer support

Now that you are the proud owner of a Packt book, we have a number of things to help you to get the most from your purchase.

Downloading the example code and data

You can download the example code and data files for all Packt books you have purchased from your account at http://www.packtpub.com. If you purchased this book elsewhere, you can visit http://www.packtpub.com/support and register to have the files e-mailed directly to you.

Downloading the color images of this book

We also provide you a PDF file that has color images of the screenshots/diagrams used in this book. The color images will help you better understand the changes in the output. You can download this file from https://www.packtpub.com/sites/default/files/downloads/4367OS_ColoredImages.pdf.

Errata

Although we have taken every care to ensure the accuracy of our content, mistakes do happen. If you find a mistake in one of our books—maybe a mistake in the text or the code—we would be grateful if you could report this to us. By doing so, you can save other readers from frustration and help us improve subsequent versions of this book. If you find any errata, please report them by visiting http://www.packtpub.com/submit-errata, selecting your book, clicking on the **Errata Submission Form** link, and entering the details of your errata. Once your errata are verified, your submission will be accepted and the errata will be uploaded to our website or added to any list of existing errata under the Errata section of that title.

To view the previously submitted errata, go to https://www.packtpub.com/books/content/support and enter the name of the book in the search field. The required information will appear under the **Errata** section.

Piracy

Piracy of copyright material on the Internet is an ongoing problem across all media. At Packt, we take the protection of our copyright and licenses very seriously. If you come across any illegal copies of our works, in any form, on the Internet, please provide us with the location address or website name immediately so that we can pursue a remedy.

Please contact us at `copyright@packtpub.com` with a link to the suspected pirated material.

We appreciate your help in protecting our authors, and our ability to bring you valuable content.

Questions

You can contact us at `questions@packtpub.com` if you are having a problem with any aspect of the book, and we will do our best to address it.

1
The R Environment

In this chapter, we are going to introduce the R environment, learn how to install and use it, and introduce some of the main concepts related to writing R code. First, the technical issues of setting up the work environment are covered. After that, we will have R running and ready to receive instructions from the user. The basic concepts related to working in the R environment are also introduced.

In this chapter, we'll cover the following topics:

- Installing R
- Using R's command line
- Editing code using text editors
- Executing simple commands
- Arithmetic operations
- Logical operations
- Calling functions
- Understanding errors and warning messages
- Checking which class a given object belongs to

Installing R and using the command line

In this section, we'll cover the installation of R before getting started with the R command line.

Downloading R

The R software can be downloaded from the R Project website at http://www.r-project.org/. The following screenshot shows the main page of this website:

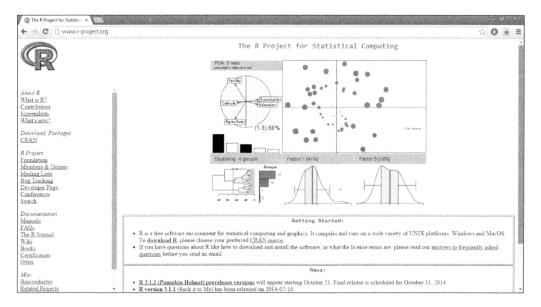

Perform the following steps to download R from the R Project website:

1. Under the **Getting Started** section, select the **download R** link.

2. Select one of the download sources (it does not matter which one).

3. Choose the appropriate version for your operating system, such as Linux, Mac OS, or Windows.

4. If you are using Windows, which is the option we will cover from now on, select **install R for the first time**.

5. Finally, click on the download link. This may vary according to the name of the current R version, such as **Download R 3.1.0 for Windows**.

Installing R

After downloading the file, follow the installation instructions. Note that if you are using a 64-bit version of Windows, you will be asked to select whether to install a 32-bit version, 64-bit version, or both. It is recommended that you use the 64-bit version in this case since it allows a single process to take advantage of more than 4 GB of RAM (this is helpful, for example, when loading a large raster file into memory).

Using R as a calculator

Start R by navigating to **Start | All Programs | R** and choose the appropriate shortcut from there (such as **R x64 3.1.0** when running the 3.1.0 64-bit version of R).

The main screen of the **R Graphical User Interface** (**RGui**) looks like the following screenshot:

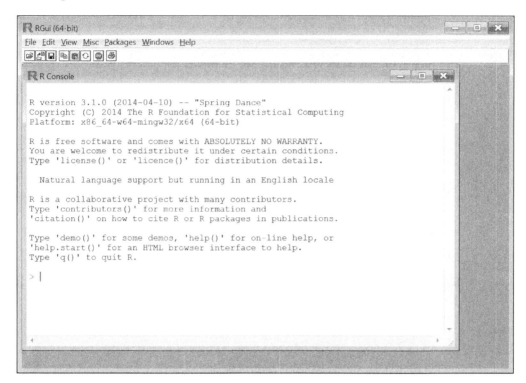

The window you see when starting the program, **R Console**, is the command line. The > symbol followed by a flashing cursor indicates that the system is waiting for instructions from the user. When the user types an expression into the command line and presses *Enter*, that expression is interpreted from the R language into the language that the computer processor understands, and the respective operation that expression entails is performed. As you may have noted, very few point-and-click menu options are found within the R environment as almost all operations are only accessible through code.

First, we will try simple calculations. For example, type the expression 5+5. The result 10 will appear on the next line followed by the > symbol, indicating that all instructions have been executed and the system is waiting for new ones:

```
>  5+5
[1]  10
```

What has just happened is that the expression 5+5 was interpreted and the respective instruction (add 5 and 5) was sent to the processor. The processor found the result (which is 10), which was then returned and printed in the command-line window. As we will see later, the result was saved neither in the RAM nor in the long-term computer memory, such as the hard disk. The meaning of the [1] part is that the result is a vector, with the first member being the number 10. Vectors will be covered in the next chapter.

Note that an R expression can be several lines long. For example, if we type 5* and press *Enter*, the symbol + appears on the next line, indicating that R is waiting for the remaining part of the expression (5 multiplied by ...):

```
>  5*
+  2
[1]  10
```

If you change your mind and do not wish to complete the expression, you can press *Esc* to cancel the + mode and return to the command line. Pressing *Esc* can also be used to terminate the current process that is being executed. (We didn't get a chance to try that out yet since simple operations such as 5+5 are executed very quickly.)

While using the command line, you can scroll through the history of previously executed expressions with the ↑ and ↓ keys. For example, this can be useful to modify a previously executed expression and run it once more.

You can clear all text from the command-line window by pressing *Ctrl + L*.

Throughout this book, code sections display both the expressions that the user enters (following the > symbol) and the resulting output. Reading both the inputs and the outputs will make it easier to follow the code examples. If you wish to execute the code examples in R and to investigate what happens when modifying them (which is highly recommended), only the input expressions should be entered into the R interpreter (these are the expressions followed by the >, or + if the expression spans several lines, symbols). Therefore, copying and pasting the entire content of code sections directly from the book into the interpreter will result in errors, since R will try to execute the output lines. The input, in fact, will not be correctly interpreted either since input expressions include > and + symbols that are not part of the code. To make things easier, all code sections from this book are provided on the book's website as plain R code files.

Coding with R beyond the command line

Working in R exclusively through the command line is rarely appropriate in practice, except when running short and simple commands (such as those introduced in this chapter) or when experimenting with new functions. For more complicated operations, we will save our code to a file in order to have the capability, for example, to work on it on several instances or to share it with other users. This section introduces approaches to editing and saving R code.

Approaches to editing R code

Typing the expression 5+5 into the command line was easy enough. However, if we perform more complicated operations, we'll have to edit and save our code for later use. There are three main approaches to edit R code:

- Using R's built-in editor
- Using a text editor
- Using an **Integrated Development Environment** (IDE)

Using R's built-in editor is the simplest way to edit R code. In this case, you don't need to use any software other than R. To open the code editor, simply navigate to **File | New script** from R's menu. A blank text window will open. You can type code in this window and execute it by clicking on *Ctrl + R*, either after selecting the code section that you want to execute (the selected section will be sent to the interpreter) or by placing the cursor on the line that you want to execute (that line will be sent to the interpreter).

The following screenshot shows the way RGui appears with both a command-line window and a code editor window:

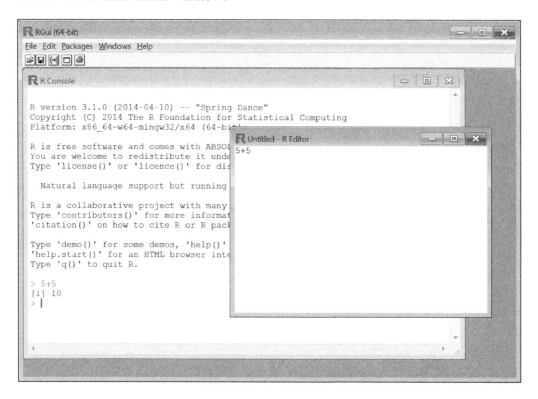

You can save the R code that you have written to a file at any time (**File | Save as...**) in order to be able to work on it another day. An R code file is a plain text file, usually with the suffix `.R`. To open an existing R code file, simply select it after navigating to the **File | Open script...** menu.

It is sometimes easier to use other text editors since they provide more options than R's basic text editor. For example, one can edit R code in the all-purpose Notepad++ text editor, which is available for free at `http://notepad-plus-plus.org/`. Notepad++ can be customized to edit code written in different programming languages (including R). By selecting the appropriate language, the specific function names and operators of that language will be highlighted in different colors for easier interpretation by the user.

The following screenshot shows Notepad++ with the menus used to select the R programming language:

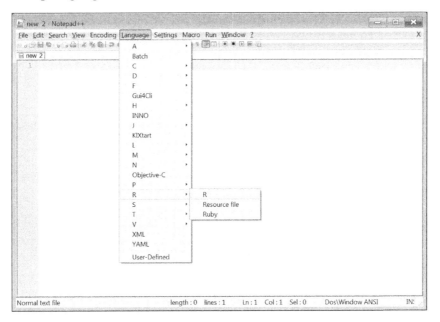

A code section can be transferred to the R interpreter simply by copying it from the text editor and then pasting into the R command line. To automatically pass code into the R interpreter (such as by clicking *Ctrl + R*), it might be necessary to install an add-on component such as the NppToR software for Notepad++ (which is freely available at `http://sourceforge.net/projects/npptor/`), or use a text editor such as Tinn-R (which is freely available at `http://sourceforge.net/projects/tinn-r/`) that has this capability built in.

The most sophisticated way of editing R code is to use an IDE, where an advanced text editor and the R interpreter portions are combined within a single window (much like in RGui itself), in addition to many other advanced functions that may be of help in programming and are not found in RGui. These can include automatic code completion, listings of libraries and functions, automatic syntax highlighting (to read code and output more easily), debugging tools, and much more.

Note that word processors such as Microsoft Word or OpenOffice Writer are not appropriate to edit computer code. The reason is that they include many styles and symbols that will not be recognized by R (or by any programming language for that matter), and this may cause problems. For example, the quote symbol " (into which the word processor may automatically convert to the symbol ") will not be recognized by R, resulting in an error.

Installation of RStudio

RStudio is an IDE designed specifically for R, and it is the recommended way of editing R code. You will quickly discover that even without using any of the advanced options, code editing in RStudio is more convenient than the previously mentioned alternatives. RStudio can be freely downloaded from www.rstudio.com.

Using RStudio

When you open RStudio, you will see the R command-line window and several additional utility panes that can display the code editor, help files, graphic output, and so on, during the course of working in R. To open a new R code file, navigate to **File | New File | R Script**. A code editing window, such as the one shown in the following screenshot, will appear:

In RStudio, code can be sent from the editor window into the command-line window in the same way as in RGui, that is, by pressing *Ctrl + R* either on a code section or on a single line of code. You can quickly switch to the code editor or to the command-line pane by clicking on it with the mouse or by pressing *Ctrl + 1* or *Ctrl + 2*, respectively. You can also have several R code files open in different tabs within the code editor pane.

More details can be found on the RStudio website (www.rstudio.com) or in other resources such as Mark P.J. van der Loo and Edwin de Jonge's book *Learning RStudio for R Statistical Computing*, *Packt Publishing* (2012).

> All references mentioned in this book are collectively provided in *Appendix B*, *Cited References*.

Evaluating expressions

We now know how to enter code for R to interpret, whether directly entering it into R's command line or sending it to the command line from a code editor. Our next step will be to see how to use the simplest operations: arithmetic and logical operators and functions.

Using arithmetic and logical operators

The standard arithmetic operators in R are as follows:

- +: Addition
- -: Subtraction
- *: Multiplication
- /: Division
- ^: Power

The following examples demonstrate the usage of these operators:

```
> 5+3
[1] 8
> 4-5
[1] -1
> 1*10
[1] 10
> 1/10
[1] 0.1
> 2^3
[1] 8
```

Parentheses can be used to construct more elaborate expressions, as follows:

```
> 2*(3+1)
[1]  8
> 5^(1+1)
[1]  25
```

It is better to use parentheses even when it is not required to make the code clearer.

Another very useful symbol is #. All code to the right of this symbol is not interpreted. Let's take a look at the following example:

```
> 1*2 # *3
[1]  2
```

The # symbol is helpful for adding comments within the code to explain what each code segment does, for other people (or oneself, at a later time of reference) to understand it:

```
> 5+5 # Adding 5 and 5
[1]  10
```

Note that R ignores spaces between the components of an expression:

```
> 1+  1
[1]  2
```

Conditions are expressions that have a yes/no answer (the statement can be either true or false). When interpreting a conditional expression, R returns a logical value, either TRUE for a true expression or FALSE for a false expression. A third option, NA, which stands for Not Available, is used when there is not enough information to determine whether the expression is true or false (NA values will be discussed in the next chapter).

The logical operators in R are summarized as follows:

- ==: Equal to
- >: Greater than
- >=: Greater than or equal to
- <: Smaller than
- <=: Smaller than or equal to
- !=: Not equal to

- &: *and*
- |: *or*
- !: *not*

For example, we can use condition operators to compare between two numbers as follows:

```
> 1<2
[1] TRUE
> 1>2
[1] FALSE
> 2>2
[1] FALSE
> 2>=2
[1] TRUE
> 2!=2
[1] FALSE
```

The and (&) and or (|) operators can be used to construct more complex expressions as follows:

```
> (1<10) & (10<100)
[1] TRUE
> (1<10) & (10>100)
[1] FALSE
> (1<10) | (10<100)
[1] TRUE
> (1<10) | (10>100)
[1] TRUE
```

As you can see in the preceding examples, when the expressions at both the sides of the & operator are true, TRUE is returned; otherwise, FALSE is returned (refer to the first two expressions). When at least one of the expressions at either side of the | operator is true, TRUE is returned; otherwise, FALSE is returned (refer to the last two expressions).

Two other useful conditional operators (== and !=) are used for testing equality and inequality, respectively. These operators are opposites from one another since a pair of objects can be either equal or non-equal to each other.

```
> 1 == 1
[1] TRUE
> 1 == 2
[1] FALSE
> 1 != 1
[1] FALSE
> 1 != 2
[1] TRUE
```

As you can see in the preceding examples, when using the == operator, TRUE is returned if the compared objects are equal; otherwise FALSE is returned (refer to expressions 1 and 2). With != it is the other way around (refer to expressions 3 and 4).

The last operator that we are going to cover is the not operator (!). This operator reverses the resulting logical value, from TRUE to FALSE or from FALSE to TRUE. This is used in cases when it is more convenient to ask whether a condition is *not* satisfied. Let's take a look at the following example:

```
> 1 == 1
[1] TRUE
> !(1 == 1)
[1] FALSE
> (1 == 1) & (2 == 2)
[1] TRUE
> (1 == 1) & !(2 == 2)
[1] FALSE
```

Using functions

In mathematics, a function is a relation between a set of inputs and a set of outputs with the property that each input is related to exactly one output. For example, the function $y=2*x$ relates every input x with the output y, which is equal to x multiplied by 2. The function concept in R (and in programming in general) is very similar:

- The function is composed of a code section that knows how to perform a certain operation.
- Employing the function is done by *calling* the function.
- The function receives one object, or several objects, as input (for example, the number 9).

- The function returns a single object as output (for example, the number 18). Optionally, it can perform other operations called *side effects* in addition to returning the output.

- The type and quantity of the objects that a function receives as input has to be defined in advance. These are called the function's parameters (for example, a single number).

- The objects that a function receives in reality, at a given function call, are called the function's *arguments* (for example, the number 9).

The most common (and the most useful) expressions in R are function calls. In fact, we have been using function calls all along, since the arithmetic operators are functions as well, which becomes apparent when using a different notation:

```
> 3*3
[1] 9
> "*"(3,3)
[1] 9
```

A function is essentially a predefined set of instructions. There are plenty of built-in functions in R (functions that are automatically loaded into memory when starting R). Later, you will also learn how to use functions that are not automatically loaded, and how to define your own functions.

As you might have guessed from the previous example, a function call is composed of the function name, followed by the function's arguments within parentheses and separated by commas. For example, the function sqrt returns the square root of its argument:

```
> sqrt(16)
[1] 4
```

R is case sensitive. For example, Sqrt and sqrt are treated as two different names:

```
> Sqrt(16)
Error: could not find function "Sqrt"
```

When trying the first option, we receive an error message stating that there is no function named Sqrt in memory.

Dealing with warning and error messages

Error messages are printed when for some reason it is impossible to execute the expression that we have sent to the interpreter. For example, this can happen when one of the objects we refer to does not exist (refer to the preceding information box). Another example is trying to pass an inappropriate argument to a function. In R, character values are delimited by quotes. Trying to call a mathematical function on a character understandably produces an error:

```
> "oranges" + "apples"
Error in "oranges" + "apples" : non-numeric argument to binary op$
```

The $ symbol at the end of the text message indicates that we need to scroll rightwards in the command-line window to see the whole message.

Warning messages are returned when an expression can be interpreted but the system suspects that the respective employed method is inappropriate. For example, the square root of a negative number does not yield a number within the real number system. A Not a Number (NaN) value is returned in such a case, along with a warning:

```
> sqrt(-2)
[1] NaN
Warning message:
In sqrt(-2) : NaNs produced
```

R has a set of predefined symbols to represent special constant values, most of which we already mentioned:

- NaN: Not a number
- NA: Not available
- NULL: An empty object
- TRUE and FALSE: Logical values
- Inf: Infinity (for example, try typing 1/0)

Unnecessary warnings and information messages, such as an indication that a given operation has been successfully carried out, are omitted from the code sections in this book to save space. However, readers who reproduce the examples will occasionally see such messages on the screen.

Getting help

A help page on every function in R can be reached by using the ? operator (or the help function). For example, the following expression opens the help page for the sqrt function:

```
> ?sqrt
```

The same result is achieved by typing help(sqrt).

> On the other hand, the ?? operator searches the available help pages for a given keyword (corresponding to the help.search function).
>
> Another useful expression regarding the official R help pages is help.start() that opens a page with links to R's official introductory manuals.

The structure of all help files on functions is similar, usually including a short description of what the function does, the list of its arguments, usage details, a description of the returned object, references, and examples. The help pages can seem intimidating at first, but with time they become clearer and more helpful for reminding oneself of the functions' usage details.

Another important source of information on R is the Internet. Entering a question or a task that we would like to perform (such as Googling *r read raster file*) into a web search engine usually yields a surprising amount of information from forums, blogs, and articles. Using these resources is inevitable when investigating new ways to utilize R.

Exploring the basic object types in R

So far, we have encountered two types of objects in R: numeric values (numeric vectors, to be precise, as we will see in *Chapter 2, Working with Vectors and Time Series*) and functions. In this section, we are going to introduce the key concept that an object is an instance of a certain class. Then, we will distinguish between, for operational purposes, the classes that are used to store data (data structures) and classes that are used to perform operations (functions). Finally, a short sample code that performs a simple GIS operation in R will be presented to demonstrate the way themes introduced in this chapter (and those that will be introduced in *Chapter 2, Working with Vectors and Time Series*, and *Chapter 3, Working with Tables*) will be applied for spatial data analysis in the later chapters of this book.

Everything is an object

R is an object-oriented language; accordingly, everything in R is an object. Objects belong to classes, with each class characterized by certain properties. The class to which an object belongs to determines the object's properties and the actions we can do with that object. To use an analogy, a gray Mitsubishi Super-Lancer model 1996 object belongs to the class car. It has specific attributes (such as color, model, and manufacturer) for each of the data fields a car object has. It satisfies all criteria that the car class entails; thus, the actions that are applicable to cars (such as igniting the engine and accelerating or using the breaks) are also meaningful with that particular object. In much the same way, a multi-band raster object in R will obligatorily have certain properties (such as the number of rows and columns, and resolution) and applicable actions (such as creating a subset of only the first band or calculating an overlay based on all bands).

All objects that are stored in memory can be accessed using their names, which begin with a character (without quotes; some functions, such as all arithmetic and logical operators can be called using their respective symbol within quotes, such as in "*" as we saw earlier). For example, sqrt is the name of the square root function object; the class to which this object belongs is function. When starting R, a predefined set of objects is loaded into memory, for example, the sqrt function and logical constant values TRUE and FALSE. Another example of a preloaded object is the number π:

```
> pi
[1] 3.141593
```

The class function returns the class name of the object that it receives as an argument:

```
> class(TRUE)
[1] "logical"
> class(1)
[1] "numeric"
> class(pi)
[1] "numeric"
> class("a")
[1] "character"
> class(sqrt)
[1] "function"
```

Storing data in data structures

From the point of view of a typical R user, all objects we handle in R can be divided into two groups: data structures (which hold data) and functions (which are used to perform operations on the data).

The basic components of all data structures are constant values, usually numeric, character, or logical (the last code section shows examples of all three). The simplest data structure in R is a vector, which is covered in *Chapter 2, Working with Vectors and Time Series.* Later, we'll see how more complex data structures are essentially collections of the simpler data structures. For example, a raster object in R may include two numeric vectors (holding the raster values and its dimensions) and a character vector (holding the **Coordinate Reference System** (**CRS**) information). The object-oriented nature of the language makes things easier both for the people who define the data structure classes (since they can build upon predefined simpler classes, rather than starting from the beginning) and for the users (since they can utilize their previous knowledge of the simpler data structure components to quickly understand more complex ones).

Calling functions to perform operations

Objects of the second type—functions—are typically used to perform operations on data structures. A function may have its influence limited to the R environment, or it may invoke side effects affecting the environment outside of R. All functions we have used until now affect only the R environment; a function to save a raster file, for example, has an external effect—it influences the data content of the hard drive.

A short sample session

Finally, let's take a look at a complete code section that performs a simple spatial analysis operation:

```
> library(raster)
> r = raster("C:\\Data\\rainfall.tif")
> r[120, 120] = 1000
> writeRaster(r, "C:\\Data\\rainfall2.tif")
```

The task that this code performs is to read a raster file, `rainfall.tif`, from the disk (look at the following screenshot to see its visualization in QGIS), change one of its values (the one at row 120 line 120, into `1000`) and write the resulting raster to a different file.

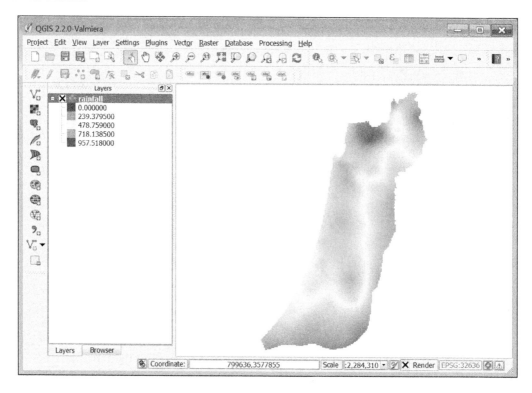

 The `rainfall.tif` file, as well as all other external data files used in this book, is provided on the book's website so that the reader can reproduce the examples and experiment with them. Refer to *Appendix A, External Datasets Used in Examples*, for a summary of all data files encountered throughout the book. R code files, containing all code sections that appear in the book, are also provided on the book's website for convenience.

Do not worry if you do not understand all the lines of code given in the beginning of this section. They will become clear by the time you finish reading *Chapter 4, Working with Rasters*. Briefly, the first line of code tells R to load the set of functions that are used to work with rasters (called the `raster` package), such as the `raster` and `writeRaster` functions that we use here to read and write raster files. In the second line, we read the requested file and load it into memory. In the third line of code, we assign the value `1000` to the specified pixel of that raster. The fourth line of code writes the new (modified) raster to the disk.

The task indeed sounds simple, but when we use desktop GIS software, it may not be easy to perform through the menus and dialog box system (where direct access to raster values may be unavailable). For example, we may have to create a new point feature over the pixel that we want to change (120,120) in raster A, convert it to a raster B (with the value of 1 at the (120,120) pixel and 0 in all other pixels), and then use an overlay tool to say that we want the pixel in raster A that overlays the value of 1 in raster B to have the value of 1000, while all other pixels retain their original values. Finally, we might need to use an additional toolbox to export the new raster. However, what if we need to perform this operation on several files or repeatedly on a given file as new information comes in?

Generally speaking, when we use programming rather than menu-based interfaces, the steps we have to take may seem less intuitive (writing code rather than scrolling, clicking with the mouse, and filling out dialog boxes). However, we have much more power with giving the computer specific instructions. The beauty of using programming for data analysis, and using R for geospatial analysis in particular, is not only that we gain greater efficiency through automation, but also that we get closer to the data and discover a wide range of new possibilities to analyze it, some of which may not even come to mind when we use a predefined set of tools or menus.

Summary

In this chapter, we covered the basics of using R. At this point, you should have R installed and you should be able to write and execute several basic commands from the command line or from the text editor of your preference. The concepts of classes and objects were also introduced, which are both important for the rest of the topics that you will learn in this book. We are now ready to proceed to more complex data structures and operations used in spatial data analysis.

The next chapter will be devoted to vectors, the basic data structures in R. Then, we will introduce more complex data structures to represent nonspatial data in *Chapter 3, Working with Tables,* and spatial data in *Chapter 4, Working with Rasters,* and *Chapter 5, Working with Points, Lines, and Polygons.*

2
Working with Vectors and Time Series

In this chapter, we are going to cover the basic data structure in R—a vector. Understanding vectors is the foundation for all the subsequent chapters. You will learn how to perform efficient operations on numeric and logical vectors and how to create subsets. After this, you will learn how to write custom functions in order to expand and customize R's capabilities. Working with dates and time series and the use of graphical functions are introduced at the end of this chapter.

In this chapter, we'll cover the following topics:

- Creating, saving, and examining the three main types of vectors
- The principles of performing operations on vectors in R
- Using functions that have more than one argument
- Creating subsets of vectors
- Dealing with missing values in vectors
- Writing new functions
- Working with dates
- Displaying and saving graphical output

Vectors – the basic data structures in R

A vector is an ordered collection of values of the same type (or mode, in R terminology). As mentioned in the previous chapter, the three types of values that are useful for most purposes (including the topics of this book) are numeric, character, and logical. In this section, you are going to learn about several methods to create vectors, check the properties of interest for the given vectors, and perform operations involving pairs of vectors. You are also going to learn how to save the objects we create in the temporary computer memory via assignment.

Different types of vectors

Vectors are the most basic data structures in R since single elements (such as the number 10) are also represented in R by vectors (of length 1). As we have previously seen, when we enter a numeric value on the command line, it is printed on the screen. The number in square brackets to the left of the value is, in fact, the position of the leftmost element in the respective printed line. For example, the [1] part in the following output means the first (and only) printed element, 10, of the particular vector is at position 1:

```
> 10
[1] 10
```

> Entering a value on the command line is, in fact, a shortcut for the
> print function:
> ```
> > print(10)
> [1] 10
> ```

Vectors can be created from individual elements with the c function, which stands for combine. Let's take a look at the following examples:

```
> c(1,5,10,4)
[1]  1  5 10  4
> c("cat","dog","mouse","apple")
[1] "cat"   "dog"   "mouse" "apple"
```

Sequential numeric vectors can be easily created with the : operator. Such vectors have many uses in R. The : operator creates an ordered vector starting at the value to the left of the : symbol and ending at the value to the right of the : symbol, as follows:

```
> 7:20
[1]  7  8  9 10 11 12 13 14 15 16 17 18 19 20
```

Or, when the first argument is larger than the second one:

```
> 33:24
[1] 33 32 31 30 29 28 27 26 25 24
```

A logical vector can also be created with the c function. Remember that TRUE and FALSE are special values and not characters. Therefore, these values should be typed without quotes:

```
> c(TRUE,FALSE,TRUE,TRUE)
[1]  TRUE FALSE  TRUE  TRUE
```

However, in practice, the creation of logical vectors is usually associated with employing a conditional operator on a vector rather than manually typing a sequence of logical values. We will elaborate on this later.

There are several functions that we can use to convert between vector types. The two most useful ones are as.numeric and as.character, which are used to convert a vector to a numeric or character vector, respectively. There are other functions to convert objects of a particular class into another, which we'll see in subsequent chapters. Let's take a look at the following examples:

```
> 33:24
[1] 33 32 31 30 29 28 27 26 25 24
> as.character(33:24)
[1] "33" "32" "31" "30" "29" "28" "27" "26" "25" "24"
> as.numeric(as.character(33:24))
[1] 33 32 31 30 29 28 27 26 25 24
```

A factor is a special type of encoding for a vector, where the vector has a defined set of acceptable values or levels. Such an encoding is most common in statistical uses of R, for example, when defining categorical variables to identify treatments in an experiment. Using factors is not essential for the purposes of this book. However, encountering factors is inevitable when working with R (for example, when reading a table from a file, character columns are encoded as factors by default), so at the very least, we need to be aware of this data structure.

The factor function can be used to convert a vector into a factor:

```
> factor(c("cat","dog","dog"))
[1] cat dog dog
Levels: cat dog
> factor(c("cat","dog","dog","mouse"))
[1] cat   dog   dog   mouse
Levels: cat dog mouse
```

As you can see, the acceptable levels of the resulting `factor` object (which are, by default, defined as a set of unique values that the vector has) are printed along with its values.

Using the assignment operator to save an object

So far we have used R by entering standalone expressions on the command line. As mentioned in the previous chapter, the returned objects are not saved anywhere this way. Therefore, we cannot make sequential operations with each created object serving as an input for the next step(s). However, saving intermediate result is essential to automate processes.

Saving objects to the temporary memory is called assignment. By temporary, we mean that the objects are deleted when we shut down the computer (or quit R), as opposed to writing to a file on the hard drive, where the information will permanently remain unless it's deleted. Assignment is performed by an assignment expression, which is composed of the object we would like to save, the assignment operator =, and the name we would like to give the new object. For example, we can save the `1:10` sequential vector to an object named v as follows:

```
> v = 1:10
```

We can then access our newly created object using its name the same way we accessed predefined objects (such as `pi`) in the previous chapter:

```
> v
[1]  1  2  3  4  5  6  7  8  9 10
```

There is another assignment operator in R, namely <-:

```
> v <- 1:10
```

Throughout this book, the = operator is used since it is easier to type.

Also, note the difference between the assignment operator = and the equality conditional operator == (see the previous chapter). The = operator is used for assignment:

```
> one = 1
> two = 2
> one = two
> one
[1] 2
> two
[1] 2
```

The == operator is used to compare:

```
> one = 1
> two = 2
> one == two
[1] FALSE
```

When assigning an object with a name that already exists in memory, the older object is deleted and replaced by the new one:

```
> x = 55
> x
[1] 55
> x = "Hello"
> x
[1] "Hello"
```

The ls function returns a character vector with the names of all the user-defined objects (in a given environment, with the default one being the global R environment). For example, so far we have assigned four objects in memory:

```
> ls()
[1] "one" "two" "v"   "x"
```

Removing objects from memory

We can remove objects from memory by using the `rm` function. Let's take a look at the following examples:

```
> rm("v")
> ls()
[1] "one" "two" "x"
```

It is sometimes useful to remove all objects from memory. For example, if we want to run a given code section without worrying that the previously defined objects will interfere, this can be done by passing the whole list of objects currently in memory to the `rm` function as follows:

```
> rm(list = ls())
> ls()
character(0)
```

The `character(0)` output indicates an empty character vector.

Removing all objects can be achieved by navigating to **Misc** | **Remove all objects** (RGui) or **Session** | **Clear workspace...** (RStudio). The reason for writing the `list=ls()` part will become evident after reading the *Using functions with several parameters* section in this chapter.

Summarizing vector properties

Many functions in R are intended to work with vectors. The current section reviews some commonly used functions that are used to find out vectors' properties.

For example, we may be interested in the mean, minimal, and maximal values of a given vector. To get these, we can use the `mean`, `min`, and `max` functions, respectively:

```
> v = 1:10
> mean(v)
[1] 5.5
> min(v)
[1] 1
> max(v)
[1] 10
```

We can also get both the minimal and maximal values at once with the `range` function:

```
> range(v)
[1] 1 10
```

The `length` function returns the number of elements a given vector has:

```
> v = c(4,2,3,9,1)
> length(v)
[1] 5
```

With logical vectors, we sometimes would like to know whether they contain at least one TRUE value or whether all of their values are TRUE. This can be achieved with the `any` and `all` functions, respectively:

```
> l = c(TRUE, FALSE, FALSE, TRUE)
> any(l)
[1] TRUE
> all(l)
[1] FALSE
```

If we would like to know how many TRUE values a vector contains, we can utilize the default transformation from logical to numeric vectors when arithmetic functions are used on the former:

```
> l = c(TRUE, FALSE, FALSE, TRUE)
> sum(l)
[1] 2
```

In this example, each TRUE value was first converted to 1 and each FALSE value to 0. Therefore, the vector `c(TRUE,FALSE,FALSE,TRUE)` became the vector `c(1,0,0,1)` and the sum of this vector's elements is 2.

The `which` function returns the positions of all the TRUE elements within a logical vector:

```
> which(l)
[1] 1 4
```

Here, a vector of length 2 was returned since there are two TRUE values in the vector l. The two values of this vector are 1 and 4 since the first TRUE value occupies the first position in the vector l, while the second TRUE value occupies the fourth position.

The related functions `which.min` and `which.max` return the position of the minimal or maximal element in a numeric vector:

```
> which.min(v)
[1] 5
> which.max(v)
[1] 4
```

We are going to see another example with `which.min` later in this book.

The last useful function we will mention is the `unique` function, which returns the unique elements of a vector; that is, it returns a set of elements the vector consists of without repetitions. Let's take a look at the following examples:

```
> v = c(5,6,2,2,3,0,-1,2,5,6)
> unique(v)
[1]  5  6  2  3  0 -1
```

Element-by-element operations on vectors

As opposed to functions that treat the vector as a single entity (as seen in the previous section), some functions work on each element of the vector as if it was a separate entity and return a vector of the results (which, therefore, has the same number of elements as the input vector). In fact, all arithmetic and logical operators work this way, as shown in the following examples (we did not have a chance to witness this since we always used vectors of length 1):

```
> 1:10 * 2
 [1]  2  4  6  8 10 12 14 16 18 20
> 1:10 - 10
 [1] -9 -8 -7 -6 -5 -4 -3 -2 -1  0
> sqrt(c(4,16,64))
[1] 2 4 8
```

In the first expression, we multiplied the vector (1, 2, ..., 10) by 2, which resulted in a vector of 10 elements where the first element is equal to *1*2*, the second is equal to *2*2*, the third is equal to *3*2*, and so on, up to *10*2*.

Logical operators function in the same way, shown as follows:

```
> x = 1:5
> x
[1] 1 2 3 4 5
> x >= 3
[1] FALSE FALSE  TRUE  TRUE  TRUE
```

Here, for each of the values 1, 2, 3, 4, 5, it has been evaluated whether the value is larger or equal to 3, giving FALSE for 1 and 2 and TRUE for 3, 4, and 5.

If we want to check whether a given value from one vector is present in another, we can use the %in% operator. With %in%, we basically ask whether the value(s) of a vector on the left match any of the values of a vector on the right:

```
> 1 %in% 1:10
[1]  TRUE
> 11 %in% 1:10
[1]  FALSE
```

For these simple examples, we can do without the %in% operator (see the following examples). Its utility will become apparent towards the end of this chapter, when we want, for instance, to look for each element of a long vector A and check whether it has a match in a long vector B. Here are the alternatives to the preceding expressions:

```
> any(1:10 == 1)
[1]  TRUE
> any(1:10 == 11)
[1]  FALSE
```

In these two examples, we encompass the logical operation within the any function to check whether the resulting logical vector has at least one TRUE value.

Now, let's move on to character vectors. When working with character values, the paste function can be useful to combine separate elements into a single character string. The sep parameter of this function determines which characters will be used to separate the values (a single space is the default). Let's take a look at the following example:

```
> paste("There are", "5", "books.")
[1]  "There are 5 books."
```

The paste function also works with vectors that have more than one element:

```
> paste("Image", 1:5)
[1]  "Image 1" "Image 2" "Image 3" "Image 4" "Image 5"
```

Note that the paste function automatically converts numeric values into characters if characters are supplied:

```
> x = 80
> paste("There are", x, "books.")
[1]  "There are 80 books."
```

The paste0 function does the same thing as paste, with the default value for the sep parameter being nothing:

```
> paste(1, 2, 3, sep = "")
[1] "123"
> paste0(1, 2, 3)
[1] "123"
```

The recycling principle

In the previous chapter, we only used operators on two vectors of length 1. In this chapter, so far, we have used operations involving one vector of length 1 and another of length >1. What happens when we perform an operation involving two vectors of length >1?

If we have two vectors of exactly the same length, the operation is performed on each consecutive pair of elements taken from the two vectors, as follows:

```
> c(1,2,3) * c(10,20,30)
[1] 10 40 90
```

In this example, 1 is multiplied by 10, 2 is multiplied by 20, and 3 is multiplied by 30, and the three results are combined into a single vector of length 3.

In case when the lengths of the two vectors are unequal, the shorter vector is recycled before the operation is performed. In other words, values at the beginning of the shorter vector are attached to its end, sequentially and as many times as necessary, until the lengths of both vectors match. The simplest case, which we witnessed in the previous section, is the one that involves one vector of length 1 and another vector of length greater than 1. We can describe what happens in such a case as the recycling of the vector that has one element until it matches the length of the longer vector. For example, when executing the first of these two expressions, it is as if we are performing the second:

```
> 1:4 * 3
[1]  3  6  9 12
> 1:4 * c(3,3,3,3)
[1]  3  6  9 12
```

The same way, in the following example, the vector c(3,5) is recycled until it is of length 4, to c(3,5,3,5). The result is c(1,2,3,4) multiplied by c(3,5,3,5):

```
> c(1,2,3,4) * c(3,5)
[1]  3 10  9 20
```

When the length of the longer vector is not a multiple of the shorter vector, recycling is incomplete and we receive a warning message. Nevertheless, the operation is carried out. In the next example, the vector `c(1,10,100)` is of length 3, while the vector `1:5` is of length 5. The vector `c(1,10,100)` is recycled to `c(1,10,100,1,10)`, which is the same length as the vector `c(1,2,3,4,5)`, as follows:

```
> 1:5 * c(1,10,100)
[1]   1  20 300   4  50
Warning message:
In 1:5 * c(1, 10, 100) :
   longer object length is not a multiple of shorter object length
```

Using functions with several parameters

A function in R can have more than one parameter. In this section, we are going to get acquainted with supplying several arguments to such functions. At the same time, several new functions that take more than one argument will be introduced.

Supplying more than one argument in a function call

When specifying several arguments in a function, we need to assign each argument to the respective parameter using the usual assignment operator = during the function call, separating the assignment expressions for different parameters with commas.

For example, let's examine the `seq` function. Its most useful three parameters are `from`, `to`, and `by` (you can see in the function's help page that it has several more parameters). The `seq` function creates a sequential vector based on the input, as follows:

- `from`: This parameter specifies from where to begin
- `to`: This parameter specifies where to end
- `by`: This parameter specifies the step size

Let's take a look at the following examples:

```
> seq(from = 100, to = 150, by = 10)
[1] 100 110 120 130 140 150
> seq(from = 190, to = 150, by = -10)
[1] 190 180 170 160 150
```

The : operator we previously encountered is, in fact, used to create sequences of special cases (where the step size is 1 or -1), while the seq function is more general.

There are several important rules regarding function calls involving more than one argument:

- The names of the parameters can be omitted as long as the arguments are entered in the default order, which is specified in the function definition. Therefore, the following two expressions are equivalent:

```
> seq(from = 5, to = 10, by = 1)
[1]  5  6  7  8  9 10
> seq(5, 10, 1)
[1]  5  6  7  8  9 10
```

  We have, in fact, used this property already. For example, the name of the first argument of the mean function (the vector to compute the mean for) is x, but we can omit it during the function call:

```
> mean(1:10)
[1] 5.5
> mean(x = 1:10)
[1] 5.5
```

- On the contrary, if the parameter names are specified, the arguments order can be altered:

```
> seq(to = 10, by = 1, from = 5)
[1]  5  6  7  8  9 10
```

- Arguments can be skipped as long as they have a default value in the function definition. For example, the by parameter has the default argument of 1, therefore the following two expressions are equivalent:

```
> seq(5, 10, 1)
[1]  5  6  7  8  9 10
> seq(5, 10)
[1]  5  6  7  8  9 10
```

Creating default vectors

New vectors populated with default values (0 for numeric, " " for characters, and FALSE for logical vectors) can be created via the vector function, specifying the mode (vector type) and length:

```
> vector(mode = "numeric", length = 2)
[1]  0 0
> vector(mode = "character", length = 10)
 [1] "" "" "" "" "" "" "" "" "" ""
> vector(mode = "logical", length = 3)
[1]  FALSE FALSE FALSE
```

Creating repetitive vectors

You have already learned the two ways to create consecutive vectors with : and seq. Another special type of vector, a repetitive vector, can be created with the rep function (which stands for replicate). We simply need to specify what to replicate and how many times to replicate it:

```
> rep(x = 22, times = 10)
[1]  22 22 22 22 22 22 22 22 22 22
```

The rep function can operate on vectors longer than 1 as well:

```
> x = c(18, 0, 9)
> rep(x, 3)
[1]  18  0  9 18  0  9 18  0  9
```

Substrings

Another useful function with characters is substr, which is used to extract subsets of character strings, that is, we create a subset of the characters within an individual element of a vector (substring), rather than a subset of the vectors elements (see the next section). The function requires the start and stop values. Let's take a look at the following examples:

```
> x = "Subsetting strings"
> substr(x, start = 1, stop = 14)
[1] "Subsetting str"
> substr(x, 6, 14)
[1] "tting str"
> substr(x, 1, 3)
[1] "Sub"
```

As we can see, the start and stop values are considered inclusive. For example, the last expression, where `start` is equal to `1` and `stop` is equal to `3`, gives us the three characters occupying places 1 to 3 within the character string `x`.

Creating subsets of vectors

Creating subsets of data is one of the fundamental operations in data analysis. In this section, we will cover the two basic ways to create subsets of a vector. The first way involves numeric vectors, which specify the requested indices to be included in the subset. The second way involves using logical vectors, which specify for each element whether we would like to keep it or not.

Subsetting with numeric vectors of indices

Subsetting using numeric vectors of indices is done using the square brackets operator `[`, by providing the vector of indices within the square brackets. For example, we can select a single element of a vector by putting the value of the required index within brackets, as follows:

```
> x = c(5,6,1,2,3,7)
> x[3]
[1] 1
> x[1]
[1] 5
> x[6]
[1] 7
```

If we would like to, for example, find out the value of the last element in a given vector, we can use the `length` function, which returns its length (the index of the vectors' last element), as follows:

```
> x[length(x)]
[1] 7
```

We can also assign new values to a subset of a vector, as follows:

```
> x = 1:3
> x
[1] 1 2 3
> x[2] = 300
> x
[1]   1 300   3
```

We can create a subset that is more than one element long, when the length of our vector of indices is larger than 1:

```
> x = c(43,85,10)
> x[1:2]
[1] 43 85
> x[c(3,1)]
[1] 10 43
```

As seen in the last expression, the indices vector, which we placed in the square brackets, does not need to be composed of consecutive values, nor do its values need to have an increasing order. For example, we can reverse the order of values in a vector by using a vector of indices going from the position of the last element down to 1:

```
> x = 33:24
> x
 [1] 33 32 31 30 29 28 27 26 25 24
> x[length(x):1]
[1] 24 25 26 27 28 29 30 31 32 33
```

The vector of indices can also include repetitive values, as follows:

```
> x = c(43,85,10)
> x[rep(3,4)]
[1] 10 10 10 10
```

In this example, the `rep(3,4)` expression creates the vector `c(3,3,3,3)`. The latter then results in the creation of a subset (which is longer than the original vector), where the third element of the vector is repeated four times.

The recycling rule also applies to assignment into subsets:

```
> x = 1:10
> x[3:8] = c(15,16)
> x
[1]  1  2 15 16 15 16 15 16  9 10
```

In this example, the values `15` and `16` were alternated until the six-element long subset in the vector `x` is filled.

Subsetting with logical vectors

Another method to create a subset of a vector is by supplying a logical vector within the `[` operator. The logical vector points out to the elements that need to be kept within the subset; the elements to be kept are those whose indices match the indices of the TRUE values in the logical vector. It is frequently useful to create the logical vector that is used for subsetting by applying a conditional operator on the same vector we wish to subset. Let's take a look at the following example:

```
> x = seq(85, 100, 2)
> x
[1] 85 87 89 91 93 95 97 99
> x > 90
[1] FALSE FALSE FALSE  TRUE  TRUE  TRUE  TRUE  TRUE
> x[x > 90]
[1] 91 93 95 97 99
```

Here, we created a logical vector x>90, which like the vector x has eight elements (since the operation was carried out element by element as we saw previously). The values in this vector are either TRUE or FALSE depending on whether the vector x has a value larger than 90 at the respective position. When we create a subset of the vector x using the logical vector x>90, we get a vector containing those five values in x that occupy the same position that the TRUE values occupy in the x>90 vector. These are the positions where the values of x are greater than 90.

We can even apply more complex conditions to select some very specific values:

```
> x
[1] 85 87 89 91 93 95 97 99
> x[x>85 & x<90]
[1] 87 89
> x[x>92 | x<86]
[1] 85 93 95 97 99
```

Note that when subsetting with logical vectors, the order of values in the subset matches their order in the original vector, since the first element in the subset will be the first element that has TRUE in the logical vector, the second will be the second element that has TRUE in the logical vector, and so on.

If none of the elements satisfies the required condition (which results in the logical vector having all FALSE values), we will get an empty vector as a result. For example, no values in the vector x (or in any other vector) are larger as well as smaller than 90 at the same time:

```
> x>90 & x<90
[1] FALSE FALSE FALSE FALSE FALSE FALSE FALSE FALSE
> x[x>90 & x<90]
numeric(0)
```

Dealing with missing values

In this section, we are going to introduce the representation of missing values in R and ways to deal with them. Missing values can arise in many situations during data collection and analysis, either when the required information could not be acquired for some reason or when, due to certain circumstances, we would like to exclude some data from an analysis by marking them as missing. In the spatial data analysis context, it can be that some districts in an area we surveyed were inaccessible for data collection by the researcher or some parts of an aerial image were clouded and we could not digitize features of interest there.

Missing values and their effect on data

The special value that marks missing values in R is NA. As briefly mentioned in the previous chapter, NaN values represent cases when the resulting value cannot be represented within the real system number. NaN values function in the same way as NA in all respects that are relevant here.

The same way that NaN values can result from inappropriate calculations (such as 0 divided by 0), NA values are created when there is not enough information to provide a result. For example, the 100th element of a vector that has only 10 elements is not available:

```
> x = 1:10
> x[100]
[1] NA
```

The average of a set of numbers including at least one NA is NA since the average can be ascertained only when all of the values it is based upon are known:

```
> x = c(2,5,1,0)
> mean(x)
[1] 2
> x[2] = NA
> x
[1]   2 NA  1  0
> mean(x)
[1] NA
```

At times, we will be interested in marking certain types of values as NA. For example, if we have a dataset of a car's driving speeds with one of the values being 900 km/h we will likely mark it as a typing error. Other times, the data we get to analyze will have a specific encoding to mark the missing values that people who created the data decided upon (for example -9999), and we would like to convert those values to NA in R. We will see an example of this later.

Detecting missing values in vectors

The is.na function indicates whether a given element of a vector is NA (in which case TRUE is returned) or not (in which case FALSE is returned). Let's take a look at the following examples:

```
> x = c(2,5,1,0)
> x[2] = NA
> x
[1]   2 NA  1  0
> is.na(x)
[1] FALSE  TRUE FALSE FALSE
```

At times, it is more convenient to check which values in a vector are not NA, rather than to check which are. To do this, we can use the ! operator, which we encountered in the previous chapter, to transpose the resulting logical vector:

```
> !is.na(x)
[1]  TRUE FALSE  TRUE  TRUE
```

For example, if we would like to have a subset of only the non-missing elements in x, we can type the following code:

```
> x[!is.na(x)]
[1] 2 1 0
```

Performing calculations on vectors with missing values

Continuing the previous example, the mean of the non-missing elements in x can be computed if we subset only the non-missing values:

```
> mean(x[!is.na(x)])
[1] 1
```

To save us the need of manually removing missing values from a vector prior to such calculations, many functions that require all values to be non-missing (such as mean, min, and max) have a parameter called na.rm to indicate whether we would like to remove the missing values before executing the calculation. The default for this parameter is FALSE (which means that we do not remove the NA values); if we would like the opposite, we need to specify na.rm=TRUE:

```
> x = c(3,8,2,NA,1,7,5,NA,9)
> mean(x)
[1] NA
> mean(x, na.rm = TRUE)
[1] 5
> max(x)
[1] NA
> max(x, na.rm = TRUE)
[1] 9
```

Writing new functions

A function is an object loaded into the computer's temporary memory and can be activated (usually with specific arguments) to perform a certain action. So far, we have used predefined functions (from R's base packages; starting in *Chapter 3, Working with Tables,* we are going to use functions from other contributed packages). In this section, we will describe the structure of a function's definition and see how we can write our own functions.

Note that in this book you are not going to define that many functions and the functions you will define are going to be rather simple. The reason for this is that most of the time you will be learning new methods, rather than repeatedly applying a given method you developed (which would justify writing a function for it). However, in practice, wrapping your code to a function form is frequently useful in cases where you have developed a certain procedure you would like to apply routinely to different datasets.

Defining our own functions

Let's review the components of a function's definition using an example. In the following example, we define a new function called `add_five`, which adds 5 to the provided argument and returns the result:

```
> add_five = function(x) {
+ x_plus_five = x + 5
+ return(x_plus_five)
+ }
```

The components of the definition are as follows:

- The function's name (for example, `add_five`)
- The assignment operator (`=`)
- The function definition operator (`function`)
- The function's parameters, possibly with default values, within brackets (for example, `(x)`)
- Opening brackets for the code section (`{`)
- The function's body of code (for example, `x_plus_five=x+5`)
- The definition of the returned value (for example, `return(x_plus_five)`)
- Closing brackets for the code section (`}`)

The idea is that the code that constitutes the function's body will run every time the function is called:

```
> add_five(5)
[1] 10
> add_five(7)
[1] 12
```

When we perform a function call, the objects that we provide as arguments are assigned to local objects within the function's environment so that the function's code can use them. These objects exist only while the function runs and are inaccessible from the global environment after the function is terminated:

```
> x_plus_five
Error: object 'x_plus_five' not found
```

Every function returns a value that we would frequently like to preserve for subsequent calculations. This is done by assignment in the same way we saw earlier in this chapter for predefined functions:

```
> result = add_five(3)
> result
[1] 8
```

The `return(x_plus_five)` expression can be skipped since by default, the function returns the last created object (which is `x_plus_five`). Therefore, in fact, we do not even need to assign the result to the `x_plus_five` object. In addition, when the code section contains a single expression, we can omit the parentheses. Therefore, an identical function can be defined simply, as follows:

```
> add_five = function(x) x + 5
```

Setting default values for the arguments

We can assign default arguments to parameters during the function's definition. This way, we will be able to skip some (or all) of the parameters during a function call. In other words, we can provide no arguments for some of the parameters, in which case the function will use the default arguments:

```
> add_five = function(x) x + 5
> add_five()
Error in add_five() : argument "x" is missing, with no default
> add_five = function(x = 1) x + 5
> add_five()
[1] 6
```

In the preceding example, in the first case, we got an error message since we tried calling the `add_five` function without providing an argument for the x parameter, which had no default value. In the second case, the function call was successful since this time the function was defined with a default value for x (which was equal to 1 and thus, the returned value was 6).

Many of the predefined functions in R have default arguments for some of the parameters. For example, the default arguments for the `mode` and `length` parameters of the `vector` function are `"logical"` and 0:

```
> vector()
logical(0)
```

Therefore, by default, it creates an empty logical vector (the default arguments can be found on the respective function's help page). There are no limitations for the class each argument in a function call must belong to as long as we (or the person who wrote the function) have not defined such limitations. However, if one of the expressions in the function's code results in an error given the particular set of arguments, the execution of the function will terminate and we will get no returned value. For example, our `add_five` function will trigger an error when supplying a character vector as an argument:

```
> add_five("one")
Error in x + 5 : non-numeric argument to binary operator
```

Working with dates and time series

In this section, we'll cover a concept closely related to vectors—time series. A time series is a sequence of values, each associated with a time index. For convenience, the values are usually ordered from the earliest to latest. The time difference between consecutive time indices can be fixed (in which case we have a regular time series) or variable (in which case we have an irregular time series), although an irregular time series can also be considered as a regular time series with missing data. For example, daily rainfall amounts in New York or Dollar to Euro currency exchange rates for the period of January 1, 2014 to January 15, 2014 would comprise two different time series.

Following its definition, the simplest way to represent a time series would be to have a separate vector of data values and a separate vector of time, with the same length, with each element of the data values vector corresponding to the respective element in the time vector. The only thing you need to learn in order to do this in R is to represent time, which is the topic of the present section.

Specialized time series classes in R

Several special classes to represent time series exist in R. Basically, such classes encompass the time and data values parts of a time series within a single object. For example, `ts`, `zoo`, and `xts` are different time series classes in R. The `ts` class is defined in the base packages, whereas the `zoo` and `xts` classes are defined in the contributed packages of the same respective names. The concept of working with packages in R will be introduced in the next chapter.

Working with time series objects has certain advantages such as having the ability to use specialized functions (for example, linear or spline interpolation of missing values in a time series using a single function call) or making sure that every object satisfies the class rules (for example, the number of data values and time indices in a time series must be equal). For the purposes of this book, we will stick to the basic manual representation of a time series. This way, we will have a chance to gain a better understanding of R's general principles, while the next step towards specialized time series classes would be easily executed by interested readers. There are numerous resources devoted to the time series analysis with R; for example, Paul S.P. Cowpertwait and Andrew V. Metcalfe in their book *Introductory Time Series with R, Springer*, (2009), provide an excellent applied introduction on this subject.

Reading climatic data from a CSV file

You are now going to learn how to use dates in R using our very first real-world example. We are going to use the **comma separated values (CSV)** file named `338284.csv`, which was downloaded from the **National Oceanic and Atmospheric Administration (NOAA)** National Climatic Data Center. This file contains daily rainfall and temperature data from a meteorological station at the Albuquerque International Airport, New Mexico, from March 1, 1931 to May 15, 2014.

A CSV file is used to store plain tabular data with no additional features that are common in spreadsheet files such as XLS. This is how the file looks when opened in Excel:

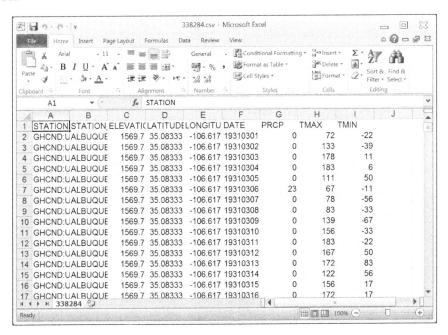

The following three lines of code read the file into R and assign the values in the DATE and TMAX columns to two separate vectors named `time` (since the data in the DATE column represents time) and `tmax` (which stands for maximum temperature). This involves operations on tables, which will be explained in the next chapter. They are provided here only for completeness:

```
> dat = read.csv("C:\\Data\\338284.csv", stringsAsFactors = FALSE)
> time = dat$DATE
> tmax = dat$TMAX
```

The important point is that we now have two vectors to work with, `time` and `tmax`, as an exercise summarizing most of the topics we dealt with in this chapter.

Converting character values to dates

Dates can be represented in R (as in many other types of software) using a special format. This allows certain special operations (such as finding the time difference between two dates) to be performed, which is not possible when dates are represented by simply using characters. There are several classes for date and time data in R. The simplest class (and the only one we will use in this book) is called Date, and it is used to represent calendar dates. Other classes exist to represent longer intervals of time (for example, monthly) or shorter (for example, date plus the time of day) intervals.

 Note that the Date and factor objects are not vectors in R terminology since they have additional attributes not present in the vector class. However, from the user's perspective, working with them often follows the same principles as seen in vectors. For example, creating subsets of Date objects works the same way as creating subsets of vectors.

For example, the Sys.Date and Sys.time functions return the current date or date plus the time of day, respectively. The object returned by Sys.Date belongs to class Date, while the object returned by Sys.time is an object of a different class (POSIXct). Let's take a look at the following examples:

```
> x = Sys.Date()
> x
[1] "2014-05-22"
> class(x)
[1] "Date"
> y = Sys.time()
> y
[1] "2014-05-22 10:04:56 IDT"
> class(y)
[1] "POSIXct" "POSIXt"
```

As we can see in the first half of the previous example, a Date object is printed the same way as a character vector holding the value "2014-05-22" would. However, as already mentioned, we can conduct calculations involving time intervals with the Date class, which make it worthwhile to represent dates in such a specialized format. For example, we can tell what date it will be seven days from today or what the date was 1,000 days ago:

```
> x + 7
[1] "2014-05-29"
> x - 1000
[1] "2011-08-26"
```

We can switch between the character vector and `Date` classes, using the
`as.character` and `as.Date` functions. For example, we can convert our `Date` object
`x` to a character vector using `as.character`:

```
> x = as.character(x)
> x
[1] "2014-05-22"
> class(x)
[1] "character"
```

We can convert the character vector back to `Date` using `as.Date`:

```
> x = as.Date(x)
> x
[1] "2014-05-22"
> class(x)
[1] "Date"
```

We can create a sequence of consecutive dates using `seq`, since this function accepts
`Date` objects as well:

```
> seq(from = as.Date("2013-01-01"),
+ to = as.Date("2013-02-01"),
+ by = 3)
 [1] "2013-01-01" "2013-01-04" "2013-01-07" "2013-01-10"
 [5] "2013-01-13" "2013-01-16" "2013-01-19" "2013-01-22"
 [9] "2013-01-25" "2013-01-28" "2013-01-31"
```

This gives us consecutive dates separated by three days from each other, from
January 1, 2013 to February 1, 2013.

The latter conversions, from character to date, were made possible so easily since
the `"2014-05-22"` configuration is a default one. This way, the `as.Date` function
knew that the first four characters in `"2014-05-22"` represent the *year*, the next two
characters (following a hyphen) represent the *month*, and the last two characters
represent the *day*. When we have characters representing a date in a different
configuration, we need to use the format parameter of `as.Date`, where we specify the
encoding types of the elements, their order, and the characters separating them (if any).

The common encoding types of the year, month, and day elements, and their respective symbols in R, are summarized in the following table:

Symbol	Meaning
%d	Day (for example, 15)
%m	Months in number (for example, 08)
%b	The first three characters of a month (for example, Aug)
%B	The full name of a month (for example, August)
%y	The last two digits of a year (for example, 14)
%Y	The full year (for example, 2014)

Using this symbology, along with the format parameter of the `as.Date` function, we can convert character values of other formats to dates. Let's take a look at the following examples:

```
> as.Date("07/Aug/12")
Error in charToDate(x) :
  character string is not in a standard unambiguous format
> as.Date("07/Aug/12", format = "%d/%b/%y")
[1] "2012-08-07"
> as.Date("2012-August-07")
Error in charToDate(x) :
  character string is not in a standard unambiguous format
> as.Date("2012-August-07", format = "%Y-%B-%d")
[1] "2012-08-07"
```

In each of these two example pairs, the first expression resulted in an error since we were trying to convert a character value of a non-standard date format to a `Date` without specifying the format, while the second expression worked since we did specify the format.

Once we have a `Date` object, we can extract one or two (or all) of its three elements (year, month, and day), and encode them as we wish using the `format` function, specifying the required format the same way as shown earlier. Note that the results are no longer `Date` objects, but character vectors:

```
> d = as.Date("1955-11-30")
> d
[1] "1955-11-30"
> format(d, "%d")
[1] "30"
> format(d, "%B")
```

```
[1] "November"
> format(d, "%Y")
[1] "1955"
> format(d, "%m/%Y")
[1] "11/1955"
```

We are now ready to proceed with our example involving the `time` and `tmax` vectors. First, we can find out that both vectors are numeric (integers, numbers without a fractional component, to be precise) as follows:

```
> class(time)
[1] "integer"
> class(tmax)
[1] "integer"
```

Then, let's see what the values of these vectors look like by printing the first 10 values from each one of them:

```
> time[1:10]
 [1] 19310301 19310302 19310303 19310304 19310305 19310306
 [7] 19310307 19310308 19310309 19310310
> tmax[1:10]
 [1]   72 133 178 183 111  67  78  83 139 156
```

The `time` vector contains dates in the `%Y%m%d` configuration (year, month, and day indicated by full numeric values, without separating characters). Therefore, we can convert it to a `Date` object, as follows:

```
> time = as.Date(as.character(time), format = "%Y%m%d")
> time[1:10]
 [1] "1931-03-01" "1931-03-02" "1931-03-03" "1931-03-04"
 [5] "1931-03-05" "1931-03-06" "1931-03-07" "1931-03-08"
 [9] "1931-03-09" "1931-03-10"
> class(time)
[1] "Date"
```

Note that we first needed to convert the `time` vector from numeric to character since the `as.Date` function works on character vectors. Now that `time` is a vector of dates, we have more freedom to treat the data as a time series.

Examining our time series

Looking into the documentation on climatic data from NOAA (which is also provided on the book's website), we can see that the temperature is provided in tenths of Celsius degree, with missing values marked as -9999. First, we will convert the -9999 values to NA by selecting the respective subset and making an assignment:

```
> tmax[tmax == -9999] = NA
```

Then, to convert the data into degrees Celsius units, we will divide each of the values by 10:

```
> tmax = tmax / 10
> tmax[1:10]
 [1]   7.2 13.3 17.8 18.3 11.1  6.7  7.8  8.3 13.9 15.6
```

Now, let's check the range of values each vector contains:

```
> range(time)
[1] "1931-03-01" "2014-05-15"
> range(tmax, na.rm = TRUE)
[1] -14.4  41.7
```

This means that the range of the measured maximum daily temperatures from March 1, 1931 to May 15, 2014 was -14.4 to 41.7 degrees Celsius.

Regarding the dates of measurement, looking at the first few values of the time vector (or at the original CSV file in a spreadsheet, for that matter), it seems that the days are consecutive. However, we may want to make sure that all days of the respective period are indeed present in the file. We can do this by comparing a consecutive sequence all_dates covering the time period from March 1, 1931 to May 15, 2014 with our time vector:

```
> range_t = range(time)
> all_dates = seq(range_t[1], range_t[length(range_t)], 1)
> length(all_dates)
[1] 30392
> length(time)
[1] 30391
```

This already indicates that we have an incomplete agreement. Our time vector contains the 30391 values, while there are 30392 dates during the time period from March 1, 1931 to May 15, 2014. Therefore, the CSV file is missing at least one date.

We will next check how many dates (and which ones) are missing. First, we will verify that, indeed, not all dates appear in the `time` vector using the `%in%` operator (asking for each element in `all_dates` whether it appears in the `time` vector) and the `all` function (asking whether all of the values in the resulting logical vector are `TRUE`).

```
> all(all_dates %in% time)
[1] FALSE
```

The answer is no; at least one of the dates in the range of March 1, 1931 to May 15, 2014 is indeed missing from the `time` vector. The next question would be which one is missing, or which ones are missing? We can get the indices of the dates that appear in `all_dates` but not in `time` with the `which` function:

```
> which(!(all_dates %in% time))
[1] 5499
```

The missing date is the 5499th element of the `all_dates` vector. Its value is as follows:

```
> all_dates[which(!(all_dates %in% time))]
[1] "1946-03-20"
```

Manually examining the CSV file in a spreadsheet software will confirm that indeed the date March 20, 1946 was skipped for some reason.

Another interesting question we can ask is on what day the highest temperature (which was 41.7 degree Celsius, as we saw earlier) has been observed:

```
> max(tmax, na.rm = TRUE)
[1] 41.7
time[which.max(tmax)]
[1] "1994-06-26"
```

The highest maximum daily temperature was observed on June 6, 1994.

Creating subsets based on dates

If we are interested in a particular subset of the time series, say the period from December 31, 2005 to January 1, 2014, we could create a subset of the dates in that period based on the `time` vector and a respective subset of data values based on the `tmax` vector. We can do this in two steps. First, we will create a logical vector, w, pointing at those dates we would like to keep:

```
> w = time > as.Date("2005-12-31") & time < as.Date("2014-1-1")
```

To find out the ratio between the number of days we would like to keep in the subset and the number of days in the complete series, we can type the following expression:

```
> sum(w) / length(w)
[1] 0.09614689
```

The amount of data within the subset we are interested in (December 31, 2005 to January 1, 2014) is about 9.6 percent of the total amount of data since the proportion of the TRUE values count in the logical vector, w, from the total number of values is 0.096 (remember that before summing a logical vector, it is converted to a numeric one with ones instead of TRUE and zeroes instead of FALSE).

Secondly, we will use the w vector to create subsets of both the time and tmax vectors:

```
> time = time[w]
> tmax = tmax[w]
```

Note that the selection was non-inclusive of the end dates since we used the > and < operators:

```
> range(time)
[1] "2006-01-01" "2013-12-31"
```

If we wanted to include the first and last dates (December 31, 2005 and January 1, 2014), we would rather use the >= and <= operators.

Introducing graphical functions

The graphical representation of data is a central feature, or even the main purpose, of data analysis in general and of spatial data analysis in particular. This section serves as a basic introduction to the procedure of creating graphical output in R. Such an introduction is necessary before moving on to the later chapters, where we would like to quickly be able to display intermediate products during various spatial data analysis steps. In *Chapter 9, Advanced Visualization of Spatial Data*, we will devote some additional time to the subject of visualization in R, and see how graphical output can be customized when producing publication-quality plots as the end product of spatial data analysis.

Displaying vectors using base graphics

We can graphically display a vector's values using the plot function. For example, the following expression opens a new window within the R environment with a plot of the vector values:

```
> plot(tmax)
```

The following screenshot shows what the graphical output looks like, and where it appears, when using RGui and RStudio:

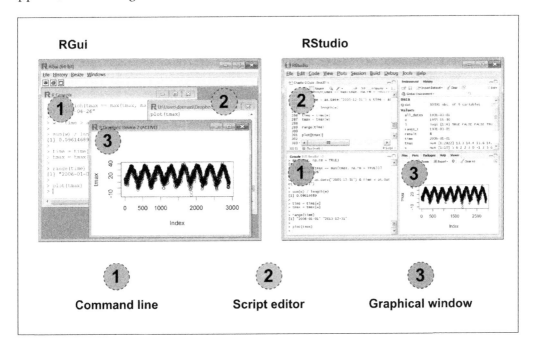

This output is the default one for the `plot` function; the values of the `tmax` vector are plotted on the *y* axis as a function of their index on the *x* axis, with open circles marking data points.

When plotting a time series, we would usually like to have the time of observation on the *x* axis (rather than the indices) and see a line connecting the data points from left to right (rather than unconnected circles). This can be done as follows:

```
> plot(time, tmax, type = "l")
```

When plotted, we will see what is shown in the following screenshot:

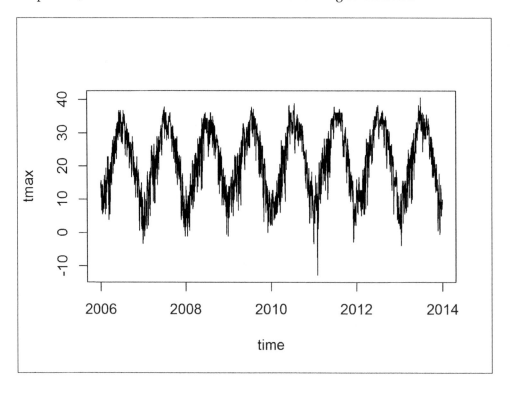

The `"l"` argument for the `type` parameter indicates we want a line plot, while the first and second arguments are treated as vectors of coordinates on the *x* and *y* axes, respectively. We also see that the `time` vector is automatically formatted so that year breakpoints are labeled on the *x* axis. There are many additional ways in which we can further customize this plot (and other types of plots we will produce in subsequent chapters). However, we will usually limit ourselves to the default plots until we reach *Chapter 9, Advanced Visualization of Spatial Data*, where we will elaborate on the subject of graphical output customization within the context of spatial data.

The last plot can also be produced using the following expression:

```
> plot(tmax ~ time, type = "l")
```

In this form of calling the `plot` function, the specification of the *x* and *y* axes is indicated by the `tmax~time` expression. The ~ operator creates a special type of object, a formula object. In this particular case, the formula indicates that `tmax` is the dependent variable (to the left of the ~ operator and thus plotted on the *y* axis) and `time` is the independent variable (to the right of the ~ operator and thus, plotted on the *x* axis). Formula objects are most common in statistical applications of R (we shall see an example of this in *Chapter 8, Spatial Interpolation of Point Data*), and in some other cases as well (as we shall see in the next chapter).

Saving graphical output

With the graphical window selected, we can save the image we see in a file through the menus (by navigating to **File | Save as** in RGui). Several raster (such as `*.png`) and vector (such as `*.pdf`) file formats are available for the output. However, sometimes we would like to embed the instructions to save a graphical output within our code to save ourselves the trouble of clicking on the menu buttons when constantly updating an image or when saving multiple images. This is possible by specifying a different graphical device—a file—instead of the graphical window—and closing it afterward. For example, the following code creates a PDF file (named `time_series.pdf`) with the plot we just saw in the `C:\Data` directory:

```
> pdf("C:\\Data\\time_series.pdf")
> plot(tmax ~ time, type = "l")
> dev.off()
```

The last expression, `dev.off()`, turns the PDF graphics device off, thereby returning to the default device (which is the graphical window) for the subsequent plots.

> Note that path indications in R are character values with directories separated by \\. The / symbol can also be used, but not the usual Windows symbol \ (which is used for a different purpose in R).

There are several functions analogous to the pdf function to write graphical output in other formats, such as `bmp`, `jpeg`, `png`, and `tiff`. All of these functions have several parameters (in addition to the file path) to modify the output, such as specifying image width, height, and resolution; see the help pages of these functions for more information.

The main graphical systems in R

There are three main graphics systems in R: base graphics (which we just used to create the previous plot), `lattice`, and `ggplot2`. For example, the following code produces the previous plot as well as two analogous plots using `lattice` and `ggplot2`. The code includes some functions that will be made clear later, and requires installation of additional packages (which we will cover in the next chapter).

```
> dat = data.frame(time = time, tmax = tmax)
# Base graphics
> plot(tmax ~ time, dat, type = "l")
# lattice
> library(lattice)
> xyplot(tmax ~ time, data = dat, type = "l")
# ggplot2
> library(ggplot2)
> ggplot(dat, aes(x = time, y = tmax)) +
+ geom_line()
```

The graphs this code produces are sequentially shown in the following screenshot, from left to right, with the name of the respective graphics system indicated at the top of each panel:

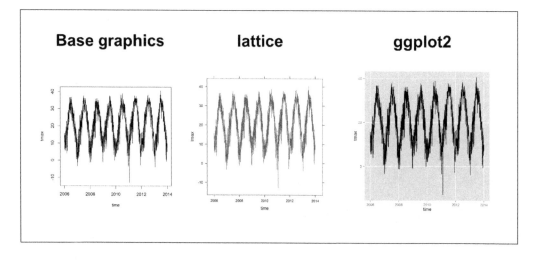

Many types of plots (such as the time series plot we just created) can be produced using any of the three systems. Therefore, choosing one in many cases is a matter of taste. However, some non-overlapping features do exist among the graphics systems. For example, faceting (which produces a series of plots for different portions of the data side by side) cannot be achieved using base graphics, while 3D plots cannot be produced using `ggplot2`. As seen in the preceding screenshot, there are also some small differences in the default styling of the plots. Finally, as we can see in the preceding code section, the `ggplot2` system has quite a different syntax compared to base graphics and `lattice`.

In the upcoming chapters, we are going to use base graphics (and sometimes `lattice`) to quickly visualize the products we get at various steps of spatial data analysis. In *Chapter 9*, *Advanced Visualization of Spatial Data*, we are going to concentrate on customizing graphical output in R, mostly using `ggplot2`.

Summary

In this chapter, we covered the basic subjects that we are going to use in almost every operation from now on. First, you learned the fundamental methods of working with vectors, including the creation of three common types of vectors, subsetting them, and dealing with missing values in them. You also saw how dates are represented in R, and how such a representation can be useful when working with time series. In addition, we expanded on the function call structure in R, discussed how to define custom functions, and saw how a graphical output can be produced and saved.

In the next chapter, we are going to discuss working with tables in R. We will see that the common tabular data class in R (`data.frame`) is a direct extension of the vector class. Thus, many of the operations to work with tables will be intuitive once we know how to work with vectors. Later, we will move on to working with spatial data classes, where the principles of working with vectors and tables are also directly applicable.

3
Working with Tables

Working with tables is central to programming in R, both with regards to spatial analysis (for example, working with attribute tables of geometries) and more generally. In this chapter, we will learn how to work with tables on their own, while in the subsequent chapters, we will see the ways that spatial data analysis involves dealing with tables. At the same time, two central subjects, which we will have to be familiar with for the subsequent chapters, will be introduced. These are working with contributed packages in R and controlling code execution.

As a central example, we will work with real-world data (monthly climatic records for Spain, which were downloaded from the NOAA archive) so that we can witness several very common cleaning and reshaping procedures of tables.

In this chapter, we'll cover the following topics:

- Working with `data.frame` objects to represent tables in R
- Controlling code execution through conditional statements and loops
- Automated calculations on tables and vectors using the `apply` functions
- Installing and using contributed packages in R
- Reshaping tables into different forms
- Joining tables

Using the data.frame class to represent tabular data

In this section, you will learn how tables are represented in R and how you can work with tabular objects. In particular, you will learn two common ways to create table objects (from vectors or by reading a file from the disk). Afterwards, you will learn how to examine, subset, and make calculations with tables.

Creating a table from separate vectors

The data.frame class is the basic class to represent tabular data in R. A data.frame object is essentially a collection of vectors, all with the same length. However, the vectors do not have to be of the same type. They may also include one-dimensional objects that are not strictly vectors, such as Date or factor objects (see the previous chapter). Therefore, data.frame objects are particularly suitable to represent data with different variables in columns and different cases in rows. Thus, variables may be of different types; for example, a table storing climatic data may have one character variable to store meteorological station names, another Date variable to represent measurement dates, and a third numeric variable to represent the measured values such as rainfall amounts or temperatures.

One way to create a data.frame object is to combine several vectors that are already present in the R environment. This can be achieved with the data.frame function with the arguments being the names of the vector objects we would like to combine. Let's take a look at the following examples:

```
> num = 1:4
> lower = c("a","b","c","d")
> upper = c("A","B","C","D")
> df = data.frame(num, lower, upper)
> df
  num lower upper
1   1     a     A
2   2     b     B
3   3     c     C
4   4     d     D
```

Here, we created a `data.frame` object named `df` by combining the vectors `num`, `lower`, and `upper`. The previously independent vectors now comprise columns in `df`. As we can see, the names of the columns appear on the first line of the printed output of a `data.frame` object. These are the names of the original vectors, `num`, `lower`, and `upper`. Rows have names as well; these are automatically assigned with the characters `1`, `2`, `3`, and `4` (as it appears to the left of the first column in the printed output).

We can also create the `data.frame` object in a single step by performing the vector assignments within the `data.frame` function call itself:

```
> df = data.frame(
+ num = 1:4,
+ lower = c("a","b","c","d"),
+ upper = c("A","B","C","D"))
```

Note that in this example, vector types were different (`num` is numeric, whereas `lower` and `upper` are characters). However, the vectors had the same length; otherwise, an error would have occurred since all columns of `data.frame` must have the same length.

An important parameter of the `data.frame` function (and several other functions such as `read.csv`, which will be introduced in the next section) is `stringsAsFactors`. The `stringsAsFactors` parameter controls whether character columns are automatically converted to factors (the default value is `TRUE`). Within the context of this book, we would usually like to keep the character vectors as characters for greater flexibility (we can always make the conversion to factors ourselves when necessary with the `factor` function; see the previous chapter for more information). Therefore, a function call preserving character columns will be as follows:

```
> df = data.frame(num, lower, upper,
+ stringsAsFactors = FALSE)
> df
  num lower upper
1   1     a     A
2   2     b     B
3   3     c     C
4   4     d     D
```

The way our table is printed on screen is identical when compared to the previous example. However, using methods, which will be introduced later, we will be able to see that columns 2 and 3 now consist of character vectors rather than factors.

We can add rows or columns to an existing data.frame object using the rbind (row bind) and cbind (column bind) functions, respectively. For example, we can add a fifth row to our df table using rbind as follows:

```
> row5 = c(5,"e","E")
> rbind(df, row5)
  num lower upper
1   1     a     A
2   2     b     B
3   3     c     C
4   4     d     D
5   5     e     E
```

Alternatively, we could add a fourth column using cbind as follows:

```
> word = c("One","Two","Three","Four")
> cbind(df, word, stringsAsFactors = FALSE)
  num lower upper  word
1   1     a     A   One
2   2     b     B   Two
3   3     c   C Three
4   4     d   D  Four
```

In the previous example, we had to specify, once again, that we do not want the character vector, word, to be converted into a factor vector.

Creating a table from a CSV file

Another common method to create a data.frame object is to read tabular data from the disk. For example, we can read a CSV file using the read.csv function (which was briefly mentioned earlier). The first parameter of this function, and the one with no defaults, is a file indicating the path to the CSV file. For example, the following expression reads the contents of the 343452.csv file and assigns it to a data.frame object called dat (remember that directories should be separated with \\ or /):

```
> dat = read.csv("C:\\Data\\343452.csv")
```

The `343452.csv` file contains monthly records of precipitation, minimum temperature, and maximum temperature from Spain for a period of 30 years. It was downloaded from the NOAA climatic archive and provided as is. Since we will use data from this file in several of our examples, in this and the upcoming chapters, let's examine its contents. Because the table is very large, to see what it looks like, we can print only the first several rows with the `head` function, as follows (similarly, with the `tail` function, we can print the several last rows):

```
> head(dat)
            STATION STATION_NAME ELEVATION LATITUDE LONGITUDE
1 GHCND:SP000060010      IZANA SP      2371  28.3089  -16.4992
2 GHCND:SP000060010      IZANA SP      2371  28.3089  -16.4992
3 GHCND:SP000060010      IZANA SP      2371  28.3089  -16.4992
4 GHCND:SP000060010      IZANA SP      2371  28.3089  -16.4992
5 GHCND:SP000060010      IZANA SP      2371  28.3089  -16.4992
6 GHCND:SP000060010      IZANA SP      2371  28.3089  -16.4992
      DATE TPCP MMXT MMNT
1 19840101  514   56   -5
2 19840201    0   98   28
3 19840301  687   72    2
4 19840401  136  122   35
5 19840501  214  118   30
6 19840601   65  196  105
```

The column's contents are as follows:

- `STATION`: This is the meteorological station identification code
- `STATION_NAME`: This is the meteorological station name
- `ELEVATION`: This is the elevation of the station above sea level (meters)
- `LATITUDE`: This is the latitude of the station (decimal degrees)
- `LONGITUDE`: This is the longitude of the station (decimal degrees)
- `DATE`: This is the date of measurement
- `TPCP`: This is the total monthly precipitation (0.1 mm units)
- `MMXT`: This is the mean monthly maximum temperature (0.1 degree Celsius units)
- `MMNT`: This is the mean monthly minimum temperature (0.1 degree Celsius units)

The complete documentation for the CSV file is provided along with the data from NOAA (and can also be downloaded from the book's website).

According to what you learned in the previous chapter, the dates are recorded in the %Y%m%d format (in Date objects terminology). However, since the data is monthly, the day component is not informative (we can see that all days are coded as 01). The missing values of measurements are marked as -9999, a commonly encountered convention.

Examining the structure of a data.frame object

We can get the number of rows and columns in our data.frame object using the nrow and ncol functions, respectively. For example, our small table df has four rows and three columns, while dat (containing the monthly climatic data) has 28,536 rows and nine columns:

```
> nrow(df)
[1] 4
> ncol(df)
[1] 3
> nrow(dat)
[1] 28536
> ncol(dat)
[1] 9
```

We can, if the table is not too long, print the table's contents and see how many columns (or rows) are there, according to the row names. However, it is generally advisable to get the properties of an object using functions (such as ncol), rather than typing a specific number manually (such as 9). This way, our code is going to be transferable to an analysis of any object and not just the specific object we are currently working on.

We can get the lengths of both row and column dimensions using the dim function. If our argument is a data.frame object (we will see later that the dim function works with other classes as well; such a function is called a generic function in R terminology), a vector of length 2 is returned with the first element being the number of rows and the second being the number of columns, as follows:

```
> dim(dat)
[1] 28536     9
```

We can also get the names of the rows and columns (getting column names is often more useful) as a character vector using the functions `rownames` and `colnames`, as shown in the following example:

```
> colnames(dat)
[1] "STATION"       "STATION_NAME" "ELEVATION"    "LATITUDE"
[5] "LONGITUDE"     "DATE"         "TPCP"         "MMXT"
[9] "MMNT"
```

Assignment into column names can be made to replace the existing names with new ones. For example, to change the name of the third column from ELEVATION to Elev, we can use the `colnames(dat)[3]="Elev"` expression. Similarly, we can convert all column names of the `data.frame` object from uppercase to lowercase using the `tolower` function so that it will be easier to type:

```
> colnames(dat) = tolower(colnames(dat))
> colnames(dat)
[1] "station"       "station_name" "elevation"    "latitude"
[5] "longitude"     "date"         "tpcp"         "mmxt"
[9] "mmnt"
```

It is frequently useful to examine the structure of a given object using the `str` function. This function (which is also generic) prints the structure of its argument showing the data types of its components and the relations between them. In the case of a `data.frame` object, a list of the column names and types is printed, along with the table dimensions, and the first several values (or all values, if the table is very short). For example, the output for the small table `df` shows that we have a table with three columns (the variables) and four rows (the observations). It also shows that the first column is numeric and the last two are characters. Here is how the output looks like:

```
> str(df)
'data.frame':   4 obs. of  3 variables:
 $ num  : int  1 2 3 4
 $ lower: chr  "a" "b" "c" "d"
 $ upper: chr  "A" "B" "C" "D"
```

Subsetting data.frame objects

There are two principal ways to create a subset of a `data.frame` object. The first involves accessing separate columns, using the column names, with the $ operator. The second involves providing the two vectors of indices, names or logical values, with the [operator.

Using the $ operator, we can gain access to separate columns in a `data.frame` object. To do this, we simply insert the name of the `data.frame` to the left of the $ operator and the name of the required column to the right, as follows:

```
> df$num
[1] 1 2 3 4
> df$lower
[1] "a" "b" "c" "d"
> df$upper
[1] "A" "B" "C" "D"
```

Since the columns of a `data.frame` object are basically vectors, we can employ all the previously presented vector methods in columns of a `data.frame` object the same way we would in independent vectors. For example, we can replace the -9999 values (which mark the missing data) with NA, for each of the three measured variables in dat, as follows:

```
> dat$tpcp[dat$tpcp == -9999] = NA
> dat$mmxt[dat$mmxt == -9999] = NA
> dat$mmnt[dat$mmnt == -9999] = NA
```

The only difference from how we did this operation in the previous chapter is the dat$ part. This means that we refer to columns of the `data.frame` object (dat), rather than independent vectors. Now, let's convert the tpcp values to mm units and mmxt and mmnt values to degree Celsius units by dividing each value in the respective columns by 10, as follows:

```
> dat$tpcp = dat$tpcp / 10
> dat$mmxt = dat$mmxt/ 10
> dat$mmnt = dat$mmnt / 10
```

Note that if we would have made the division by 10 before encoding the -9999 values as NA, we would have got the -999.9 values, while now that we have NA values, they will remain NA since NA/10 gives NA. This highlights the importance of representing missing data with NA to reduce the chance of mistakes.

Using the [operator, we can obtain a subset of a data.frame object, which will include the intersection of any number of rows and columns. This works the same way as vectors subsetting with one difference, that is, a data.frame is a two-dimensional object while a vector is a one-dimensional object. Therefore, we need to provide two indices rather than just one.

Remember that when subsetting with the [operator in data.frame, the first index refers to rows and the second index refers to columns. This arrangement is going to appear in other contexts as well (for example, in matrices and rasters).

The two vectors of indices, used in order to create a subset of a data.frame object, can include any combination of the following:

- A numeric vector, in which case the numeric vector refers to the indices of rows/columns to retain in the subset
- A character vector, in which case the character vector indicates the names of rows/columns to retain
- A logical vector, in which case the logical vector indicates whether to retain each row/column of data.frame

We have been extensively using methods 1 and 3 in vectors (see the previous chapter), so extending the methods to the two-dimensional case should be intuitive. In fact, method 2 can also be used with vectors since vectors can have element names the same way that a data.frame object has row names and column names (but we are not going to use that here).

For example, the following expression gives us the element populating the second row and the third column of df:

```
> df[2, 3]
[1] "B"
```

Leaving an empty space instead of the row's or column's index indicates we are interested in all the elements of the respective dimension (all rows or all columns). For example, the following expressions return all elements of the second row and the third column of df:

```
> df[2, ]
  num lower upper
2   2     b     B
> df[ ,3]
[1] "A" "B" "C" "D"
```

By default, a subset of a `data.frame` object is converted into a simpler class if values from a single column are involved. For example, the `df[2, 3]` and `df[ ,3]` expressions returned (character) vectors. The `df[2, ]` expression returned a `data.frame` object since three columns are involved. In fact, the second row of `df` contains both numeric and character values, while we already know that a vector can only contain values of the same type. If we wish, we can suppress the `data.frame` simplification by using the `drop` parameter, indicating `FALSE` (instead of the default value, `TRUE`), and then the subset will remain a `data.frame` object no matter what:

```
> df[ ,3, drop = FALSE]
  upper
1     A
2     B
3     C
4     D
```

Compare the output to the one from the previous example. Using `drop=FALSE` in the previous expression, we got a `data.frame` object (with four rows and one column) instead of a vector.

The other two methods of subsetting a `data.frame` object are using logical and character vectors as indices. Let's take a look at the following example:

```
> df[df$lower %in% c("a","d"), c("lower","upper")]
  lower upper
1     a     A
4     d     D
```

In this expression, if we put it in plain language, we are requesting to get the subset of `df` with the rows being where the values of the `lower` column are either `"a"` or `"d"`, and the columns are both `lower` and `upper`.

One very helpful function to use with `data.frame` objects is `complete.cases`. This function returns a logical vector, the same length as the number of rows in the `data.frame` object, indicating whether each row (case) is complete (has no `NA` values in it). When a given row is complete, the respective element in the logical vector will be `TRUE`; when a row is incomplete, the value will be `FALSE`. Then, the resulting logical vector can be used to remove the incomplete rows from a table as follows (note that the output is not printed here to save space):

```
> dat[complete.cases(dat), ]
```

Note that in this expression, we use the vector returned by `complete.cases` as a logical vector indicating the selection of rows in `dat` to be retained.

Calculating new data fields

As previously shown, we can assign new values to a column of a table (or to a subset of a column) using the $ operator. If the column name we assign does not exist in the table, a new column will be created to accommodate the data. Let's take a look at the following examples:

```
> df
  num lower upper
1   1     a     A
2   2     b     B
3   3     c     C
4   4     d     D
> df$word[df$num == 2] = "Two"
> df
  num lower upper word
1   1     a     A <NA>
2   2     b     B  Two
3   3     c     C <NA>
4   4     d     D <NA>
```

Here, we made an assignment of the character value "Two" to a subset of the word column (which did not previously exist in df) corresponding to the rows where the value of column num is equal to 2. As a result, a new column has been created, which contains the assigned value (and NA for all the other elements). Note that <NA> is simply the character representation of NA (the column word is a character vector).

As another example with our climatic data, we are going to create two new columns, holding the year and month of each measurement. For this purpose, we will first convert the date column to a Date object. Then, we will extract the years and months from the data in this column as follows (see the previous chapter for details):

```
> dat$date = as.Date(as.character(dat$date), format = "%Y%m%d")
> dat$month = as.numeric(format(dat$date, "%m"))
> dat$year = as.numeric(format(dat$date, "%Y"))
> head(dat)
            station station_name elevation latitude longitude
1 GHCND:SP000060010     IZANA SP      2371  28.3089  -16.4992
2 GHCND:SP000060010     IZANA SP      2371  28.3089  -16.4992
3 GHCND:SP000060010     IZANA SP      2371  28.3089  -16.4992
4 GHCND:SP000060010     IZANA SP      2371  28.3089  -16.4992
5 GHCND:SP000060010     IZANA SP      2371  28.3089  -16.4992
6 GHCND:SP000060010     IZANA SP      2371  28.3089  -16.4992
        date tpcp mmxt mmnt month year
```

```
1 1984-01-01 51.4   5.6 -0.5     1 1984
2 1984-02-01  0.0   9.8  2.8     2 1984
3 1984-03-01 68.7   7.2  0.2     3 1984
4 1984-04-01 13.6 12.2  3.5     4 1984
5 1984-05-01 21.4 11.8  3.0     5 1984
6 1984-06-01  6.5 19.6 10.5     6 1984
```

Using the first expression, we converted the `dat$date` vector to a `Date` object (and assigned it back to `dat$date`). In the second and third expressions, we extracted the month and year components, as numeric vectors, out of `dat$date` and assigned them to the new columns, `dat$month` and `dat$year`, respectively.

Writing a data.frame object to a CSV file

A `data.frame` object can be written to a CSV file with the `write.csv` function. The two first (and most important) parameters for this function indicate the name of the `data.frame` object, which we would like to save, and the path to the new file (including the new filename). These parameters have no defaults, so we need to specify them. For example, the following expression writes the `data.frame` object `df` to the `df.csv` file in the `C:\Data` directory:

```
> write.csv(df, "C:\\Data\\df.csv")
```

The newly created file when opened in Excel looks like the following screenshot:

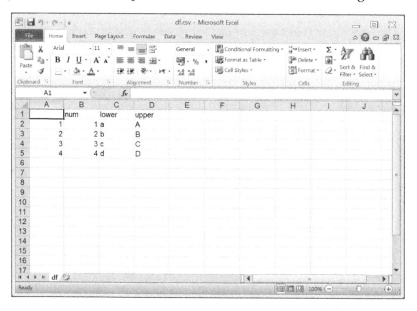

Note that row names (the numbers **1** to **4** in column **A**) and column names have been added; this behavior can be disabled when required.

Controlling code execution

So far, all of the code sections we have written were executed once in the same order as they were sent to the command line. However, one of the most important themes in programming is the flow control—operations that are used to control the sequences of our code execution. For example, we may want to induce the execution of a certain code section only if a condition is met (these are called conditional statements), or we may wish to execute a code section several times, over and over again (these are called loops). In this section, you will learn about three flow control commands: two to construct conditional statements and one to construct loops.

Conditioning execution with conditional statements

The purpose of conditional statements is to condition the execution of a given code section. For example, the second expression in the following code section is a conditional statement using the `if` operator:

```
> x = 3
> if(x > 2) {print("x is large!")}
[1] "x is large!"
```

A conditional statement is composed of the following elements:

- The conditional statement operator (`if`)
- The condition in parentheses (for example, `(x>2)`)
- Code section opening brackets (`{`)
- The code section to execute when the condition is met (for example, `print("x is large!")`)
- Code section closing brackets (`}`)
- Optionally, the `else` operator (`else`)
- Optionally, code section opening brackets (`{`)
- Optionally, the code to execute when the condition is not met
- Optionally, code section closing brackets (`}`)

Importantly, the condition should be an expression that returns a single logical value. The code section following this condition will then be executed if the value is TRUE or ignored if the value is FALSE. For example, if x is not larger than 2, nothing will happen since the print("x is large!") expression will not be executed:

```
> x = 0
> if(x > 2) {print("x is large!")}
```

Nothing is printed on screen.

The same way as with function definitions (see the previous chapter) and for loops (see the next section), code with only one expression does not have to be encompassed in parentheses {.

Optionally, we can use the else operator to add another code section. The code section after the else operator will be executed when the condition in if is FALSE as follows:

```
> x = 3
> if(x > 2) {print("x is large!")} else {print("x is small!")}
[1] "x is large!"
> x = 1
> if(x > 2) {print("x is large!")} else {print("x is small!")}
[1] "x is small!"
```

There is another conditional operator, specialized in working on vectors element by element, called ifelse. With ifelse, we need to supply three arguments: a logical vector, a value for TRUE (the yes parameter), and a value for FALSE (the no parameter). What we receive is a new vector with the same length as the input logical vector, where the TRUE and FALSE values have been replaced with the alternative values we supplied.

Regarding the replacement values for TRUE and FALSE, the most useful modes of operation are either to have them as vectors of length 1 (and then they are recycled to fill the entire length of the logical vector) or to have them as vectors of the same length as the logical vector (and then the elements of the logical vector are replaced with the respective elements either from the yes or no vector).

For example, the first mode of operation is useful when we want to classify the values of a given vector into two categories, according to a condition:

```
> dat$mmxt[1:7]
[1]  5.6  9.8  7.2 12.2 11.8 19.6 24.1
> ifelse(dat$mmxt[1:7] < 10, "cold", "warm")
[1] "cold" "cold" "cold" "warm" "warm" "warm" "warm"
```

Here, we used a condition on the first seven values of the mmxt column in dat, to produce a logical vector, and then classified its values into "cold" (temperature below 10 degrees) or "warm".

The second mode of operation is useful, for example, when we would like to perform either one of the two operations on each element of a vector (and to select which one, according to the value of the respective element). For example, we can use ifelse to get a vector of absolute values, if we reverse the sign of only the negative values in that vector as follows:

```
> x = c(-1,-8,2,5,-3,5,-9)
> ifelse(x < 0, -x, x)
[1] 1 8 2 5 3 5 9
```

Here, each element of x that is smaller than 0 (that is, negative) has been replaced by its respective opposite -x, while positive values were left as is, giving a vector of absolute values for all elements. By the way, a function to find the absolute values of a vector already exists (the abs function).

Repeatedly executing code sections with loops

Loops are used when we need a code section to be executed repeatedly. The way the number of times a code section is to be executed is determined distinguishes the different types of loops. We are going to introduce the for loop, which is especially useful in many data analysis tasks.

In a for loop, a code section is executed a predetermined number of times. This number of times is equal to the number of elements in a vector that we supply when we initiate the loop. The code section is thus executed once for each element in the vector; in each such run of the loop, the assignment of the current element in that vector is made to an object that we can then use in the code within the loop.

For example, the following expression executes a for loop:

```
> for(i in 1:5) {print(i)}
[1] 1
[1] 2
[1] 3
[1] 4
[1] 5
```

A `for` loop expression includes the following components:

- The `for` loop operator (`for`)
- The name of the object that will get the consecutive vector elements in each run (for example, `i`)
- The `in` operator (`in`)
- The loop vector (for example, `1:5`)
- The code section to be executed repeatedly (for example, `print(i)`)

In the preceding example, the code `print(i)` was executed five times as the number of elements in the vector `1:5`. In each run, the `i` object was assigned to the next element in `1:5`, and since the code section consists of the expression `print(i)`, we got the integers 1 to 5 printed consecutively.

Using conditional expressions and loops, we can construct more complex code where operations are applied to numerous objects (using loops) and adjustments of these operations are automatically being made, on the fly, for each of these objects (using conditional statements). However, as we shall see in the upcoming sections of this chapter, there are many functions in R that can bypass the necessity of explicitly defining loops in situations when a (simple) function needs to be repeatedly applied on subsets of our data. It is advisable to use such functions when possible, instead of loops, for the sake of code compactness and clarity. In situations when the operation we would like to repeatedly execute is more complex, however, possibly having several branches of decisions, using loops and conditional statements again becomes essential. We shall see such examples in *Chapter 8, Spatial Interpolation of Point Data*.

Automated calculations using the apply family of functions

In this section, you are going to learn about two very useful functions to apply an operation on the subsets of data. The two functions, `tapply` and `apply`, along with a few others, form a collection of functions called `apply` functions. The functions in the collection are used to apply (hence the name) a function we choose over subsets of an object, and then join the results to form a single object once again. The `apply` functions are a defining feature of R; they replace the necessity to write explicit loops in many common situations in data analysis, which makes the code shorter and more elegant.

Applying a function on separate parts of a vector

The `tapply` function is used to apply a function over different sections of a vector and then combine the results into a single object. To do this, we need to provide three arguments for the following three parameters:

- Vector A, which the function will operate upon (X)
- Vector B, which defines the subsets of vector A (INDEX)
- A function that will be applied to the subsets of vector A (FUN)

As an example, we shall use a short table, which is a random subset of six rows (out of the original 150) in the `iris` dataset (available in R by typing `iris`). These are measurements of four floral traits (first four columns) on different plants (rows) that belong to three different iris species (fifth column, `Species`). You can create a `data.frame` object such as the following example with `iris=iris[sample(1:nrow(iris),6),]` (note that since it is a random sample, the exact values will be different each time). The exact table being used in the examples is provided on the book's website (`iris2.csv`). Here is the `iris` dataset subset we are going to use:

```
> iris
    Sepal.Length Sepal.Width Petal.Length Petal.Width    Species
100          5.7         2.8          4.1         1.3 versicolor
45           5.1         3.8          1.9         0.4     setosa
90           5.5         2.5          4.0         1.3 versicolor
34           5.5         4.2          1.4         0.2     setosa
38           4.9         3.6          1.4         0.1     setosa
101          6.3         3.3          6.0         2.5  virginica
```

Using `tapply`, we can quickly find out, for example, the average petal width per species, as follows:

```
> x = tapply(iris$Petal.Width, iris$Species, mean)
> x
    setosa versicolor  virginica
 0.2333333  1.3000000  2.5000000
```

The first argument, `iris$Petal.Width`, is the vector on which we apply our function. The second argument, `iris$Species`, is the vector that defines the subsets in `iris$Petal.Width`. Basically, all elements in `iris$Petal.Width` at the positions with a unique value in `iris$Species` are treated as groups. The last argument is the function that we apply on the subsets of `iris$Petal.Width`; in this case, the `mean` function. Thus, the `iris$Petal.Width` vector was split into three subsets, a mean was calculated for each subset, and the results were combined once again.

The returned object of `tapply` is an `array`, which is a vector with an additional attribute stating the number and size of its dimensions. A one-dimensional array, which is what we have here, is identical to a vector in its usage. The reason that the returned object of `tapply` is an array, however, is that in some cases (which we will not cover here), the returned object will have more than one dimension, and thus cannot be represented by a vector (for example, when the function we apply returns more than one value, such as the `range` function). We will further elaborate on two-dimensional (`matrix`) and three-dimensional (`array`) vector-like objects in the next chapter.

Note that the array is named using the values in the grouping vector, so we can access any value of interest using its name as follows:

```
> x["setosa"]
   setosa
0.2333333
```

Also, if we wish, we can transform the result to a vector using `as.numeric` as follows:

```
> as.numeric(x)
[1] 0.2333333 1.3000000 2.5000000
```

As previously mentioned, the `apply` functions are similar to loops in purpose and concept, although simpler and clearer in their syntax. For example, the preceding operation can be performed using a `for` loop, although the code would be longer (and, arguably, less clear):

```
> x = NULL
> for(i in unique(iris$Species)) {
+ x = c(x, mean(iris$Petal.Width[iris$Species == i]))
+ }
> names(x) = unique(iris$Species)
> x
versicolor     setosa   virginica
 1.3000000  0.2333333   2.5000000
```

Here, we create an empty object (with `NULL`, the special value that denotes an empty object in R) and then go through the unique values in `iris$Species` using a loop, each time adding the mean of `iris$Petal.width` to the respective species in x. Finally, we edit the names attribute of the resulting vector, using the `names` function, to add the unique species names.

Let's see another example with `tapply` involving our climatic data. Say we are interested in finding out how many stations are there (and which ones) with at least one missing value within its respective time series of precipitation amount. For an individual station (such as the one named `"IZANA SP"`), we could check whether its `tpcp` column contains at least one `NA` value as follows:

```
> any(is.na(dat[dat$station_name == "IZANA SP", "tpcp"]))
[1] TRUE
```

The returned value is `TRUE`, meaning the answer is yes. Note that the operation consisted of three steps. We first created a subset of `dat` (consisting of the rows for which the station name is `"IZANA SP"` and the column name is `"tpcp"`). Since the subset is created from a single column, it was automatically simplified to a vector. Secondly, we looked for each element whether it is `NA` with the `is.na` function. Finally, we checked whether at least one element in the resulting logical vector is `TRUE`, with the `any` function.

To instantly perform this operation on all stations, we can use `tapply`:

```
> result = tapply(
+ dat$tpcp,
+ dat$station_name,
+ function(x) any(is.na(x)))
```

This time the values vector we use the `tapply` function upon is `dat$tpcp` (since we want to look for missing values in the precipitation data) and the vector that defines the subsets is `dat$station_name` (since we want to apply the function on data from each station separately). Finally, the function that we apply is a user-defined one; its definition is encompassed within the `tapply` function call for compactness. The function takes one argument (x) and returns `TRUE` or `FALSE` depending on whether x does or does not contain at least one `NA` value, respectively, the same way that we did in the previous code section.

The resulting array indicates, for each station, whether at least one precipitation measurement is missing. Here are its first ten elements:

```
> result[1:10]
          A CORUNA ALVEDRO SP              A CORUNA SP
                       FALSE                    FALSE
      ALBACETE LOS LLANOS SP         ALBACETE OBS. SP
                       FALSE                    FALSE
       ALMERIA AEROPUERTO SP       ASTURIAS AVILES SP
                       FALSE                    FALSE
                    AVILA SP BADAJOZ TALAVERA LA REAL SP
```

```
                     FALSE                          FALSE
        BARCELONA AEROPUERTO SP            BARCELONA SP
                     FALSE                          FALSE
```

To check how many stations have at least one missing value, we can simply use the sum function (see the previous chapter):

```
> sum(result)
[1] 11
```

The answer is that 11 stations have at least one NA value in their tpcp column. To see which stations these are, we can subset the result array with the array itself (NOT) since the TRUE values in that array exactly define the subset we are looking for:

```
> result[result]
  COLMENAR VIEJO FAMET SP      CORDOBA AEROPUERTO SP
                    TRUE                       TRUE
         GUADALAJARA SP                    IZANA SP
                    TRUE                       TRUE
                 JAEN SP PALENCIA OBSERVATORIO SP
                    TRUE                       TRUE
PAMPLONA OBSERVATORIO SP                PAMPLONA SP
                    TRUE                       TRUE
                 ROTA SP      SANTANDER CENTRO SP
                    TRUE                       TRUE
               TARIFA SP
                    TRUE
```

The values of the array are now unimportant (since they are all TRUE); we are actually interested only in the elements' names. The names attribute of an array (or of a vector for that matter) can be extracted with the names function, which we already met, as follows:

```
> names(result[result])
 [1] "COLMENAR VIEJO FAMET SP"   "CORDOBA AEROPUERTO SP"
 [3] "GUADALAJARA SP"            "IZANA SP"
 [5] "JAEN SP"                   "PALENCIA OBSERVATORIO SP"
 [7] "PAMPLONA OBSERVATORIO SP" "PAMPLONA SP"
 [9] "ROTA SP"                   "SANTANDER CENTRO SP"
[11] "TARIFA SP"
```

These are the names of the stations we were looking for, in the form of a character vector.

Applying a function on rows or columns of a table

The second function of the apply family that we will meet is `apply`. This function is also used to apply a certain function on subsets of data, but instead of operating on subsets defined by a grouping object, it does this on the margins of an array (or an object that is analogous to an array, such as a `data.frame` object with numeric values only). Applying a function on each row or each column of a table is, for example, such an operation. We will limit ourselves to this type of two-dimensional operation for now. In *Chapter 6, Modifying Rasters and Analyzing Raster Time Series*, we will see an example of `apply` involving three dimensions.

Similar to `tapply`, the first parameter of `apply` is the object we would like to base our calculation on (`X`), and the third parameter is the function we would like to apply (`FUN`). The second parameter (`MARGIN`), however, defines the dimension across which we would like to apply the function (rather than which subsets of the input, as in `tapply`). For example, the `data.frame` objects (and matrices, which will be introduced in the next chapter) have two dimensions: rows (dimension number 1) and columns (dimension number 2). When the input has more than two dimensions (such as in a three-dimensional array), we can apply a function on the third dimension as well and so on, although having an array of more than three dimensions is not common in practice.

Let's return to our `iris` example to see how `apply` works. Using `apply`, we can find out the mean measured value for each of the five individual plants by averaging the values on the first dimension (that is, the rows) as follows:

```
> apply(iris[, 1:4], 1, mean)
  100    45    90    34    38   101
3.475 2.800 3.325 2.825 2.500 4.525
```

We can also find the mean measured value for each of the four measured traits by averaging the values of the second dimension (that is, the columns) as follows:

```
> apply(iris[, 1:4], 2, mean)
Sepal.Length  Sepal.Width Petal.Length  Petal.Width
   5.5000000    3.3666667    3.1333333    0.9666667
```

Note that we are working only with the numeric part of the `iris` object (columns 1 to 4) since the function that we apply (`mean`) operates on numeric vectors.

We can also pass additional arguments to `apply`, which will, in turn, be passed to the specific function that we apply. For example, the `mean` function has an additional parameter, `na.rm`, which we can set to `FALSE` within the `apply` function call. In that case, we will be able to, for example, find out the column means excluding the missing values:

```
> iris[3,2] = NA
> iris
    Sepal.Length Sepal.Width Petal.Length Petal.Width    Species
100          5.7         2.8          4.1         1.3 versicolor
45           5.1         3.8          1.9         0.4     setosa
90           5.5          NA          4.0         1.3 versicolor
34           5.5         4.2          1.4         0.2     setosa
38           4.9         3.6          1.4         0.1     setosa
101          6.3         3.3          6.0         2.5  virginica
> apply(iris[, 1:4], 2, mean)
Sepal.Length  Sepal.Width Petal.Length  Petal.Width
   5.5000000           NA    3.1333333    0.9666667
> apply(iris[, 1:4], 2, mean, na.rm = TRUE)
Sepal.Length  Sepal.Width Petal.Length  Petal.Width
   5.5000000    3.5400000    3.1333333    0.9666667
```

Here, we first introduced an `NA` value to our `iris` table and then applied the `mean` function on the columns, first with the default arguments (`na.rm=FALSE`) and then with `na.rm` set to `TRUE`. Note that passing additional arguments can be done the same way in `tapply` as well.

Inference from tables by joining, reshaping, and aggregating

In this section, you will learn several more advanced operations involving tables. These include, in particular, reshaping of tables and joining the information from table pairs. The presented methods, together with the ones presented earlier, will compose quite a powerful toolbox, which will suffice for all table-related operations that you will use in this book. Since you will be using functions from contributed packages, you will first learn how to download and install them. The following three sections will then introduce functions to reshape, aggregate, and join tables, respectively.

Using contributed packages

All predefined objects in R (such as the functions and classes we have been using so far) are collected in libraries or *packages* (in R terminology). In order to use an object defined in a certain package, it first needs to be loaded into memory. This is done using the `library` function. So far, we did not use the `library` function, so how come we could use all of the functions we have been using? The answer is that several packages are distributed with the R installation file (~30 of them as of May 2014), and some of them are automatically loaded into computer memory when starting R (these are called base R packages); otherwise, we will need to load a package into memory if we would like to use its functions. For example, if we would like to use graphical functions from the `lattice` package (see the previous chapter), which is automatically installed with R, we need to execute the following expression first:

```
> library("lattice")
```

The argument for the `library` function is the name of the required package that we would like to load.

 By default, the `library` function can also accept package names without parentheses, so we can type `library(lattice)` instead of the previous expression.

In addition to the preinstalled packages, many contributed packages (~5500 as of May 2014) are located on the **Comprehensive R Archive Network (CRAN)**, which is a network of FTP and web servers storing up-to-date versions of official R packages (unofficial packages or packages currently under development are available from various other online sources, such as GitHub). To use one of the packages on CRAN, we first have to download it to our computer, which can be automatically done in R using the `install.packages` function. For example, to install the `reshape2` package (which we are going to use shortly), we need to execute the following expression:

```
> install.packages("reshape2")
```

Another contributed package we are going to use in this chapter is called `plyr`. Thus, it is necessary that you download both `reshape2` and `plyr` (using the `install.packages` function for each one) and load them into memory (using the `library` function, again for each one) before executing the upcoming examples of code.

To save space, from now on, the `install.packages` commands will not be written as part of the code sections, nor will commands loading packages using `library` be replicated in each and every instance the package is used. Instead, every time a code section requires a newly contributed package, you should make sure the respective package is loaded.

Remember that downloading a package (using the `install.packages` function) is a one-time procedure (unless a new version of the package came out and we would like to reinstall it). On the other hand, loading the package into memory (using the `library` function) is something we need to do in each new R session.

Here are a few more tips concerning the installation of packages:

- Packages installation is also accessible through the menus in both RGui and RStudio
- When packages installation is triggered, the user is prompted to select one of the CRAN Mirrors to download the package from
- When installing a new version of R, all packages will need to be reinstalled

Shifting between long and wide formats using melt and dcast

In this section, and the following one, you are going to learn several useful methods to reshape data. Reshaping operations are an inevitable step of every data analysis process since a lot (if not most) of the time, data we get to work with will be structured differently from what is required to use a given function or type of software. In data reshaping, we change the form our data takes (possibly also reducing its amount, by aggregation), but not the data itself. An example of a tool used for data reshaping, from other software, is the PivotTable tool in Excel.

The functions we are going to use in this and the upcoming sections belong to the contributed packages reshape2 and plyr. There are other ways to perform the presented operations in R; some of them use only base packages. However, the methods shown here are considered more intuitive and flexible. Introduction to these two packages, by their author Hadley Wickham, can be found in the *Journal of Statistical Software* (see *Appendix B, Cited References*). Note that one of these papers addresses the reshape package (rather than the more efficient reshape2 package, which was developed later), but the principles of reshape and reshape2 are the same, so the paper is well relevant to reshape2 users. A good introduction to data manipulation with R using (mostly) base packages can be found in the excellent book *Introduction to Data Technologies* (2009) by Paul Murrell (which is also available online).

The first operation you are going to learn about is the transformation between wide and long formats. A wide table consists of columns for each measured variable. For example, our dat table is in a wide format since it has a column for the station name, a column for the precipitation amount, a column for the minimum temperature, and so on. A long table is one where a single column holds the variable names and another holds the measured values. When switching from wide to long formats, we will usually be interested in intermediate forms, where some of the variables are in columns, and others are identified in a single column holding variables names. In reshape2 terminology, the former are called identifier variables (id.vars), while the latter are called measured variables (measure.vars). This will become clearer using an example.

The iris dataset we saw earlier is also in a wide format. To convert it to a long format, we can use the melt function, which is used to convert wide formats to long formats. When using melt, we need to specify the data.frame object to reshape, and the identity of the ID and measure variables (as character vectors). In fact, we can specify either the ID or measure variables, and the function will assume that the rest of the columns belong to the other kind. For example, the most reasonable approach in this particular case would be to use the species as an ID variable (since it describes each measured unit) and the flower dimensions traits as measure variables (since they are independent measurements conducted on each measured unit). Let's take a look at the following example:

```
> library(reshape2)
> iris_melt = melt(iris, id.vars = "Species")
```

The first several rows of the resulting table are printed as follows:

```
> head(iris_melt)
      Species     variable value
1 versicolor Sepal.Length   5.7
2     setosa Sepal.Length   5.1
3 versicolor Sepal.Length   5.5
4     setosa Sepal.Length   5.5
5     setosa Sepal.Length   4.9
6  virginica Sepal.Length   6.3
```

We can see that the ID variable (in this case there was only one, `Species`) retained its status as one of the columns. The rest of the columns, the measure variables (in this case there were four), disappeared; instead, two new columns were created (`variable` and `value`), holding the measure variables names and values, respectively. The number of rows is now 24 (four times the original number of rows, six), since the ID part is replicated four times, once for each of the measure variables.

Similarly, we can use the `melt` function to convert the climatic data table `dat` to a long format, specifying that the `tpcp`, `mmxt`, and `mmnt` columns contain measured variables. We shall assign it to a different object named `dat_melt`:

```
> dat_melt = melt(dat, measure.vars = c("tpcp","mmxt","mmnt"))
> head(dat_melt)
            station station_name elevation latitude longitude
1 GHCND:SP000060010     IZANA SP      2371  28.3089  -16.4992
2 GHCND:SP000060010     IZANA SP      2371  28.3089  -16.4992
3 GHCND:SP000060010     IZANA SP      2371  28.3089  -16.4992
4 GHCND:SP000060010     IZANA SP      2371  28.3089  -16.4992
5 GHCND:SP000060010     IZANA SP      2371  28.3089  -16.4992
6 GHCND:SP000060010     IZANA SP      2371  28.3089  -16.4992
        date month year variable value
1 1984-01-01     1 1984     tpcp  51.4
2 1984-02-01     2 1984     tpcp   0.0
3 1984-03-01     3 1984     tpcp  68.7
4 1984-04-01     4 1984     tpcp  13.6
5 1984-05-01     5 1984     tpcp  21.4
6 1984-06-01     6 1984     tpcp   6.5
```

We can check and see that the molten table `dat_melt` has exactly three times more rows than the original table `dat`.

The long format is useful in its own right in many cases; for example, when we make a plot with three panels, one for each measured variable, we need to have the panel IDs in a single column, which is exactly what we have now. In addition, molten tables serve as an input to another function in the `reshape2` package called `dcast`, which is used to cast the data back into a wide format. However, this time we do not have to return exactly to the original table (on which we previously applied `melt`). Instead, we can specify exactly what we would like to have in the rows and columns. The way we specify the variables to appear in rows and columns is through a `formula` object (see the previous chapter), which may have the form: `var1+var2+var3~var4+var5`. The variables to the left of the ~ operator (in this case, `var1`, `var2`, and `var3`) are going to appear as single columns in the new table; the variables to the right of the ~ operator (in this case, `var4` and `var5`) are going to populate new columns, with the values going back from the `value` column to these new columns. For convenience, we can use the . symbol to indicate no variable or the . . . symbol to indicate all remaining variables, either to the left or right of the ~ operator.

The behavior of `dcast` can be best demonstrated through examples (for additional examples, see the 2007 paper by Hadley Wickham). For example, to get back our original table, we can indicate that we would like the values in the variable column to form new columns as follows:

```
> dat2 = dcast(dat_melt, ... ~ variable)
```

The order of the columns in the resulting table is slightly different; otherwise, the table is identical to the original `dat` table:

```
> head(dat2)
          station station_name elevation latitude longitude
1 GHCND:SP000060010      IZANA SP      2371  28.3089  -16.4992
2 GHCND:SP000060010      IZANA SP      2371  28.3089  -16.4992
3 GHCND:SP000060010      IZANA SP      2371  28.3089  -16.4992
4 GHCND:SP000060010      IZANA SP      2371  28.3089  -16.4992
5 GHCND:SP000060010      IZANA SP      2371  28.3089  -16.4992
6 GHCND:SP000060010      IZANA SP      2371  28.3089  -16.4992
        date month year tpcp mmxt  mmnt
1 1984-01-01     1 1984 51.4  5.6  -0.5
2 1984-02-01     2 1984  0.0  9.8   2.8
3 1984-03-01     3 1984 68.7  7.2   0.2
4 1984-04-01     4 1984 13.6 12.2   3.5
5 1984-05-01     5 1984 21.4 11.8   3.0
6 1984-06-01     6 1984  6.5 19.6  10.5
```

Alternately, we can have the months form new columns, as follows:

```
> dat2 = dcast(dat_melt, station+station_name+variable+year~month)
> head(dat2)
          station      station_name variable year    1    2    3
1 GHCND:SP000003195 MADRID RETIRO SP     tpcp 1984 25.3 37.2 58.0
2 GHCND:SP000003195 MADRID RETIRO SP     tpcp 1985 67.8 45.1  6.0
3 GHCND:SP000003195 MADRID RETIRO SP     tpcp 1986 10.6 57.0 22.2
4 GHCND:SP000003195 MADRID RETIRO SP     tpcp 1987 93.3 42.9  6.7
5 GHCND:SP000003195 MADRID RETIRO SP     tpcp 1988 60.0 20.9  1.1
6 GHCND:SP000003195 MADRID RETIRO SP     tpcp 1989  9.9 19.5 23.8
     4    5    6    7    8    9   10    11    12
1 39.2 82.4 35.6  0.0  7.1  7.1 30.1 161.0  11.3
2 36.8 29.9 24.1  5.4  0.0  0.0  0.0  39.9  83.8
3 57.3 12.0  1.0 37.1 16.4 47.5 93.8  13.6  19.0
4 63.1 58.4  7.8 43.9 14.5 11.9 58.5  64.8  79.1
5 96.6 46.5 49.8  9.5  0.0  0.0 79.2  50.1   0.2
6 52.2 97.7 12.7 13.3  3.2 37.5  5.9 146.4 138.6
```

Note that this time we omitted some of the variables from the resulting table (elevation, latitude, and so on), and made the months' levels (there are 12 of these) appear in separate columns, with the values of the respective climatic variable for each month in the cells of the given column. This form is ideal to answer questions such as which month is the warmest in each station (using apply, for example).

The casting operations we have performed so far involved the retention of all original data in the resulting table. What happens when we instruct the creation of a table that cannot contain all of our original data? In this case, aggregation takes place and we need to specify the function that will be used for aggregation (otherwise, the default function length will be used). For example, we can calculate the mean climatic conditions in Spain per year, as follows:

```
> dat2 = dcast(dat_melt, year ~ variable, mean, na.rm = TRUE)
> head(dat2)
  year     tpcp     mmxt       mmnt
1 1984 54.34180 19.38194  9.381115
2 1985 45.13103 20.31096  9.793890
3 1986 47.55329 19.75327  9.681250
4 1987 57.09826 20.31684 10.350206
5 1988 47.78863 20.07662  9.934514
6 1989 54.82944 20.97615 10.654617
```

A disadvantage of aggregation with dcast is that we must apply the same function across all variables. In the next section, you will learn about a more flexible aggregation method.

Aggregating with ddply

There are several functions in the plyr package that are used to apply operations on the subsets of data and then combine the subsets once again into a single object. This may sound familiar; indeed the plyr package was intended to comprise an alternative, in many cases an easier one, to apply and other base R functions. One of the most commonly used functions from this package, and the one you are going to learn about in this section, is called ddply.

> New packages namely dplyr and tidyr have recently appeared on CRAN; they are intended to serve as even faster and more efficient alternatives to plyr and (partially) reshape2. Since these packages are currently under development, they are not used in the examples in this book.

The ddply function operates on a data.frame object returning a new data.frame. It first splits the table to subsets according to the unique levels in one or more columns. The data from each subset is then used to calculate a single value, for each of the new columns in the new data.frame object. The user specifies exactly how this will be done; more importantly, the new columns in the resulting table can be calculated based on values from more than one column in the original table.

Let's demonstrate the functionality of ddply on iris. We will calculate the average area size of a flower's petals and sepals, as per species:

```
> library(plyr)
> ddply(iris,
+ .(Species),
+ summarize,
+ sepal_area = mean(Sepal.Length * Sepal.Width),
+ petal_area = mean(Petal.Length * Petal.Width))
     Species sepal_area petal_area
1     setosa      20.04  0.3933333
2 versicolor         NA  5.2650000
3  virginica      20.79 15.0000000
```

As we can see, the `ddply` function call contains several arguments:

- The input `data.frame` (for example, `iris`).
- The name(s) of the column(s), which defines subsets, in parentheses and preceded by `.` (for example, `.(Species)`). If there is more than one name, they will be separated by commas.
- The mode of operation; possible methods are as follows:
  - `summarize`: The new columns form a new, aggregated, table
  - `transform`: The new columns are appended back to the input table
- The fourth argument and onward (fifth, sixth, and so on) are the user-specified expressions for calculation of new columns based on values in the original columns.

The preceding function call thus indicates that we would like to break the `iris` table into subsets based on the unique values in the `Species` column, and create a new `data.frame` object with a column that specifies the levels (`Species`) and two new columns, `sepal_area` and `petal_area`. These columns will contain the means of the products of length and width for the respective trait. Note that the `NA` value for the `sepal_area` column of species, `versicolor`, is due to the `NA` value we previously inserted.

The instruction to create a new table is given by the word `summarize`. If we would have replaced the word `summarize` with `transform`, the values from the new columns would have been added to the input table, rather than creating a new (aggregated) table, as follows:

```
> ddply(iris,
+ .(Species),
+ transform,
+ sepal_area = mean(Sepal.Length * Sepal.Width),
+ petal_area = mean(Petal.Length * Petal.Width))
  Sepal.Length Sepal.Width Petal.Length Petal.Width    Species
1          5.1         3.8          1.9         0.4     setosa
2          5.5         4.2          1.4         0.2     setosa
3          4.9         3.6          1.4         0.1     setosa
4          5.7         2.8          4.1         1.3 versicolor
5          5.5          NA          4.0         1.3 versicolor
6          6.3         3.3          6.0         2.5  virginica
  sepal_area petal_area
1      20.04  0.3933333
2      20.04  0.3933333
```

```
3      20.04  0.3933333
4         NA  5.2650000
5         NA  5.2650000
6      20.79 15.0000000
```

As you can see, the original table has been preserved; just that our two newly calculated columns (`sepal_area` and `petal_area`) have been joined to it on the right. Note that the values in these columns are the averages of the subsets (the species). Thus, within each subset, the values are duplicated.

As another example, we will now use `ddply` in order to aggregate our climatic data table, from a monthly to an annual timescale. In other words, we would like to obtain annual averages (in case of temperature) or annual sums (in case of precipitation) for climatic variables. For this, we will first filter out those variable/year combinations where not all the 12 months are present. For example, if the minimum monthly temperature data at the `"IZANA SP"` station for 1985 is available only for 11 (rather than 12) months, we would like to remove the minimum temperature data for that year and from that station altogether, to reduce the bias in the annual average. To do this, we need to find out how many non-missing values we have for every station/year/variable combination. We will use `ddply` to our molten `dat_melt` table:

```
> dat3 = ddply(dat_melt,
+ .(station, year, variable),
+ transform,
+ months_available = length(value[!is.na(value)]))
> head(dat3)
             station      station_name elevation latitude longitude
1 GHCND:SP000003195 MADRID RETIRO SP         667  40.4117   -3.6781
2 GHCND:SP000003195 MADRID RETIRO SP         667  40.4117   -3.6781
3 GHCND:SP000003195 MADRID RETIRO SP         667  40.4117   -3.6781
4 GHCND:SP000003195 MADRID RETIRO SP         667  40.4117   -3.6781
5 GHCND:SP000003195 MADRID RETIRO SP         667  40.4117   -3.6781
6 GHCND:SP000003195 MADRID RETIRO SP         667  40.4117   -3.6781
        date month year variable value months_available
1 1984-01-01     1 1984     tpcp  25.3               12
2 1984-02-01     2 1984     tpcp  37.2               12
3 1984-03-01     3 1984     tpcp  58.0               12
4 1984-04-01     4 1984     tpcp  39.2               12
5 1984-05-01     5 1984     tpcp  82.4               12
6 1984-06-01     6 1984     tpcp  35.6               12
```

The new table `dat3`, which we just created, contains all of the data from `dat_melt` (since `transform` was used), in addition to the new `months_available` column, which contains the number of non-NA elements for the respective `.(station,year,variable)` subset. Using this column, we can now remove those station/year/variable subsets that have less than 12 months of data:

```
> nrow(dat3)
[1] 85608
> dat3 = dat3[dat3$months_available == 12, ]
> nrow(dat3)
[1] 80976
```

Overall 4,632 rows have been removed. Now we can aggregate the `dat3` table, knowing that the annual values will always be based on 12 months of data. We will do it in two steps.

First, we will create a table to only hold the location data (`latitude`, `longitude`, and `elevation` columns) for each meteorological station. It is frequently useful to have a table such as this, for example, to plot the stations' spatial locations (which we are going to do in *Chapter 7, Combining Vector and Raster Datasets*):

```
> spain_stations = ddply(dat3,
+ .(station),
+ summarize,
+ latitude = latitude[1],
+ longitude = longitude[1],
+ elevation = elevation[1])
> head(spain_stations)
            station latitude longitude elevation
1 GHCND:SP000003195  40.4117   -3.6781       667
2 GHCND:SP000004452  38.8831   -6.8292       185
3 GHCND:SP000006155  36.6667   -4.4881         7
4 GHCND:SP000008027  43.3075   -2.0392       251
5 GHCND:SP000008181  41.2928    2.0697         4
6 GHCND:SP000008202  40.9592   -5.4981       790
```

Here, the aggregation was performed by the `station` column only; therefore, we obtain a rather short table with one row for each meteorological station (96 rows in total):

```
> nrow(spain_stations)
[1] 96
```

Note that with `latitude=latitude[1]` we say, in plain language: take the first latitude value you see and assign it to the aggregated table, per station. Since the location of a given station should be constant over time, we can take any of the latitude values. However, we do not know exactly how many rows of data each station has (actually, in this particular case, we do know it is at least 12 since otherwise the data for that station could not have formed a complete 12 months series and would have been removed altogether); therefore, selecting the first one is a reasonable option.

We will save this `data.frame` object to a file since we will use it in subsequent chapters:

```
> write.csv(spain_stations, "C:\\Data\\spain_stations.csv",
+ row.names = FALSE)
```

The additional parameter `row.names` indicates whether we would like row names to be saved as an additional column in the CSV file (in this case, we do not).

Next, we will aggregate the climatic data itself, per station/variable/year combination. Here, our purpose is to find the sum of each month (in case of rainfall) or the average of each month (in case of temperature). We will use `ifelse` to assign a sum of the 12 values when the variable is `tpcp` or the average otherwise (when the variable is either `mmxt` or `mmnt`). Let's take a look at the following example:

```
> spain_annual = ddply(dat3,
+ .(station, variable, year),
+ summarize,
+ value = ifelse(variable[1] == "tpcp",
+ sum(value, na.rm = TRUE),
+ mean(value, na.rm = TRUE)))
> head(spain_annual)
          station variable year value
1 GHCND:SP000003195    tpcp 1984 494.3
2 GHCND:SP000003195    tpcp 1985 338.8
3 GHCND:SP000003195    tpcp 1986 387.5
4 GHCND:SP000003195    tpcp 1987 544.9
5 GHCND:SP000003195    tpcp 1988 413.9
6 GHCND:SP000003195    tpcp 1989 560.7
```

Note that, once again, we consider only the first element in the variable column (`variable[1]`) to make the decision on whether to use the `sum` or `mean` function since all values of the column variable are, by definition, identical within a given station/year/variable combination.

We will save this `data.frame` object to a file for later use:

```
> write.csv(spain_annual, "C:\\Data\\spain_annual.csv",
+ row.names = FALSE)
```

Our final exercise related to the processing of tabular data would be to see how we can join the `spain_stations` and `spain_annual` tables into a single table, containing both the station coordinates and climatic data. For this, you first have to learn how to join tables, which we shall do in the next section.

Joining tables with join

Joining tables is another common operation in data analysis. Those working with spatial data may be familiar with the task of joining data from an external table (such as an Excel file) with the attribute table of a spatial dataset (such an ESRI Shapefile), which is an example of a join operation.

The `plyr` library offers a very convenient function called `join`, to join `data.frame` objects. Note, once again, that there are other ways to perform the task in R, such as using the `merge` function from the base packages. However, in addition to its simplicity, an important advantage of `join` is that it always preserves the original order of rows in the `data.frame` object we join to. This feature will be especially important later, when performing the previously mentioned task of joining tables to attributes of spatial datasets (see *Chapter 5, Working with Points, Lines, and Polygons*).

The first two parameters of the `join` function are x and y, which indicate the names of the two `data.frame` objects to join, and the third parameter is by, which indicates by which column(s) to join. The other two parameters indicate, by default, that we would like to perform a left join (`type="left"`, retaining all rows of x, as opposed to a `"right"` join where we retain all rows of y) and retain all records if there are duplicates (`match="all"`), which is what we would like to do in most cases (see `?join` for more details).

For example, let's say we have a table where each row corresponds to a date, and we would like to create a new column that indicates the season that date belongs to (winter, spring, summer, or fall). One way of doing this is to create a table indicating the season each month belongs to, and then join the second table to the first one, according to the common month columns.

For this example, we will read another CSV file with a series of dates. The `dates` table looks as follows:

```
> dates = read.csv("C:\\Data\\modis_dates.csv")
> head(dates)
  image day month year
1     1  18     2 2000
2     2   5     3 2000
3     3  21     3 2000
4     4   6     4 2000
5     5  22     4 2000
6     6   8     5 2000
```

This table indicates the dates of the MODIS satellite images acquisition with the `image` column corresponding to bands in a multiband raster, which we will work with later (see the next chapter).

As another exercise of working with dates, we will create a column of the `Date` class from the `day`, `month`, and `year` columns as follows:

```
> dates$date = as.Date(
+ paste(dates$year, dates$month, dates$day, sep = "-"))
> head(dates)
  image day month year       date
1     1  18     2 2000 2000-02-18
2     2   5     3 2000 2000-03-05
3     3  21     3 2000 2000-03-21
4     4   6     4 2000 2000-04-06
5     5  22     4 2000 2000-04-22
6     6   8     5 2000 2000-05-08
```

Let's now create a table of seasons. To do this, we will use the `rep` function with a parameter we have not used so far, `each`, which indicates that we want to repeat each element of a given vector several times (rather than repeat the whole vector):

```
> month = c(12, 1:11)
> month
 [1] 12  1  2  3  4  5  6  7  8  9 10 11
> season = rep(c("winter","spring","summer","fall"), each = 3)
> season
 [1] "winter" "winter" "winter" "spring" "spring" "spring"
 [7] "summer" "summer" "summer" "fall"   "fall"   "fall"
> seasons = data.frame(month, season)
> seasons
  month season
```

```
1      12 winter
2       1 winter
3       2 winter
4       3 spring
5       4 spring
6       5 spring
7       6 summer
8       7 summer
9       8 summer
10      9  fall
11     10  fall
12     11  fall
```

The seasons table now indicates which season a given month belongs to. The final step will be to join the two tables: dates and seasons. The following expression states that we would like to join the seasons table to the dates table by month:

```
> dates = join(dates, seasons, "month")
> head(dates)
  image day month year       date season
1     1  18     2 2000 2000-02-18 winter
2     2   5     3 2000 2000-03-05 spring
3     3  21     3 2000 2000-03-21 spring
4     4   6     4 2000 2000-04-06 spring
5     5  22     4 2000 2000-04-22 spring
6     6   8     5 2000 2000-05-08 spring
```

We will use this table in several examples in the subsequent chapters.

Returning to our climatic data example, we will now join the two tables we got in the previous section: the stations, coordinates summary (spain_stations) and the aggregated annual climatic data (spain_annual). The resulting data.frame object will be named combined, as shown in the following expression:

```
> combined = join(spain_stations,
+ spain_annual,
+ by = "station",
+ type = "right")
```

Note that here we use the type="right" option since we would like to retain all rows in the second table spain_annual (rather than retain all the rows in the first table, as shown in the previous example).

The table looks as follows:

```
> head(combined)
          station latitude longitude elevation variable year
1 GHCND:SP000003195  40.4117   -3.6781       667     tpcp 1984
2 GHCND:SP000003195  40.4117   -3.6781       667     tpcp 1985
3 GHCND:SP000003195  40.4117   -3.6781       667     tpcp 1986
4 GHCND:SP000003195  40.4117   -3.6781       667     tpcp 1987
5 GHCND:SP000003195  40.4117   -3.6781       667     tpcp 1988
6 GHCND:SP000003195  40.4117   -3.6781       667     tpcp 1989
  value
1 494.3
2 338.8
3 387.5
4 544.9
5 413.9
6 560.7
```

As the output shows, this table contains duplicated data since the latitude, longitude, and elevation records are identical in each station/variable/year combination. In such cases, it is more efficient to keep two separate tables (such as spain_stations and spain_annual) rather than join all the data into a single table (such as combined).

Summary

In this chapter, you learned how tabular data is represented in R. We covered many of the basic (such as subsetting and calculating new columns) and more advanced (such as reshaping and joining) techniques related to tables. We also met several operators used to control code execution, specifically to condition code execution or induce repeated code execution.

In the remaining chapters of this book, we are going to focus on working with spatial data in R. However, we shall utilize the methods presented in this chapter regarding the data.frame class, the flow control functions and the apply functions, quite frequently.

4

Working with Rasters

In this chapter, we move on to the realm of spatial data analysis in R. We begin by introducing the properties and usage principles of the classes used to store raster data in R. For that matter, we are going to first introduce the simpler (nonspatial) structures that are conceptually related to rasters: matrices and arrays. We then cover the more sophisticated classes defined in the `raster` package to represent spatial raster data. You will learn to create, subset, and save objects of these classes as well as to query the characteristics of rasters we have at hand. Afterwards, you will learn two basic operations involving rasters: overlay and reclassification. At the same time, we will see some examples of visualizing raster data in R to help us get a better understanding of the data we have.

In this chapter, we'll cover the following topics:

- Using matrices to represent two-dimensional sets of numeric values
- Using arrays to represent three-dimensional sets of numeric values
- Using classes for single band and multiband rasters in the `raster` package
- Reading and writing raster files
- Exploring the properties of a given raster object
- Basic visualization of rasters in R
- Subsetting rasters
- Converting raster objects to simpler data structures and vice versa
- Performing raster algebra operations
- Reclassifying raster values

Using the matrix and array classes

A raster is essentially a matrix with spatial reference information. Similarly, a multiband raster is essentially a three-dimensional array with spatial reference information. Therefore, before proceeding with spatial rasters, we will cover some prerequisite material on working with these (simpler) objects in this section—matrices and arrays. Moreover, as we shall see later, matrices and arrays are common data structures with many uses in R.

Representing two-dimensional data with a matrix

A matrix object is a two-dimensional collection of elements, all of the same type (as opposed to a data.frame object; see the previous chapter), where the number of elements in all rows (and, naturally, all columns) is identical. Matrix objects have many uses in R. For example, certain functions take matrices as their arguments (such as the focal function to filter rasters) or return matrices (such as the extract function to extract raster values; we will meet both these functions in the subsequent chapters).

A matrix object can be created with the matrix function by specifying its values (in the form of a vector) and dimensions as follows:

```
> matrix(1:6, ncol = 3)
     [,1] [,2] [,3]
[1,]    1    3    5
[2,]    2    4    6
```

The first four parameters of the matrix function are as follows:

- data: The vector of values for the matrix (for example, 1:6)
- nrow: The number of rows
- ncol: The number of columns (for example, 3)
- byrow: Whether the matrix is filled column by column (FALSE, which is the default value) or row by row (TRUE)

The nrow and ncol parameters determine the number of rows and columns, respectively. We can specify either one of these parameters, and the other will be calculated taking into account the overall number of elements. Let's take a look at the following example:

```
> matrix(1:6, nrow = 3)
     [,1] [,2]
[1,]    1    4
[2,]    2    5
[3,]    3    6
```

```
> matrix(1:6, nrow = 2)
     [,1] [,2] [,3]
[1,]    1    3    5
[2,]    2    4    6
```

Note that when the allocated number of cells is smaller or larger than the number of values in the vector that is being used to populate the matrix, the vector is either deprecated or recycled, respectively. Let's take a look at the following examples:

```
> matrix(12:1, ncol = 4, nrow = 2)
     [,1] [,2] [,3] [,4]
[1,]   12   10    8    6
[2,]   11    9    7    5
> matrix(12:1, ncol = 4, nrow = 4)
     [,1] [,2] [,3] [,4]
[1,]   12    8    4   12
[2,]   11    7    3   11
[3,]   10    6    2   10
[4,]    9    5    1    9
```

There are several useful functions to examine the properties of a matrix. You are familiar with them from *Chapter 1, The R Environment*, and *Chapter 2, Working with Vectors and Time Series*, since they are analogous to the functions we used with vectors and `data.frame` objects. For example, the `length` function returns the number of elements a matrix has as follows:

```
> x = matrix(7:12, ncol = 3, byrow = TRUE)
> x
     [,1] [,2] [,3]
[1,]    7    8    9
[2,]   10   11   12
> length(x)
[1] 6
```

The `nrow` and `ncol` functions return the number of rows and columns as follows:

```
> nrow(x)
[1] 2
> ncol(x)
[1] 3
```

The `dim` function returns both (the number of rows and columns) at the same time:

```
> dim(x)
[1] 2 3
```

Using the `as.vector` function, we can convert a matrix into a vector as follows (note that the values in the vector will always be ordered by columns):

```
> as.vector(x)
[1]  7 10  8 11  9 12
```

Similar to what we saw regarding `data.frame` objects, we can subset matrices using two-dimensional indices. For example, to get the values that occupy the first and third columns in matrix x, we will use the following expression:

```
> x[, c(1,3)]
     [,1] [,2]
[1,]    7    9
[2,]   10   12
```

To get the values that occupy the second row in matrix x, we will use the following expression:

```
> x[2, ]
[1] 10 11 12
```

The previous example demonstrates that the resulting object is simplified to a vector if the values are retrieved from a single row or column. Setting the `drop` parameter to `FALSE` will suppress this behavior, similar to what we saw for the `data.frame` objects (see the previous chapter):

```
> x[2, , drop = FALSE]
     [,1] [,2] [,3]
[1,]   10   11   12
```

The assignment of new values to subsets of a given matrix is also possible using the assignment operator. For example, we can create an empty 3 x 3 matrix m and then populate some of its cells as follows:

```
> m = matrix(NA, ncol = 3, nrow = 3)
> m
     [,1] [,2] [,3]
[1,]   NA   NA   NA
[2,]   NA   NA   NA
[3,]   NA   NA   NA
> m[2:3, 1:2] = matrix(1:4, nrow = 2)
> m
     [,1] [,2] [,3]
[1,]   NA   NA   NA
[2,]    1    3   NA
[3,]    2    4   NA
```

We can also use the `apply` function to make calculations on rows or columns of a matrix, in exactly the same way as with the `data.frame` objects (see the previous chapter). For example, we can calculate the means of all columns in matrix `x` as follows:

```
> apply(x, 2, mean)
[1]   8.5   9.5 10.5
```

In fact, there are two specialized functions named `rowMeans` and `colMeans` for the specific tasks of calculating row and column means, respectively. Thus, for example, the following expression gives exactly the same result as the previous one:

```
> colMeans(x)
[1]   8.5   9.5 10.5
```

Representing more than two dimensions with an array

While vectors are used to represent one-dimensional sets of elements (see *Chapter 2, Working with Vectors and Time Series*), and `matrix` is a specialized class to represent two-dimensional sets of elements (see the previous section), the `array` class is more general. It is used to represent sets of elements having any number of dimensions (including one and two).

We can create an `array` object (a three-dimensional one, for example) using the `array` function:

```
> y = array(1:24, c(2,2,3))
> y
, , 1

     [,1] [,2]
[1,]    1    3
[2,]    2    4

, , 2

     [,1] [,2]
[1,]    5    7
[2,]    6    8

, , 3

     [,1] [,2]
[1,]    9   11
[2,]   10   12
```

The first argument we entered (`1:24`) defined the values, while the second argument (`c(2,2,3)`) defined the number of dimensions and their lengths. As opposed to creating a matrix with the `matrix` function, we need to explicitly specify the lengths of all dimensions (or else a one-dimensional object will be created by default) with the `array` function. In the previous example, we were interested in having three dimensions—two rows, two columns, and three layers (using raster terminology; see the following section). Thus, we specified their lengths as (2,2,3) using a vector of length 3.

Naturally, a three-dimensional array has a three-dimensional indexing system. For example, we can reach the (2,1,3) element in our array `y` as follows:

```
> y[2,1,3]
[1] 10
```

Working with arrays is very similar to working with vectors and matrices, and the application of many of the functions we have previously seen is intuitive. For example, we can use the `apply` function to find the means of all elements in each layer (or third dimension):

```
> apply(y, 3, mean)
[1]   2.5  6.5 10.5
```

We will see an example involving the `rowMeans` function and three-dimensional array objects in *Chapter 6, Modifying Rasters and Analyzing Raster Time Series*.

Data structures for rasters in the raster package

A raster is a rectangular grid of numeric values, referenced to a certain geographical extent. As previously mentioned, spatial referencing is what differentiates a raster from the simpler data structures (matrices and arrays) we have seen previously. A raster can have a single value in each cell (a single band, or single layer, raster—analogous to a matrix) or several values (a multiband, or multilayer, raster—analogous to an array). Rasters conceptually differ from vector layers, which are data structures to represent non-gridded objects such as spatial points, lines, and polygons (these will be covered in the next chapter).

In this book, we are going to work with classes to represent rasters from the `raster` package. This package does not come with the R installation, so we first have to install it using `install.packages` (see the previous chapter). We will also need to install the `rgdal` package since functions in the `raster` package use functions defined in `rgdal` for certain tasks, such as input/output operations. Taking a look at the official overview of R packages for spatial data analysis (`http://cran.r-project.org/web/views/Spatial.html`) is highly recommended at this stage. This web page is useful to find out how the previously mentioned packages `raster` and `rgdal` (and the ones to be introduced in the upcoming chapters) fit within the broader ecosystem of spatial data analysis tools available in R.

> The `rgdal` package, which stands for **Geospatial Data Abstraction Library (GDAL)** extensions to R, is a very important one to work with spatial data, and we will cover it in several contexts. The name GDAL may be familiar to some readers; GDAL is a C library frequently used in other software (such as QGIS) and programming languages (such as Python). In fact, there are four C libraries providing the core functionality to work with spatial data in R interfaced through R functions. They are GDAL, OGR, PROJ.4 (which are available using functions in the `rgdal` package), and GEOS (which is available through functions in the `rgeos` package).

The remaining part of this chapter is going to introduce the basic usage of the `raster` package with two real-world examples of remote sensing data. More advanced functionality of this package, as well as examples with another common type of raster data, **Digital Elevation Model (DEM)**, will be introduced in subsequent chapters. We'll be creating a third type of raster—predicted surfaces from spatial interpolation—in *Chapter 8*, *Spatial Interpolation of Point Data*.

> Similarly to the GIS software, the `raster` package has the capability of working with big rasters that cannot be accommodated in the RAM (in such cases, for example, the data are automatically processed in chunks and the results are written to temporary files on disk).

A comprehensive overview of the range of capabilities the `raster` package offers can also be found in its accompanying introductory tutorial (`http://cran.r-project.org/web/packages/raster/vignettes/Raster.pdf`).

Creating single band rasters

There are three classes to represent spatial rasters in the `raster` packages. These are `RasterLayer`, `RasterStack`, and `RasterBrick`. The first class is used to represent single band rasters (see the following examples), whereas the last two classes are used to represent multiband rasters (see the next section).

The `RasterLayer` class represents a single band raster. A new `RasterLayer` object can be created using the `raster` function in several ways. For example, a `matrix` object can be converted to a `RasterLayer` object as follows:

```
> library(raster)
> r1 = raster(x)
> r1
class       : RasterLayer
dimensions  : 2, 3, 6  (nrow, ncol, ncell)
resolution  : 0.3333333, 0.5  (x, y)
extent      : 0, 1, 0, 1  (xmin, xmax, ymin, ymax)
coord. ref. : NA
data source : in memory
names       : layer
values      : 7, 12  (min, max)
```

We see that the print method for `RasterLayer` objects does something different from what we have seen so far. Rather than printing all values the object is composed of, a summary of certain properties of the particular `RasterLayer` object is given. We will see how to directly access some of these properties later. For now, it is worth repeating that a `RasterLayer` object (as opposed to a matrix) has spatial reference information, that is, a certain resolution, extent, and **Coordinate Reference System (CRS)**. Naturally, the particular raster r, which we just created from a plain numeric matrix, has no CRS, and its resolution and extent have been automatically generated by the `raster` function (the extent is between 0 and 1 on both the x and y axes; the resolution is calculated accordingly).

A more common way to create a `raster` object in R is to read the raster data from a file. For example, given that the `raster` and `rgdal` packages are installed on our system and the raster file `landsat_15_10_1998.tif` exists in the `C:\Data` directory, the following expression will read the contents of its first band and assign it to an object named `band1` of class `RasterLayer`:

```
> band1 = raster("C:\\Data\\landsat_15_10_1998.tif")
```

Reading files from disk, as mentioned earlier, is done through the `rgdal` package (which is automatically loaded, if it was not already, when trying to read a file using the `raster` function). At present, there are ~100 supported input formats (you can get a list of these by typing `getGDALDriverNames()$name` once `rgdal` is loaded). These include, for example, the frequently used GeoTIFF (`*.tif` or `*.tiff`), which we will use in the examples in this book, and ERDAS IMAGINE image (`*.img`) formats.

Printing the properties of raster `band1` and comparing them to those of `r1` from the previous example will demonstrate that this time we do have meaningful spatial reference information in the `RasterLayer` object `band1`, as shown in the following example:

```
> band1
class        : RasterLayer
band         : 1  (of  6  bands)
dimensions   : 960, 791, 759360   (nrow, ncol, ncell)
resolution   : 30, 30  (x, y)
extent       : 663945, 687675, 3459375, 3488175   (xmin, xmax, ymin$
coord. ref.  : +proj=utm +zone=36 +ellps=WGS84 +units=m +no_defs
data source  : C:\Data\landsat_15_10_1998.tif
names        : landsat_15_10_1998
values       : 0.01737053, 0.5723241   (min, max)
```

Spatial reference information is stored in the GeoTIFF file and incorporated in the `RasterLayer` object when it is created. We can see that raster `band1` has a projected CRS, specifically the UTM Zone 36N coordinate system. Thus, its resolution, 30 x 30, is in meters. We can also see that it is one of the six bands the `landsat_15_10_1998.tif` file contains.

The input file `landsat_15_10_1998.tif` is, in fact, a subset of a Landsat satellite image of central Israel, where the original values were converted to reflectance (the fraction of incident electromagnetic radiation that is reflected from the surface, for a given wavelength). The original image, taken on October 15, 1998, is available for free at `http://earthexplorer.usgs.gov/`. The `landsat_15_10_1998.tif` file has six bands (Landsat bands 1-5 and 7) and covers an area of ~24 x ~29 kilometers (out of the 170 x 183 kilometers covered by the original image). The first four bands correspond to blue, green, red, and **Near Infrared** (**NIR**), while the last two belong to the **Short Wave Infrared** (**SWIR**) portion of the electromagnetic spectrum. Two additional Landsat images of the same area, taken about 2 and 5 years after 1998, are also available as sample datasets along with this book (the `landsat_04_10_2000.tif` and `landsat_11_09_2003.tif` files).

Since the `raster` function reads, by default, the first band of a multiband raster file, object `band1` that we just created contains reflectance data from the blue band. We can point to a different band with the `band` parameter of the `raster` function. For example, we can create another `RasterLayer` object, named `band4`, that will hold the NIR data as follows:

```
> band4 = raster("C:\\Data\\landsat_15_10_1998.tif", band = 4)
```

Creating multiband rasters

Two classes to represent multiband rasters are defined in the `raster` package: `RasterStack` and `RasterBrick`. The only difference between these classes is in the flexibility of data sources. While a `RasterBrick` object must refer to a single file (either in the RAM or on disk), each layer in a `RasterStack` object can come from a different file (or a layer in a multiband file). The advantage of `RasterBrick` is in the potentially faster processing time.

A `RasterStack` object can be created using the `stack` function, for example, by combining several `RasterLayer` objects as follows:

```
> stack(band1, band4)
class       : RasterStack
dimensions  : 960, 791, 759360, 2   (nrow, ncol, ncell, nlayers)
resolution  : 30, 30  (x, y)
extent      : 663945, 687675, 3459375, 3488175  (xmin, xmax, ymin$
coord. ref. : +proj=utm +zone=36 +ellps=WGS84 +units=m +no_defs
names       : landsat_15_10_1998.1, landsat_15_10_1998.2
min values  :            0.01737053,            0.04885371
max values  :            0.5723241,             0.7096972
```

Here, we combined the two `RasterLayer` objects `band1` and `band4` into a single `RasterStack` object. We can see that a `RasterStack` object has an additional dimension: the bands or layers (in this case, there are two). A `RasterBrick` object can be created using the `brick` function in exactly the same way.

We can also use the `stack` or `brick` function to read a multiband raster file into a `RasterStack` or `RasterBrick` object. Let's read the Landsat image from 2000 into a `RasterBrick` object named `l_00`:

```
> l_00 = brick("C:\\Data\\landsat_04_10_2000.tif")
> l_00
class       : RasterBrick
dimensions  : 960, 791, 759360, 6   (nrow, ncol, ncell, nlayers)
resolution  : 30, 30  (x, y)
extent      : 663945, 687675, 3459375, 3488175  (xmin, xmax, ymin$
```

```
coord. ref. : +proj=utm +zone=36 +ellps=WGS84 +units=m +no_defs
data source : C:\Data\landsat_04_10_2000.tif
names       : landsat_04_10_2000.1, landsat_04_10_2000.2, landsat$
min values  :              3.109737e-05,          2.019792e-02,           $
max values  :                 0.6080654,             0.6905138,           $
```

This time, our `RasterBrick` object `l_00` holds all six bands the `landsat_04_10_2000.tif` file contains.

The following table summarizes the previously mentioned properties of the three classes:

Class	Function	Bands	Storage
RasterLayer	raster	1	Disk/RAM
RasterStack	stack	Greater than 1	Disk/RAM
RasterBrick	brick	Greater than 1	Disk/RAM, single file

Once we have a multiband raster object (such as `RasterStack`), we can access individual bands using the double square brackets `[[` operator. By supplying a numeric vector of band indices within double brackets, we can get a subset of bands from the multiband raster. When the index has a length of 1, we get a `RasterLayer` object holding a single band. For example, using the expression `l_00[[2]]`, we get a `RasterLayer` object that holds the second band as follows:

```
> class(l_00[[2]])
[1] "RasterLayer"
attr(,"package")
[1] "raster"
```

When the length of the index is greater than 1, we get a multiband object that holds the specific bands we selected. For example, using the expression `l_00[[1:3]]`, we get a `RasterStack` object containing only bands 1-3:

```
> class(l_00[[1:3]])
[1] "RasterStack"
attr(,"package")
[1] "raster"
```

Writing raster files

Raster objects can be written to disk with the `writeRaster` function. Writing in nine formats is currently supported. For example, to write our recently created `RasterStack` object back to disk, in a different format (say, an ERDAS IMAGINE image, `*.img`), we will run the following expression:

```
> writeRaster(l_00,
+ "C:\\Data\\landsat_04_10_2000.img",
+ format = "HFA",
+ overwrite = FALSE)
```

Note that we specified the values of four parameters:

* The object to be written (`l_00`)
* The path and name for the file to be written (`"C:\\Data\\landsat_04_10_2000.img"`)
* The format of choice (see `?writeRaster` for the list of abbreviations) (`format="HFA"`)
* Whether to overwrite when the file already exists (`overwrite=FALSE`)

Exploring a raster's properties

In this section, we are going to review some of the functions used to query the properties of raster objects, and modify those properties when appropriate. Accessing and modifying the raster values (these can also be viewed as a property the raster has) is going to be covered in the next sections.

The number of rows, columns, and layers of a raster can be obtained using functions `nrow`, `ncol`, and `nlayers`, respectively:

```
> nrow(l_00)
[1] 960
> ncol(l_00)
[1] 791
> nlayers(l_00)
[1] 6
```

As we have seen previously in other contexts, the `dim` function returns the lengths of all dimensions at once as follows:

```
> dim(l_00)
[1] 960 791   6
```

The number of cells (equal to the number of rows multiplied by the number of columns) can be obtained using the `ncell` function:

```
> ncell(l_00)
[1] 759360
```

As for the spatial reference properties, the `res` and `extent` functions return the resolution and extent of the raster, while the `proj4string` function returns the CRS information. Let's see how these functions work, one function at a time:

```
> res(l_00)
[1] 30 30
```

The output of `res` is a vector of length 2, and its values denote the resolutions on the *x* and *y* axes, respectively (these are usually equal). Here is an example of querying the raster's extent:

```
> extent(l_00)
class       : Extent
xmin        : 663945
xmax        : 687675
ymin        : 3459375
ymax        : 3488175
```

The returned object from the `extent` function is an object of the `Extent` class. Objects of this class define a rectangular bounding box and have several uses, such as cropping a raster according to the extent of another raster (using the `crop` function, as we shall see in upcoming chapters).

The returned object from the `proj4string` function is a character vector (of length 1), holding the CRS information in the PROJ.4 format:

```
> proj4string(l_00)
[1] "+proj=utm +zone=36 +ellps=WGS84 +units=m +no_defs"
```

Certain methods (such as reprojection of vector layers, which will be introduced in the next chapter), require CRS information as an object of class CRS rather than a character value. A CRS object can be created in a straightforward manner, namely applying function CRS to a PROJ.4 character string. The CRS function is defined in the sp package—another very important package to work with spatial data in R (it is automatically loaded along with the raster package) and one that is going to be covered in the next chapter.

The CRS object contains exactly the same information, only in a different form:

```
> CRS(proj4string(l_00))
CRS arguments:
 +proj=utm +zone=36 +ellps=WGS84 +units=m +no_defs
```

One of the advantages of using the CRS class is that the correspondence of a specific character string to a valid CRS is ensured (otherwise the CRS function will trigger an error).

Sometimes, we would like to modify the CRS information of a spatial object (or assign one if it is missing). For example, assignment of NA to the CRS component is equivalent to clearing the CRS information:

```
> proj4string(l_00) = NA
> proj4string(l_00)
[1] NA
```

When a raster does not have a CRS specified, we can assign it one. One way to do this is by using the appropriate PROJ.4 character string (which, in turn, can be obtained from another resource, such as http://www.spatialreference.org/). Here is an example of how this can be done:

```
> proj4string(l_00) =
+ CRS("+proj=utm +zone=36 +ellps=WGS84 +units=m +no_defs")
> proj4string(l_00)
[1] "+proj=utm +zone=36 +ellps=WGS84 +units=m +no_defs"
```

It is frequently more convenient to transfer CRS information from another spatial object (which is analogous to importing a CRS from another layer, a common procedure in a GIS software), rather than looking up its specific parameters. For example, we can assign our raster object l_00 the CRS data from another Landsat satellite image we read from the disk:

```
> l1 = raster("C:\\Data\\landsat_15_10_1998.tif")
> proj4string(l_00) = CRS(proj4string(l1))
```

A graphical display is often the most helpful way to perceive the properties of a given raster. For example, the two basic functions plot and hist can give a first impression of the raster values' distribution. The plot function, when applied to a raster object, generates a simple map of the values in each band. For more advanced visualization of this sort, we are going to use the levelplot function (in the following example) and the ggplot2 package (in *Chapter 9, Advanced Visualization of Spatial Data*). The hist function displays a histogram of the values in each band of the raster.

Prior to plotting, we will modify another property the raster 1_00 has—its band names—using the names function, so that more appropriate names will appear along with each respective image in the graphical output. The automatically generated names are often inconvenient; for example, they may be composed of the filename with sequential numbers for the different bands:

```
> names(1_00)
[1] "landsat_04_10_2000.1" "landsat_04_10_2000.2"
[3] "landsat_04_10_2000.3" "landsat_04_10_2000.4"
[5] "landsat_04_10_2000.5" "landsat_04_10_2000.6"
```

We can assign shorter names as follows:

```
> names(1_00) = paste("Band", 1:6, sep = "_")
> names(1_00)
[1] "Band_1" "Band_2" "Band_3" "Band_4" "Band_5" "Band_6"
```

Now, using the expression hist(1_00), we will generate histograms of values in each band of raster 1_00, which are shown in the following screenshot:

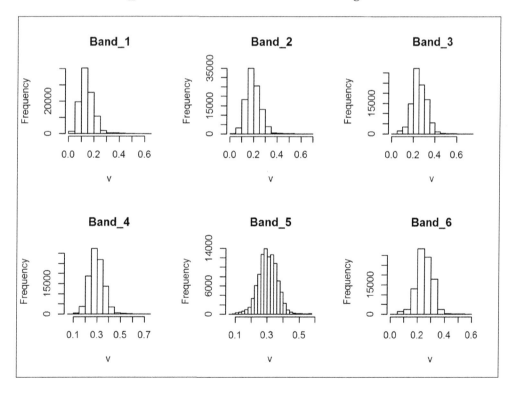

Expanded functionality in the visualization of raster data in R is available through several contributed packages. For example, the `levelplot` function from the `rasterVis` package (which is a modified version of the `levelplot` function from the `lattice` package) by default displays all bands of a given raster using a single color scale (unlike `plot`), which is something we usually want to do. Note that the `levelplot` function has numerous additional parameters to modify the plot appearance, and the `rasterVis` package contains several other useful functions to visualize rasters, that we are not going to cover (instead, you will learn how to produce customized graphical output using the `ggplot2` package in *Chapter 9, Advanced Visualization of Spatial Data*). The interested reader is referred to the tutorial of the `rasterVis` package (`http://oscarperpinan.github.io/rastervis/`) and the related book by the package author Oscar Perpinan Lamigueiro, *Displaying Time Series, Spatial, and Space-Time Data with R*, CRC Press (2014).

Two very useful parameters of `levelplot` are `par.settings`, which determines the color scale (for example, the blue-red scale is available using `RdBuTheme`), and `contour`, which determines whether to display contours. Let's take a look at the following example:

```
> library(rasterVis)
> levelplot(l_00, par.settings = RdBuTheme, contour = FALSE)
```

The following graphical output is generated:

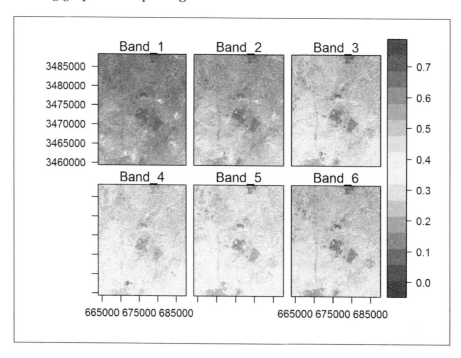

The previous screenshot shows reflectance values between 0 (completely dark) to 1 (completely reflective) for each Landsat band. To produce a so-called true color image, we would have to combine bands 1-3 (blue, green, and red), as will be shown in the next chapter.

Subsetting rasters

In many situations, we would like to access the values of a given raster either to perform calculations involving these values (for example, to calculate a frequency table) or to make an assignment (for example, to change a certain value in the raster; see the previous code section in *Chapter 1*, *The R Environment*). In this section, we are going to cover the different ways to do this.

As an example, we are going to use another multiband raster, `modis.tif`. First, we will assign it to a `RasterBrick` object named `r` and print its properties, as follows:

```
> r = brick("C:\\Data\\modis.tif")
> r
class       : RasterBrick
dimensions  : 100, 100, 10000, 280   (nrow, ncol, ncell, nlayers)
resolution  : 500, 500   (x, y)
extent      : 660000, 710000, 3445000, 3495000   (xmin, xmax, ymin$
coord. ref. : +proj=utm +zone=36 +datum=WGS84 +units=m +no_defs +$
data source : C:\Data\modis.tif
names       : modis.1, modis.2, modis.3, modis.4, modis.5, modis.$
```

The `modis.tif` file contains **Normalized Difference Vegetation Index (NDVI)** values from the MOD13A1 product of the Terra-MODIS satellite. As with Landsat, the original MOD13A1 data is available for free at http://earthexplorer.usgs. gov/. The `modis.tif` image covers an area of 2,500 km^2 at 500 meters spatial resolution. Unlike with Landsat, the bands do not refer to different wavelengths of the satellite sensor, but rather to different dates of image acquisition. In other words, we have a time series of NDVI images. There are 280 bands, corresponding to the period between February 18, 2000 and April 6, 2012 (23 images per year, each corresponding to approximately a 16-day time interval). Pixels (raster cells) with unreliable data (due to clouds, for example) were assigned with NA as part of the preprocessing.

The NDVI is a commonly used remote sensing index, quantifying the abundance of green vegetation (it has a range of -1 to 1, with values closer to 1 corresponding to more abundant vegetation). The NDVI is calculated based on reflectance in the red and NIR bands. We are going to see exactly how it is done, using the Landsat image as an example, later on in this chapter.

To examine the geographical location of the `modis.tif` raster, we can use the `plotKML` package that has a suite of functions to export the spatial data from R in the KML or KMZ formats and automatically display it in Google Earth. The simplest possible example, using nothing but defaults, would be to call the `plotKML` function on one of the bands in the raster `r` (for example, on band 1) in order to open Google Earth and display it there. The expression `plotKML(r[[1]])` will thus automatically open Google Earth, zoom in on the location of the raster `r[[1]]`, and display its values using a color scale (assuming the R packages `plotKML` and `animation` are loaded and the Google Earth software is installed). The following screenshot demonstrates what we see as a result:

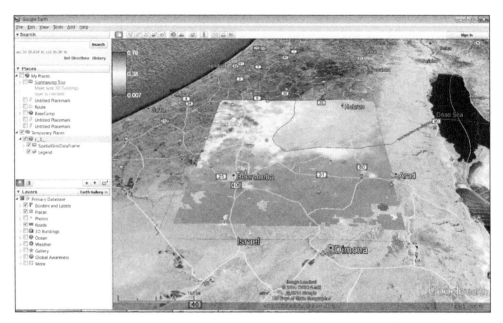

To subsequently display the result in Google Earth, the `plotKML` function has, in fact, written a KML file in the current **working directory**. The working directory is the default path that R uses to import and export files. It can be queried or modified using functions `getwd` and `setwd`, respectively. For example:

```
> getwd()
[1] "C:/Users/Michael Dorman/Documents"
> setwd("C:\\Data")
> getwd()
[1] "C:/Data"
```

Utilizing working directories can save the time spent in writing absolute file paths, but it can also make the code less concrete, so we will not use it in the present book.

Interactive visualization, over informative reference layers (for example, in Google Earth), is very helpful for the initial examination of spatial data we have at hand. For example, we can now see clearly that the NDVI gradient within the raster, from relatively high values towards north-west direction to relatively low values towards south-east direction, is due to its positioning in the transition zone between the relatively humid Mediterranean climatic region (where vegetation is more abundant) and the arid Negev desert (where vegetation is scarce).

The interested reader can refer to the paper in the Journal of Statistical Software by Hengl, Roudier, Beaudette, and Pebesma (2014), or to the online tutorial (http:// gsif.isric.org/doku.php?id=wiki:tutorial_plotkml) for further details and inspirational examples on the wide range of methods the plotKML package offers.

Accessing raster values as a vector

Returning to the subject of raster value access, the simplest way of doing that is with the [operator, exactly the same way we would with a vector. When accessing the values of a raster with [, the values will be ordered from the top-left corner rightwards, then along the second row, and so on, until the lower-right corner is reached. For example, to find out the first five values of the first layer in the r raster, we will use the following expression:

```
> r[[1]][1:5]
[1] 0.4242 0.3995 0.4190 0.4272 0.4285
```

Note that indices referring to bands with [[come first, and indices referring to cells with [come second. Either can be omitted, and then all elements from the respective dimension will be returned rather than a subset (for example, as we have seen previously, r[[1]] returns the whole first band).

When the [operator is used, but the cell value's index is omitted (as in []), we get a vector containing all of the raster values. We can use this vector, for example, to calculate the mean NDVI on the first date of acquisition (February 18, 2000).

```
> mean(r[[1]][], na.rm = TRUE)
[1] 0.2302056
```

The result is 0.23.

Accessing raster values with the matrix notation

Since a raster band is a two-dimensional object, it is frequently more useful to access its values using a two-dimensional notation. As with `matrix` objects, the first element of the two-dimensional index refers to rows and the second element refers to columns. For example, values 1-5 (in vector terms) of raster `r[[1]]` occupy row 1, columns 1-5. We can refer to these same values using a two-dimensional notation as follows:

```
> r[[1]][1, 1:5]
[1] 0.4242 0.3995 0.4190 0.4272 0.4285
```

Note that, even though we are using a two-dimensional notation to subset the raster, the values are still returned in the form of a one-dimensional numeric vector.

Subsets involving more than one layer

In the last two sections, we accessed a subset of raster values confined to a single layer. What happens when we subset both the row/column and layer dimensions of a raster? In that case, we get a `matrix` object, rather than a vector, with columns referring to layers and rows referring to raster cells. For example, using the following expression, we are referring to the values occupying row 1, columns 1-5, and layers 1-3:

```
> r[[1:3]][1, 1:5]
      modis.1 modis.2 modis.3
[1,]   0.4242   0.4518   0.4211
[2,]   0.3995   0.3334   0.4123
[3,]   0.4190   0.3430   0.4314
[4,]   0.4272   0.3430   0.4761
[5,]   0.4285   0.5814   0.4761
```

As a result, we get a matrix with three columns (corresponding to layers 1-3) and five rows (corresponding to the requested five cells, ordered from the top-left corner rightwards). Indeed, the values in the first column of the matrix are identical to the values of the vector we got in the previous two examples.

As another example, we can examine the course of NDVI over time at a single pixel—for example, in row 45, column 33—by omitting the band index this time (and thus referring to all bands at once):

```
> v = r[45, 33][1, ]
```

Note that with r[45,33], we get a matrix object with 280 columns (since we access all 280 bands of raster r) and a single row (since we access a single cell). Then, with the [1,] part, we select the first (and only) row in that matrix, containing the values of the (45,33) cell across all bands. As we witnessed earlier, a single matrix row is by default simplified to a vector. Finally, we assign the vector of NDVI values to v.

To plot the resulting NDVI time series, now held in v, we will use the date column in the dates table (see the previous chapter), which lists the dates of acquisition for each band in r. We will also specify the labels for the x and y axes, using parameters xlab and ylab of the plot function, respectively:

```
> plot(v ~ dates$date, type = "l", xlab = "Time", ylab = "NDVI")
```

The resulting graphical output is shown in the following screenshot:

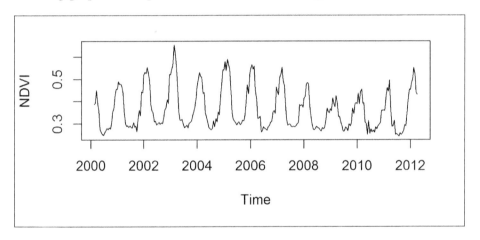

We can clearly see the periodical behavior of NDVI at the annual scale; NDVI increases in winter (the wet season), when vegetation is more abundant, and declines in summer (the dry season), when vegetation desiccates. Lower-than-usual NDVI values have been observed from 2009 to 2011 due to a drought period the region experienced at the time.

In all subset methods we have seen in the last three sections, the result was automatically converted to a simpler object, either to a vector (when dealing with values from a single band) or a matrix (when dealing with values form several bands). If we want to suppress the simplification, we can specify drop=FALSE, the same way we have seen regarding subsets of a data.frame object (see the previous chapter) and a matrix object. In the following example, using drop=FALSE yields a subset RasterBrick object named u that has the first two rows, two columns, and three layers of the original raster r:

```
> u = r[[1:3]][1:2, 1:2, drop = FALSE]
```

Plotting the object will demonstrate that u is indeed a 2 x 2 raster with three layers. The following expression plots the raster u:

```
> levelplot(u, layout = c(3,1), par.settings = RdBuTheme)
```

Using the parameter `layout`, we specified that the bands should be arranged in a single row and three columns within the plot area. The following screenshot shows what the plot will look like:

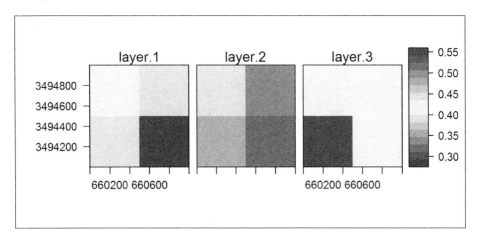

Transforming a raster into a matrix or an array

At times, it can be useful to transform a raster into a simpler data structure, such as a matrix or an array. One of the reasons to do that is to perform faster calculations (see *Chapter 6, Modifying Rasters and Analyzing Raster Time Series*). The transformations can be achieved using functions such as `as.matrix` and `as.array`, respectively.

For example, a single layer of a raster can be transformed into a matrix as follows:

```
> as.matrix(u[[1]])
        [,1]    [,2]
[1,]  0.4242 0.3995
[2,]  0.4495 0.2925
```

A multiband raster can be transformed into an array as follows:

```
> as.array(u[[1:2]])
, , 1

        [,1]    [,2]
[1,]  0.4242 0.3995
[2,]  0.4495 0.2925
```

```
, , 2

        [,1]    [,2]
[1,]  0.4518 0.3334
[2,]  0.4846 0.3223
```

If we try to convert a multiband raster into a matrix with `as.matrix`, we will get a matrix with rows representing cells and columns representing layers, as we have seen earlier in the context of raster subsetting:

```
> as.matrix(u[[1:2]])
     layer.1 layer.2
[1,]   0.4242  0.4518
[2,]   0.3995  0.3334
[3,]   0.4495  0.4846
[4,]   0.2925  0.3223
```

Overlay and reclassification of rasters

In this section, we will introduce two basic operations involving rasters: performing mathematical operations between overlapping rasters and reclassifying the values of a raster into new aggregated categories.

Raster algebra and overlay operations

In many cases, when we have two or more overlapping rasters, we would like to apply a certain function on each pair, triplet, and so on of overlapping pixels in those rasters. As a result, we will get a new raster, where the value of each pixel is the result of the latter function on the respective pixels in the input rasters. Such operations are also referred to as raster algebra, usually when using straightforward arithmetic notation (such as `r+s`, where `r` and `s` are rasters) or overlay operations.

There are numerous functions that can be used in raster algebra expressions, including arithmetic operators (such as `+`, `-`, `*`, and `/`), logical operators (such as `>`, `>=`, `<`, `<=`, `==`, and `!`), and several simple functions (such as `min`, `max`, and `sum`). Numeric values can also be combined with rasters (as long as the first object in the expression is a raster), in which case the numeric values are recycled as if to form a raster where all the values are equal to the given numeric value. For example, if `r` is a raster, `r+1` would yield a new raster, where `1` is recycled and added to each of the values in raster `r`. Similarly, the expression `r*2` would yield a raster where each value is multiplied by `2`. A single band raster can also be combined with a multiband raster, in which case the single band raster is recycled.

For example, the following expression will give us a new raster with the minimal NDVI values observed in each pixel over the 280 layers of raster r, excluding NA values:

```
> min_ndvi = min(r, na.rm = TRUE)
```

> In cases where we would like to apply a certain function on the values of the raster (rather than performing an overlay operation), we need to apply the respective function on the vector of raster values, rather than on the raster object itself.
>
> For example, to find out the minimum value among all cells in the first band of raster r, we will have to use the following expression:
>
> ```
> > min(r[[1]][], na.rm = TRUE)
> [1] 0.007
> ```
>
> Applying the min function on the raster itself, with min(r[[1]],na.rm=TRUE), is an overlay operation. It is not what we want to do in this case since an overlay would give us a new raster where each cell contains the minimal observed value among all bands of the input raster. The result will be r[[1]] itself since there is only one band to choose from.

Using the range function on the multiband raster r would give us a new raster with two bands (since the function returns a vector of length 2), one with the minimal values observed in each pixel and the other with the maximal values observed in each pixel:

```
> range_ndvi = range(r, na.rm = TRUE)
```

We can examine the range_ndvi result by plotting it with the levelplot function (this time, showing contours with contour=TRUE):

```
> levelplot(range_ndvi, par.settings = RdBuTheme, contour = TRUE)
```

The following screenshot shows the graphical output:

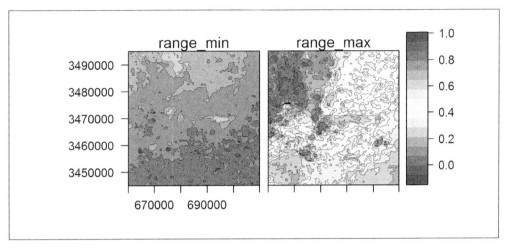

The resulting graphical output shows that NDVI minima are more spatially uniform than NDVI maxima.

Though slightly less straightforward than the raster algebra notation, the `overlay` and `calc` functions provide a more flexible way to perform overlay operations on rasters. Their main advantage is that we can supply any function (built-in or user-defined) to define the overlay operation, rather than choosing from the predefined set of functions that are applicable using the raster algebra notation. The main difference between `calc` and `overlay` is that `calc` is intended for overlay operations involving the bands of a single (multiband) raster, while overlay is intended to be used with several separate raster objects, although in many cases these functions are interchangeable (since we can always stack individual rasters into a single multiband raster). In both cases, we supply the overlay function as an argument to the `fun` parameter. The only requirement for the function we supply is that it should accept a vector and return a vector of a fixed length.

For example, we can write a function called `prop_na` that takes a numeric vector and returns the proportion of the NA values that vector contains (from 0, if the vector has no NA values, to 1, if the vector is entirely composed of the NA values). The following code section defines the `prop_na` function and demonstrates that it works as expected using a simple example:

```
> prop_na = function(x) length(x[is.na(x)]) / length(x)
> prop_na(c(10,3,NA,2))
[1] 0.25
```

We can now utilize `calc` to perform an overlay operation on all layers in `r` with the function `prop_na`, as follows:

```
> prop_na_r = calc(r, fun = prop_na)
```

The resulting object `prop_na_r` is a single band raster, where the value of each pixel reflects the proportion of missing values among the bands of the multiband raster `r`.

As another example, we will calculate an NDVI image based on our Landsat image `l_00`. NDVI is defined as the difference between NIR and red reflectances (which in Landsat correspond to bands 4 and 3, respectively) divided by their sum. We can perform the calculation by first defining a function called `ndvi` that, given a vector, calculates the NDVI based on its fourth and third elements (assuming they correspond to NIR and red, respectively).

```
> ndvi = function(x) (x[4] - x[3]) / (x[4] + x[3])
```

Then, we can apply the function on the Landsat multiband raster `l_00` with `calc`:

```
> ndvi_00 = calc(l_00, fun = ndvi)
```

We will display the result using `levelplot`. Note that when plotting a single layer, an average profile of mean values is shown for rows and columns along plot margins (this behavior can be disabled by specifying `margin=FALSE`):

```
> levelplot(ndvi_00, par.settings = RdBuTheme, contour = FALSE)
```

The following graphical output is produced:

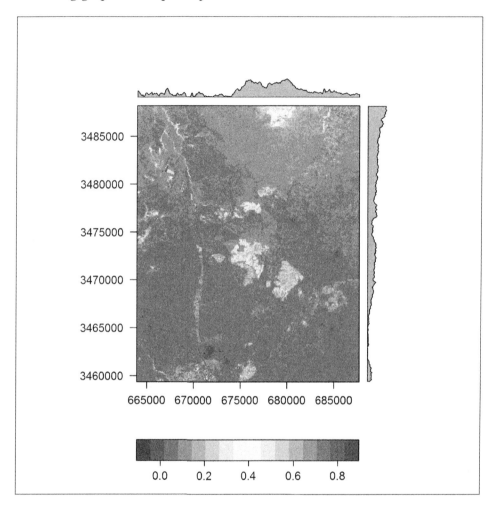

The Landsat image was taken during the dry season, and the area has a semiarid climate; thus, the green vegetation cover is scarce except in a few spots. For example, the two larger white/light blue patches, roughly in the middle of the preceding screenshot, are planted pine (mainly Aleppo pine) forests named Lahav and Kramim. Aleppo pine is an evergreen tree species; thus, the forested area retains relatively high NDVI values even during the dry season. We are going to return to these two forests in other examples later.

When applying logical operators on rasters, we get rasters with logical values (TRUE or FALSE). However, the same way as we have seen regarding logical vectors (*Chapter 2, Working with Vectors and Time Series*), when we apply an arithmetic operation on a logical raster, the logical values are converted to numeric values (1 or 0) before the operation is carried out. For example, if we would like to find out how many missing values the first layer of raster r contains, we can use the following expression:

```
> sum(is.na(r[[1]])[])
[1] 721
```

Note that with is.na(r[[1]]), we first created a logical raster, where the values are TRUE in pixels with NA in r[[1]], or FALSE otherwise. Then, with [], we obtained the vector of values from this logical raster. Finally, with sum, we found out how many TRUE values the vector contains. The answer is 721 NA values in the first layer of r.

Logical rasters can also be used to select a subset of the values of another overlapping raster and assign new values to the resulting subset. For example, if we wanted to fill the missing values in r[[1]], say with the mean of all non-missing values, we could do so as follows:

```
> temp = r[[1]]
> temp[is.na(temp)] = mean(temp[], na.rm = TRUE)
```

Note that we first assigned the first band of r to a new object named temp so that we will not alter the values of the original raster object. Then, we created a logical raster named is.na(temp) to subset the NA values in temp and assign the mean value of all the other cells to that subset. Plotting the new raster temp alongside the original one r[[1]] indeed shows that the missing values—appearing white in the left panel of the following screenshot (and transparent in the Google Earth visualization as seen in the previous screenshot)—were uniformly filled:

```
> levelplot(stack(r[[1]], temp),
+ par.settings = RdBuTheme, contour = FALSE)
```

The resulting graphical output is shown in the following screenshot:

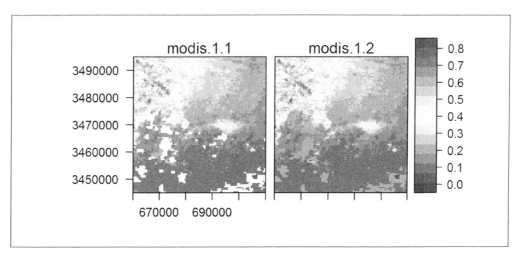

Reclassifying raster values

Reducing the amount of information a raster has for easier interpretation often involves reclassifying the values of the raster from a continuous scale into a set of discrete categories. In fact, we have already seen one method that we can use to do this in the previous section— the assignment to subsets of raster values defined by a condition. For example, we can reclassify the `ndvi_00` raster by assigning `0` to all cells where NDVI≤0.2 and 1 to all cells where NDVI>0.2, as follows:

```
> l_rec = ndvi_00
> l_rec[l_rec <= 0.2] = 0
> l_rec[l_rec > 0.2] = 1
```

The following expression that uses `plot` will show an image of `l_rec`:

```
> plot(l_rec)
```

This following screenshot shows the graphical output:

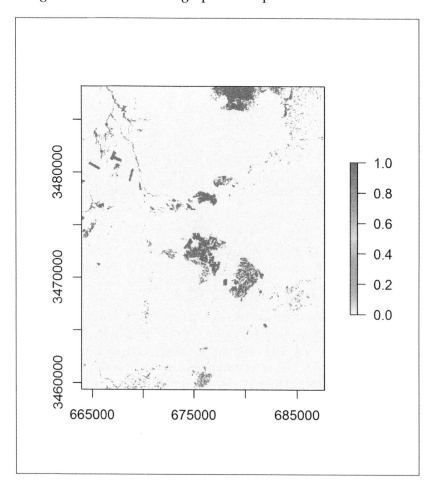

In fact, there is a specialized function for reclassification in the `raster` package called `reclassify`. The function accepts a raster (which we would like to reclassify) and a numeric vector or matrix (specifying the rules of reclassification). For example, if we supply a numeric vector, it should be composed of triplets of numeric values specifying the classification rules: from-, to-, new value, from-, to-, new value, and so on. It is often convenient to use the special value `Inf` (which stands for infinity) to specify unlimited from- or to- edges for a given range. For example, to specify the ≤0.2 range, we will say from `-Inf` to `0.2`. Therefore, for example, we could create the `l_rec` raster with the following expression, instead of the three expressions shown in the previous example:

```
> l_rec = reclassify(ndvi_00, c(-Inf, 0.2, 0, 0.2, Inf, 1))
```

Here, in plain language, we request the values from -∞ to `0.2` (closed on the right by default, thus including `0.2`, as in ≤0.2) to be converted to `0`, and the values from `0.2` to ∞ to be converted to `1`.

Summary

In this chapter, we covered the basic methods for working with raster data in R. We now know how to import and export raster data to and from the R environment, how to examine the raster objects at hand, and how to perform simple calculations to modify these objects. We also covered several ways to visually display raster data in R.

The next chapter is going to be very similar in structure and purpose to the present one; it's just that we are going to cover the other main type of spatial data—vector layers.

5

Working with Points, Lines, and Polygons

In this chapter, we will cover the basic usage of the second major type of spatial data—vector layers (points, lines, and polygons). In GIS terminology, these data are sometimes referred to as vectors, but we will use the term *vector layers* to distinguish them from vectors in R (see *Chapter 2, Working with Vectors and Time Series*). We will review the architecture of the vector layer classes defined in the sp package. Examples of the most common operations involving vector layers will then be presented using the sp, rgdal, and rgeos packages.

In this chapter, we'll cover the following topics:

- Classes for spatial vector layers (points, lines, and polygons) in the sp package
- Creating point layers by geocoding
- Reading and writing vector layer files
- Exploring the properties of vector layers
- Accessing and modifying attribute tables
- Reprojecting vector layers
- Calculating derived geometrical properties (for example, polygon area)
- Querying relations (for example, intersection) between a pair of layers
- Creating new layers based on a single layer or a pair of layers
- Joining data to an attribute table based on the location or common columns

Data structures for vector layers in R

Spatial vector layers have two components: the geometry and the attribute table. The geometry component holds the spatial coordinates and information regarding their arrangement in separate features, while the attribute table holds additional information regarding each feature. For example, in a point layer of capital cities, the record for London may be composed of a geometric component (a point coordinate, such as 51.5072°N, 0.1275°W) and a row in an attribute table holding additional data regarding each city (for example, population size, built area, and so on).

The geometry part in a vector layer is obligatory and there are three types of geometries: points, lines, and polygons. The attribute table is optional. Classes for the six spatial vector layers types, constituting all possible combinations of these two properties, have been defined in the sp package. They are summarized in the following table:

Geometry type	Attribute table	Class
Points	No	`SpatialPoints`
	Yes	`SpatialPointsDataFrame`
Lines	No	`SpatialLines`
	Yes	`SpatialLinesDataFrame`
Polygons	No	`SpatialPolygons`
	Yes	`SpatialPolygonsDataFrame`

Together with the three raster classes from the `raster` package (presented in the previous chapter), these constitute a commonly used set of classes suitable for a wide range of spatial analysis applications in R.

Additional classes for spatial vector layers (and rasters) do exist in R. They are often associated with packages intended for specialized data analysis tasks. Conveniently, however, there are usually established methods of converting objects to and from such classes, with respect to the highly popular classes in the sp and `raster` packages (which we've used throughout this book). For example, the ppp class (the `spatstat` package) is used to represent a point pattern (event locations and the window where the pattern has been observed) to employ statistical analysis tools for such patterns. A `SpatialPoints` object can be converted to a ppp object and vice versa using the `maptools` package.

In this section, we will see an example of how to create a vector layer for each of the three types of geometries—points, lines, and polygons. In the next section, methods to examine spatial vector layers will be presented, while in the last three sections of this chapter, we will see how some more advanced operations on vector layers are performed. Additional information regarding the sp package and its spatial vector classes can be found in the book *Applied Spatial Data Analysis with R*, *Springer*, whose second edition was published in 2013, by Roger Bivand, Edzer Pebesma, and Virgilio Gómez-Rubio.

Points

Points are the simplest type of spatial objects since the geometrical component of a point is just a single (x,y) coordinate. A set of (x,y) coordinates, along with CRS information, constitutes a spatial point layer, which can be represented in R with a SpatialPoints object. If we also have an attribute table where each row corresponds to a single point, the layer can be represented with a SpatialPointsDataFrame object.

In our first example, we are going to create a SpatialPointsDataFrame object by geocoding, the procedure to convert addresses to geographic coordinates. The intermediate steps we will go through are as follows:

1. Creating a vector of addresses we want to geocode.
2. Geocoding the addresses to get a data.frame object of geographic coordinates for each address.
3. Adding location names as an additional column.
4. Converting the data.frame object to a SpatialPointsDataFrame object.
5. Adding CRS information.

In the example, we will geocode the addresses of three airports in New Mexico:

- Albuquerque International Airport
- Double Eagle II Airport
- Santa Fe Municipal Airport

For the geocoding step (step 2), we are going to use the Google Maps API, accessible from R through the ggmap package. Additional functionality of the ggmap package for visualization of spatial data will be presented in *Chapter 9*, *Advanced Visualization of Spatial Data*. For an overview of package capabilities, refer to the introductory paper on ggmap (*ggmap: Spatial Visualization with ggplot2*) by Kahle, D. and Wickham, H. 2013.

Our first step is to create a character vector with the airports addresses. The addresses are ordered in accordance with the airport names listed earlier:

```
> addresses = c(
+ "2200 Sunport Blvd, Albuquerque, NM 87106, USA",
+ "7401 Paseo Del Volcan Northwest Albuquerque, NM 87121, USA",
+ "121 Aviation Dr, Santa Fe, NM 87507, USA")
```

> Note that the Google Maps API (which we will use for geocoding) can also search for location names (such as the White House) or partial addresses, but the result will be less determinate (two different places can be go by the same name, but not the same address). The exact addresses are used here to ensure that the reader will obtain the same results as in the book's text.

We are ready for the second step and will now load the ggmap package and geocode the addresses using the geocode function. This function accepts a vector of addresses (such as addresses that we just created) and returns a data.frame object of the matched geographic coordinates:

```
> library(ggmap)
> airports = geocode(addresses)
> airports
         lon      lat
1 -106.6168 35.04918
2 -106.7947 35.15559
3 -106.0731 35.62866
```

> The geocode function accesses the Google Maps API. Therefore, an Internet connection is required. Using the Google Maps API also implies agreement with the Google Maps API Terms of Service (https://developers.google.com/maps/terms) and is limited to 2,500 queries in a 24-hour time period (using the free service option). A promising alternative can be found in the geocodeHERE package providing access to the **HERE** Geocoding API (https://developer.here.com/geocoder) that has a higher threshold of 10,000 queries per day.

We now have a data.frame object named airports that holds the longitudes (lon) and latitudes (lat) of the three airports.

In our third step, we will add the airport names in an additional column called `name` in `airports` as follows:

```
> airports$name = c("Albuquerque International",
+ "Double Eagle II",
+ "Santa Fe Municipal")
> airports
         lon      lat                      name
1 -106.6168 35.04918 Albuquerque International
2 -106.7947 35.15559           Double Eagle II
3 -106.0731 35.62866        Santa Fe Municipal
```

The resulting `data.frame` object has everything we need to create a `SpatialPointsDataFrame` object, where the geometry components will be the airports' coordinates, and the attribute table will have a single column that holds the airport names. This is our fourth step. It is performed using the `coordinates` function of the `sp` package by specifying the columns that hold the coordinates with a `formula` object of the structure `~x_coord+y_coord`. In our case, the x coordinate is the longitude (`lon`) and the y coordinate is the latitude (`lat`), therefore the formula takes the following form:

```
> library(sp)
> coordinates(airports) = ~ lon + lat
```

The last expression converts `airports` from a `data.frame` object to a `SpatialPointsDataFrame` object. We can confirm the conversion took place using the `class` function as follows:

```
> class(airports)
[1] "SpatialPointsDataFrame"
attr(,"package")
[1] "sp"
```

Using the `print` method on the object shows that it holds exactly the same information as before; just that the `lon` and `lat` columns are now identified as spatial coordinates, as shown in the following output:

```
> airports
            coordinates                      name
1 (-106.6168, 35.04918) Albuquerque International
2 (-106.7947, 35.15559)           Double Eagle II
3 (-106.0731, 35.62866)        Santa Fe Municipal
```

Our last step is to specify the CRS of airports, which is a geographic CRS:

```
> proj4string(airports) = CRS("+proj=longlat +datum=WGS84")
```

The `airports` vector layer is now complete.

Writing of `Spatial*DataFrame` objects (that is, the `SpatialPointsDataFrame`, `SpatialLinesDataFrame`, and `SpatialPolygonsDataFrame` objects) can be done with the `writeOGR` function from the `rgdal` package. In the following example, as well as in most other examples in this book, we will use the popular ESRI Shapefile format for the input and output of vector layers.

We can export our `SpatialPointsDataFrame` object `airports` to a Shapefile on the disk as follows:

```
> library(rgdal)
> writeOGR(airports, "C:\\Data", "airports", "ESRI Shapefile")
```

The four arguments that were supplied to the first four parameters of the `writeOGR` function are as follows:

- `obj`: The name of the object to be written (for example, `airports`)
- `dsn`: The path of the directory where the file(s) will be written (for example, `"C:\\Data"`)
- `layer`: The layer name (for example, `"airports"`)
- `driver`: The driver name (for example, `"ESRI Shapefile"`)

Since Shapefile datasets are composed of several separate files (at least three: `*.shp`, `*.shx`, and `*.dbf`), when reading and writing with the ESRI Shapefile driver, we specify the directory (`dsn`) and filename without the extension (`layer`). In the previous example, with `dsn="C:\\Data"` and `layer="airports"`, four files were written to the `C:\Data` directory: `airports.dbf`, `airports.prj`, `airports.shp`, and `airports.shx`. The meaning of the `dsn` and `layer` parameters can be different with other drivers (see the next section and `?writeOGR`).

To read the file we just wrote back into a `SpatialPointsDataFrame` object in R, we can use the `readOGR` function (also available in the `rgdal` package). When reading vector layers, we need to provide only the `dsn` and `layer` arguments (the path and layer name, respectively). In addition, we can specify that we do not want character values in the attribute table to be converted to factors by specifying `stringsAsFactors=FALSE` (see *Chapter 3, Working with Tables*):

```
> airports = readOGR("C:\\Data",
+ "airports",
+ stringsAsFactors = FALSE)
```

Obviously, all the `airports.*` files that constitute the Shapefile need to be found in the same directory (in this case, in the `C:\Data` directory) for the layer to be properly read.

Lines

Line and polygon layers are more complex than point layers in two principal aspects. First, individual lines or polygons are defined with a set of points, rather than a single one. Specifically, a line is a set of points connected to each other from the first point to the last one. A polygon is defined similarly; just that the last point is equal to the first. The number of points in each line or polygon is not fixed, but dependable on the shape complexity (a more complex shape will be defined with more points). Secondly, a single line or polygon feature (corresponding to a single entry in an attribute table) can be composed of more than one individual line or more than one individual polygon. For example, in a layer of countries' boundaries, the USA feature will be composed of more than one polygon since the contiguous United States, Alaska, and each of the Hawaii Islands are separate from one another.

 An additional complication, specific to polygonal layers, is the existence of holes. A single feature can be composed of an external boundary polygon and hole polygons. For example, in a layer of North America's land area, hole polygons may represent the Great Lakes. Hole polygons can once again have internal polygons (such as islands inside the Great Lakes) and so on.

Due to their complexity, it is much less common to manually define line and polygon layers from raw coordinates. Instead, they are usually either imported from an external source (for example, reading a Shapefile) or created from another object (for example, contour lines created based on a DEM raster).

As an example for `SpatialLinesDataFrame`, we will read a **GPS Exchange Format (GPX)** file with a track record from a GPS device. With GPX files, unlike with Shapefiles, the `dsn` argument is the file itself, while the `layer` argument points to the data component we would like to read (such as `"tracks"` or `"track_points"`; see `?readOGR`). The particular file `GPS_log.gpx` contains the GPS log, from driving around the Lahav and Dvira forests with the GPS device in recording mode. Let's read the file as follows:

```
> track = readOGR("C:\\Data\\GPS_log.gpx","tracks")
```

Using the `class` function, we can demonstrate that `track` is a
`SpatialLinesDataFrame` object:

```
> class(track)
[1] "SpatialLinesDataFrame"
attr(,"package")
[1] "sp"
```

Polygons

As an example of polygonal data, we are going to read another external file; this
time it's a Shapefile named `USA_2_GADM_fips`. The file is composed of polygons
corresponding to the second level administrative division (counties) of the USA,
with several attributes such as county names and **Federal Information Processing
Standards (FIPS)** codes. We will assign the resulting `SpatialPolygonsDataFrame` to
an object named `county` to use in the subsequent examples in this chapter:

```
> county = readOGR("C:\\Data", "USA_2_GADM_fips",
+ stringsAsFactors = FALSE)
```

To summarize, so far we have witnessed two ways to create spatial vector layers
in R: from a set of (x,y) coordinates (relevant to points) and from a file (relevant to
points, lines, and polygons). A third way—deriving vector layers from raster data—
will be presented in *Chapter 7, Combining Vector and Raster Datasets*.

Exploring vector layer properties and subsetting

This section is going to be devoted to the examination of spatial vector layer
properties, and to subsetting them based on their attribute tables. Some of the
presented procedures will be analogous to those presented for rasters in the previous
chapter (for example, plotting and querying CRS information), while others are
generally relevant only to vector layers (for example, calculating areas and creating
subsets according to the attribute table). As will quickly become apparent, many
operations involving attribute tables of vector layers are conveniently analogous to
operations on `data.frame` objects.

Examining vector layer properties

The summary function produces a useful textual summary of the properties of a vector layer, including its class, bounding box coordinates, CRS, and attribute table column types. For example, using summary on airports produces the following textual output:

```
> summary(airports)
Object of class SpatialPointsDataFrame
Coordinates:
                   min        max
lon -106.79467 -106.07308
lat    35.04918    35.62866
Is projected: FALSE
proj4string : [+proj=longlat +datum=WGS84]
Number of points: 3
Data attributes:
    Length      Class      Mode
         3 character character
```

All of the properties listed in this output can also be accessed, and in some cases modified, using functions. For example, similar to what we already saw for rasters in the previous chapter, the proj4stpring function returns the CRS definition of a vector layer in the PROJ.4 format. Using proj4string on airports returns the definition of the WGS84 CRS:

```
> proj4string(airports)
[1] "+proj=longlat +datum=WGS84"
```

Referring to the geometry part, the length function returns the number of features the layer consists of. For example, airports contains three points (the three airports), as the following output shows:

```
> length(airports)
[1] 3
```

A spatial layer also always has row names that internally serve as ID variables to match the geometries with attribute table entries. The number of row names is thus equal to the number of features:

```
> row.names(airports)
[1] "1" "2" "3"
```

The `dimensions` function returns the number of spatial dimensions:

```
> dimensions(airports)
[1] 2
```

 In this book, we only deal with two-dimensional vector layers (geometries on a plane). Three-dimensional layers can also be useful to represent certain types of data, such as points with (x,y) coordinates and (z) elevation.

Accessing the attribute table of vector layers

The attribute table of a vector layer is, in fact, a `data.frame` object and some of the functions that work with `data.frame` objects have been defined to consistently work directly on vector layers as well. For example, the `nrow`, `ncol`, and `dim` functions applied to a vector layer refer to its attribute table to return its dimensions:

```
> nrow(county)
[1] 3145
> ncol(county)
[1] 4
> dim(county)
[1] 3145    4
```

We see that the attribute table of `county` has 3,145 rows (thus, the layer has 3,145 features) and four columns. The columns contain the following information:

* `NAME_1`: The first-level name (for example, the state name)
* `NAME_2`: The second-level name (for example, the county name)
* `TYPE_2`: The feature type (for example "County" or "Water body")
* `FIPS`: The FIPS code

Individual columns of an attribute table, or subsets of these, can be accessed with the `$` and `[` operators. For example, the second-level names (held in the `NAME_2` column) of the first 10 features in `county` can be obtained as follows:

```
> county$NAME_2[1:10]
 [1] "Litchfield" "Hartford"   "Tolland"    "Windham"
 [5] "Siskiyou"   "Del Norte"  "Modoc"      "New London"
 [9] "Fairfield"  "Middlesex"
```

As another example, we can check the types of features the county layer contains by listing the unique values in the TYPE_2 column:

```
> unique(county$TYPE_2)
 [1] "County"           "District"        "Borough"
 [4] "Census Area"      "Municipality"    "City And Borough"
 [7] "City And County"  "Water body"      "Parish"
[10] "Independent City"
```

The whole attribute table of a spatial vector layer can be accessed directly using the @ operator. The @ operator is used to extract a slot, by its name, from an object, using the notation object_name@slot_name.

 More specifically, the @ operator is applicable to objects of the so-called S4 classes, which all raster and vector layers we deal with are, as opposed to S3 classes whose components are accessed with a different method (using the $ operator). The distinction between S3 and S4 concerns the internal class structure and is beyond the scope of this book. For more information, refer to *Advanced R, Wickham, H., CRC Press, 2014* (http://adv-r.had.co.nz/OO-essentials.html).

The attribute table slot of spatial vector classes defined in the sp package is called data. Therefore, adding @data after a vector layer name will yield its attribute table (if it has one).

For example, the following expression returns the attribute table of airports:

```
> airports@data
                       name
1 Albuquerque International
2          Double Eagle II
3        Santa Fe Municipal
```

As another example, we can print the first few rows in the attribute table of county using the head function applied to county@data:

```
> head(county@data)
         NAME_1      NAME_2 TYPE_2  FIPS
0 Connecticut Litchfield County 09005
1 Connecticut    Hartford County 09003
2 Connecticut     Tolland County 09013
3 Connecticut     Windham County 09015
4  California    Siskiyou County 06093
5  California  Del Norte County 06015
```

As we shall see later in this chapter, the attribute table of a vector layer can also be modified using assignment, similar to a separate `data.frame` object. New attribute table columns can be created and populated using the `$` operator, or the whole attribute table can be modified (for example, certain columns can be deleted or joined) and reassigned to the `data` slot.

All other components of spatial vector (and raster, for that matter) objects are also contained in slots and thus, are accessible with the `@` operator. Using the `str` function, we can obtain a tree describing the object's structure. Let's take a look at the following example:

```
> str(airports)
Formal class 'SpatialPointsDataFrame' [package "sp"] with 5 slots
  ..@ data       :'data.frame': 3 obs. of  1 variable:
  .. ..$ name: chr [1:3] "Albuquerque International" "Double Eagl$
  ..@ coords.nrs : int [1:2] 1 2
  ..@ coords      : num [1:3, 1:2] -106.6 -106.8 -106.1 35 35.2 ...
  .. ..- attr(*, "dimnames")=List of 2
  .. .. ..$ : NULL
  .. .. ..$ : chr [1:2] "lon" "lat"
  ..@ bbox        : num [1:2, 1:2] -106.8 35 -106.1 35.6
  .. ..- attr(*, "dimnames")=List of 2
  .. .. ..$ : chr [1:2] "lon" "lat"
  .. .. ..$ : chr [1:2] "min" "max"
  ..@ proj4string:Formal class 'CRS' [package "sp"] with 1 slot
  .. .. ..@ projargs: chr "+proj=longlat +datum=WGS84"
```

Using such a tree, we can find our way to all the data components of an object. Then, why is the use of specialized functions (such as `proj4string`), rather than direct access to the relevant property (such as `airports@proj4string@projargs`), usually advocated in R? One reason is that working through functions makes our code more robust in the face of changes in class definition. In other words, if the internal architecture of a certain class changes in a future version of a given package (so that, for instance, the slot x is now named y), the user may not even notice since the code for all the relevant functions operating on the class will also be changed accordingly while access with `@x` will no longer work. Accessing the attribute table of a vector layer (with `@data`) is going to be the only direct access we have in this book. The exception is necessary since certain operations on an attribute table are unfeasible otherwise.

The attribute table of a vector layer can also be removed altogether, by converting a
`Spatial*DataFrame` object into a `Spatial*` object. Such a conversion can be done
with the `as` function, specifying the object name and the class we want to convert it
to. For example, we can convert `airports`, a `SpatialPointsDataFrame` object, to a
`SpatialPoints` object as follows:

```
> airports_sp = as(airports, "SpatialPoints")
```

Since a `SpatialPoints` object does not have a `data` slot, an error occurs when
trying to access it:

```
> airports_sp@data
Error: no slot of name "data" for this object of class "SpatialPo$
```

We can also use the `as` function to perform the reverse conversion from a
`SpatialPoints` object to a `SpatialPointsDataFrame` object. Naturally, the attribute
table of the resulting object is going to be empty (since `SpatialPoints` objects do not
have one):

```
> as(airports_sp, "SpatialPointsDataFrame")@data
data frame with 0 columns and 0 rows
```

Subsetting vector layers

We can subset a vector layer according to its attribute table using the same notation
as in subsetting `data.frame` objects. Selecting which features to retain can be done
by supplying a numeric or logical vector within the `[` operator.

For example, to get a subset of only those `county` features that belong to the
contiguous U.S., we need to exclude those features corresponding to the states
of Alaska and Hawaii. This can be done by creating a logical vector (applying a
condition to the `county$NAME_1` column holding state names) and supplying that
vector as the `rows` index of `county` with the `[` operator, as follows:

```
> county = county[
+ county$NAME_1 != "Alaska" &
+ county$NAME_1 != "Hawaii", ]
```

Keep in mind the following alternative that utilizes the `%in%` operator:
```
> county = county[
+ !(county$NAME_1 %in%
+ c("Alaska", "Hawaii")), ]
```

Similarly, we can retain only the land area by excluding water body polygons:

```
> county = county[county$TYPE_2 != "Water body", ]
```

Let's examine the resulting layer using the `plot` function. The expression
`plot(county)` produces the graphical output as shown in the following screenshot:

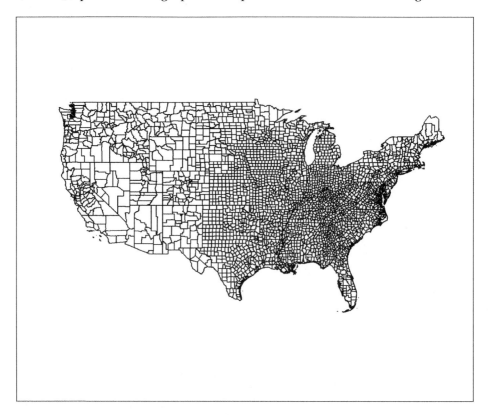

As we can see, the `plot` function, by default, draws polygon borders using black
lines. In subsequent examples, we will experiment a little bit with several parameters
of this function to modify the appearance of the plot.

Geometrical calculations on vector layers

In previous sections, we covered the querying of the immediately available properties of vector layers (for example, the CRS definition or attribute table), and the modification of vector layers involving only the attribute table component (for example, removing the attribute table or subsetting the layer according to it). In the next two sections, you will learn to examine and modify the geometrical component of vector layers. In this section, operations involving a single vector layer, such as reprojection and area calculation, will be covered. In the next section, we will deal with operations involving pairs of vector layers.

Reprojecting vector layers

Reprojection is the conversion of all the coordinates of a spatial object from one CRS to another. Note the distinction when specifying a CRS (which we previously did with `airports`), where only the CRS definition associated with the layer is modified, leaving the coordinates unaltered. The reprojection of a vector layer is done with the `spTransform` function from the `rgdal` package. The function accepts two arguments: the layer to be reprojected and the target CRS.

For example, the following expression transforms the `county` layer (currently defined in a geographical CRS) to the US National Atlas Equal Area projection:

```
> newProj = CRS("+proj=laea +lat_0=45 +lon_0=-100
+ +x_0=0 +y_0=0 +a=6370997 +b=6370997 +units=m +no_defs")
> county = spTransform(county, newProj)
```

Note that the preceding operation consisted of two steps. The first expression created an object named `newProj` of the class `CRS` by applying the `CRS` function on a PROJ.4 character string corresponding to the US National Atlas Equal Area projection. Second, the `county` layer has been reprojected to the `newProj` CRS using the `spTransform` function.

> The PROJ.4 strings can be obtained from other objects (see the previous chapter) or from databases such as http://www.spatialreference.org/. The PROJ.4 string used earlier, for example, was copied from http://spatialreference.org/ref/epsg/us-national-atlas-equal-area/proj4/.

We can evaluate the effect of reprojection by visualizing the new `county` layer with `plot(county)`. The following screenshot shows the graphical output:

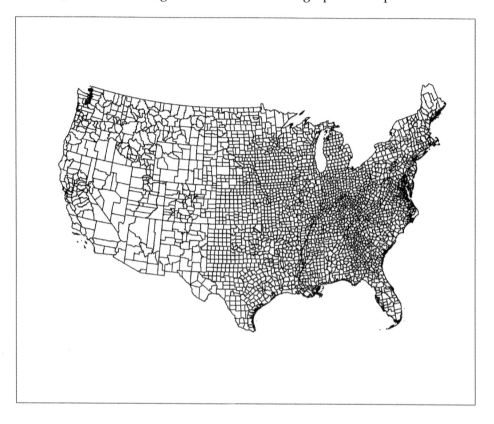

Reprojection is often used in spatial data analysis since any operation involving multiple layers (such as an overlay or map production) requires all layers to be projected onto the same CRS. For example, in order for us to display the GPS track object (see the *Lines* section in this chapter) on top of the Landsat satellite image `landsat_11_09_2003.tif` (see the previous chapter), we first need to bring them into the same CRS. For that, we can either reproject the raster to the CRS of the vector layer (WGS84, in this case) or reproject the vector layer to the CRS of the raster (UTM Zone 36N, in this case). Unless we have a special reason to prefer the CRS of the vector layer(s), it is usually better to reproject the vector layers into the CRS of the raster and leave the raster unmodified; the reason is that raster reprojection also involves resampling and thus, potential modification of its values (see the next chapter).

To plot the GPS track on top of the Landsat image, we will first read the latter into a `RasterBrick` object named `l_03`:

```
> library(raster)
> l_03 = brick("C:\\Data\\landsat_11_09_2003.tif")
```

Then, we will reproject `track`, supplying the CRS parameters of `l_03` to `spTransform`, with a single step this time:

```
> track = spTransform(track, CRS(proj4string(l_03)))
```

With the `l_03` and `track` objects in the same CRS, we can now plot them one on top of the other using two function calls. In the second function call, we need to specify `add=TRUE` so that the second layer will be plotted on top of the first, in the same graphical window (two or more layers can be plotted this way).

Regarding the satellite image, rather than plotting the values of an individual band, we will produce a true color image, using the red, green, and blue bands (which correspond to bands 3, 2, and 1 in Landsat, respectively), using the `plotRGB` function. This is done by assigning the appropriate bands to the `r` (red), `g` (green), and `b` (blue) parameters:

```
> plotRGB(l_03, r = 3, g = 2, b = 1, stretch = "lin",
+ ext = extent(track) + 10000)
> plot(track, add = TRUE, col = "yellow")
```

The following screenshot shows the graphical output with the GPS route (in yellow) on top of the true-color Landsat image, which is generated as a result of the last two expressions:

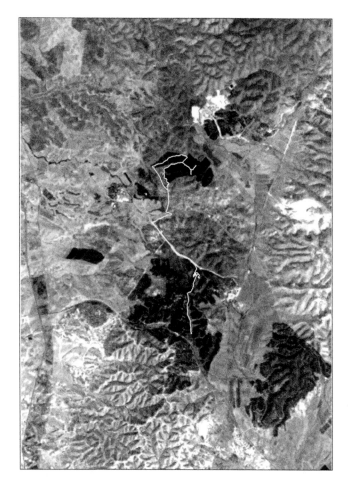

The additional `plotRGB` parameters we used, `stretch` and `ext`, specify the type of stretch and the required extent, respectively. Stretching is essentially a transformation from a raster value (which in this case is between 0 and 1) to an RGB color model value (between 0, which is the darkest, and 255, which is the brightest). The simplest option is `lin`, which specifies a linear stretch. Supplying an `Extent` object to the `ext` parameter allows us to zoom in and plot only a portion of the raster. In this case, we use the extent of the `track` layer, plus a 10 kilometer buffer on all sides, with the expression `extent(track)+10000` (note that all distance-related calculations are in CRS units; in this case, meters). When adding the second layer (`track`), we use the `col` parameter to specify the required line color; in this case, `"yellow"`.

R has excellent capabilities to use colors and color gradients in the graphical output, which are mostly beyond the scope of this book. In short, there are three main methods to specify colors in R:

- **Color name**: For example, `"yellow"`
- **Position on a color palette**: For example, `rainbow(12)[3]`, which gives the third color in a 12-color rainbow palette, which is a kind of yellow

- **Position within the RGB color model**: For example, `rgb(1,1,0)`, which returns the hex code `"#FFFF00"` that corresponds to pure yellow

For the purposes of this book, the first method, involving the predefined color names, will mostly be sufficient (a list of available colors can be obtained using the expression `colors()`). We are, in fact, also using color palettes although indirectly through graphical functions such as `levelplot` (see the previous chapter). We will see an example of how to directly use a color palette in *Chapter 9, Advanced Visualization of Spatial Data*.

Working with the geometrical properties of vector layers

Spatial objects have a wide range of properties related to their geometry; some are instantly available as part of the data structure itself (for example, the coordinates of points in a point layer); others are derivable via geometrical calculations (for example, the area sizes of polygons).

The coordinates of a point layer can be obtained using the `coordinates` function:

```
> coordinates(airports)
          lon      lat
[1,] -106.6168 35.04918
[2,] -106.7947 35.15559
[3,] -106.0731 35.62866
```

The result is a matrix object with the number of rows corresponding to the number of points the layer consists of.

To derive more complex properties, the rgeos package, which stands for R interface to **Geometry Engine Open Source (GEOS)**, offers a range of functions for geometrical operations involving vector layers. The available geometrical operations can conceptually be divided into three groups according to the output they produce:

- **Numeric values**: Obtained from functions that summarize geometrical properties (for example, calculating area sizes)

- **Logical values**: Obtained from functions that evaluate whether a certain geometrical property (for example, whether the given geometry is valid), or the relation between objects (for example, whether feature A intersects with feature B), holds true

- **Spatial layers**: Obtained from functions that create a new layer based on an input layer (for example, finding polygon centroids) or a pair of layers (for example, finding the intersecting area of feature A with feature B)

Several examples of functions for each type of these operations will be provided in this chapter, while some of the additional functions will only be mentioned for reference.

> For a complete list of functions that the rgeos package offers, refer to the help pages of the package available at http://cran.r-project.org/web/packages/rgeos/rgeos.pdf.

As an example of a function that returns numeric values, the gArea function can be used to calculate the area size of polygons. For example, we can calculate the area covered by the county polygons as follows:

```
> library(rgeos)
> gArea(county) / 1000^2
[1] 7784859
```

The area is given in the units of the projection, in this case m^2; dividing the result by 1000^2 transformed the area figure to km^2 units. According to Wikipedia, the land area of the contiguous U.S. is 7,663,942 km^2, which is close enough to our result (given that the CRS and level of detail affect the calculation).

If we want to calculate the area of each feature (each county, in this case), rather than the area of the layer as a whole, we need to specify `byid=TRUE`. The `byid` parameter determines whether we wish to perform the calculation by ID, that is, for each feature separately. This parameter is present in many of the functions in the `rgeos` package with the same functionality, as we shall see in the subsequent examples. The following expression returns a numeric vector with the area of each feature in the `county` layer in km^2. The vector is immediately assigned to a new column in the `county` layer, named `area`:

```
> county$area = gArea(county, byid = TRUE) / 1000^2
```

Now the attribute table of a `county` contains an extra column with the area size for each county. We can confirm this by printing the first few rows of the attribute table:

```
> head(county@data)
          NAME_1      NAME_2 TYPE_2  FIPS       area
0 Connecticut Litchfield County 09005  2451.876
1 Connecticut    Hartford County 09003  1941.110
2 Connecticut     Tolland County 09013  1077.789
3 Connecticut     Windham County 09015  1350.476
4  California    Siskiyou County 06093 16416.572
5  California  Del Norte County 06015  2626.707
```

As an example of an operation where a new spatial layer is created, we will dissolve the `county` polygons into state polygons. For simplicity, we will perform the dissolving on a subset of `county`, including only two states: Nevada and Utah. At first, we will create the subset and assign it to a new object named `county_nv_ut`:

```
> county_nv_ut = county[county$NAME_1 %in% c("Nevada", "Utah"), ]
```

Now, we will dissolve the `county_nv_ut` polygons using the `gUnaryUnion` function. The two arguments transferred to this function are the layer to be dissolved and the ID, a vector defining the features that should be aggregated (all features with identical levels will be dissolved into one). If the `id` argument is omitted, all polygons are dissolved into one, as we shall see in subsequent examples. Here is the code for dissolving our current layer:

```
> states = gUnaryUnion(county_nv_ut, id = county_nv_ut$NAME_1)
```

In the present case, the state name column (NAME_1) was passed as the ID and thus, all the counties that form a single state were dissolved into state polygons. Since rgeos deals with the geometrical component of vector layers, the returned object of gUnaryUnion (and, as we shall see, of other functions in this package) has no attribute table. In this case, for example, while the input county_nv_ut was a SpatialPolygonsDataFrame object, the output states is a SpatialPolygons object. Then, how will we be able to tell which polygon corresponds to which state? The answer is that the information is recorded in the ID codes of the resulting layer and can be obtained using the row.names function. Using this function, we can find out that the first feature in states corresponds to "Nevada" and the second to "Utah":

```
> row.names(states)
[1] "Nevada" "Utah"
```

To get a better understanding of what we just did, it would be helpful to visualize the dissolved states' polygons on top of the original county_nv_ut polygons. We can produce a simple plot using two plot function calls (specifying add=TRUE the second time):

```
> plot(county_nv_ut, border = "lightgrey", lty = "dotted")
> plot(states, add = TRUE)
```

Note that the border parameter of plot is used to indicate the polygon border color (rather than col, which, in the case of polygons, refers to fill color). An additional argument is lty (which stands for the line type), which specifies that we want the county borders to be dotted.

There are six line types available in R. See the full list at the entry concerning the lty parameter on the ?par help page.

The resulting output is not presented since we are not done just yet. An additional layer in our plot is going to consist of labels for county names. Text labels can be added to an image created with a plot using the text function. With text, we need to supply a set of coordinates defining where the labels will be plotted (for example, using a matrix object with two columns, for *x* and *y*), and the text to be written at each coordinate (for example, using a character vector).

The most straightforward option would be to place the labels at the centroids of each county. For this, we first have to find the centroid coordinates using yet another function from rgeos that returns a new layer based on a single input layer called gCentroid:

```
> county_ctr = gCentroid(county_nv_ut, byid = TRUE)
```

The resulting `SpatialPoints` object was assigned to `county_ctr`. Since `byid=TRUE` was specified, the layer contains the centroids of the individual counties, rather than the centroid of the whole `county_nv_ut` layer.

We can supply `county_ctr` along with the vector of labels (which we get from the `NAME_2` column of `county_nv_ut`) to the `text` function. The additional parameter `cex` defines the labels font size in relative units (1.5 times the default size):

```
> text(county_ctr, county_nv_ut$NAME_2, cex = 1.5)
```

The final graphical output, produced by the two `plot` functions and one `text` function call, is shown in the following screenshot:

The plot shows the dissolved state polygons (in black), the original `county` polygons (in dotted gray), and county names (as text labels).

Many of the functions in the `rgeos` package cannot handle geometries that are invalid from the topological point of view. For example, when referring to polygons, a valid layer does not contain self-intersecting polygons (polygons whose boundary crosses itself). Examining whether a given layer is valid or not can be done using the `gIsValid` function, which returns TRUE for valid features (either for the layer as a whole, by default, or for each feature separately when specifying `byid=TRUE`). Searching for and resolving topological errors, however, is best done interactively. Thus, GIS software (such as QGIS) is more suitable for this task than R.

Spatial relations between vector layers

In this section, you will learn how to perform operations involving pairs of vector layers. These types of operations are very common in spatial data analysis. We often want to know, for instance:

- What are the distances of different resorts from the nearest coastline?

- Which houses are within a radius x of the epicenter of an earthquake?

- Which parts of the habitat of an endangered species are contained within protected nature reserves?

All of these operations require the overlay of features from two distinct layers, although, as we have seen earlier, the result can be:

- A numeric value (the distance from a resort to the nearest coastline is 50 meters)

- A logical value (the house is within a distance of 10 kilometers of the earthquake epicenter)

- A spatial layer (a polygon defining the intersecting area between the natural distribution of the endangered species and nature reserves)

In this section, we will see examples of all three kinds of operations.

Querying relations between vector layers

Querying relations between two layers is required when we would like to do one of the following:

- Assign data from the attribute table of one feature to another (for example, polygon A gets the attribute table entry of polygon B it intersects with)

- Examine whether a specific relation exists between features (for example, we get TRUE if polygon A is completely within polygon B, or FALSE otherwise)

In GIS terminology, the first type of operation is sometimes referred to as a spatial join or a join by spatial location. The way it can be done in R will be demonstrated using the `airports` and `county` layers. The second type of operation (examining relations) will be demonstrated using another example, involving layers of buildings and natural areas in London.

The `over` function provides consistent functionality to join the attribute table data from one spatial object to another based on their intersection. All nine possible types of relations are permitted (point/line/polygon with point/line/polygon), either via the `sp` package (point-point, point-polygon, and polygon-point) or `rgeos` (all other combinations). The `over` function accepts two spatial layers (parameters x and y). The function call `over(x,y)` then returns—for all features in the first layer (x)—the attribute table entries (or indices, if the layer has no attribute table) of the second layer (y) that intersect it. The related syntax `x[y,]`, when both x and y are vector layers, serves as a shortcut to `over` when we are interested in subsetting the vector layer x according to intersection. The latter function call returns only those features in x that intersect with a feature in y.

As already mentioned, our first example of querying relations between layers will involve the `airports` and `county` layers. The first preliminary step, as always, is to bring both layers to a common CRS. In this case, we will reproject `airports` to the CRS of `county`:

```
> airports = spTransform(airports, CRS(proj4string(county)))
```

We will now plot `airports` on top of the `county` layer to visually examine their relation so that we know what to expect later. Since we already know that all three airports are located in New Mexico, we will work with a subset of `county`, called nm, containing only the counties of New Mexico:

```
> nm = county[county$NAME_1 == "New Mexico", ]
> plot(nm)
> plot(airports, col = "red", pch = 16, add = TRUE)
```

Note that we used yet another parameter of the `plot` function, pch, to choose a different point shape (16 corresponds to the filled circles, while the default argument is a plus symbol +).

 There are 26 point shapes available. The possible shapes and their code are listed in the `?points` help page.

The following screenshot shows the graphical output that is produced:

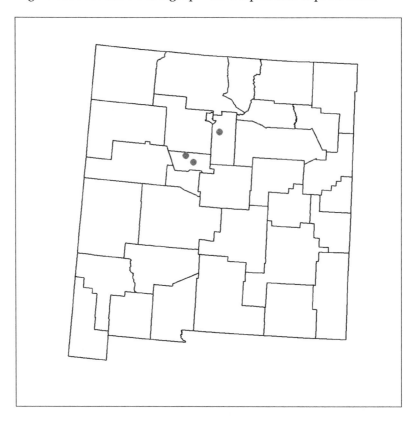

We can see that two of the airports fall within (thus, by definition, also intersect) a single county, while the third airports falls within a different county. Using over with `airports` and `nm` (in that order) will return the following output:

```
> over(airports, nm)
    NAME_1    NAME_2 TYPE_2  FIPS      area
```

```
1 New Mexico Bernalillo County 35001 3023.909
2 New Mexico Bernalillo County 35001 3023.909
3 New Mexico   Santa Fe County 35049 4944.339
```

Indeed, we see that the first two rows are identical since the first two airports are located in the same county (Bernalillo county). To examine specifically which airport falls within each county, we can bind the result of over with the attribute table of airports:

```
> cbind(airports@data, over(airports, nm))
                      name      NAME_1      NAME_2 TYPE_2  FIPS
1 Albuquerque International New Mexico Bernalillo County 35001
2            Double Eagle II New Mexico Bernalillo County 35001
3         Santa Fe Municipal New Mexico   Santa Fe County 35049
      area
1 3023.909
2 3023.909
3 4944.339
```

Now we can tell that the Albuquerque International and Double Eagle II airports are located within Bernalillo County, while the Santa Fe Municipal airport is located within Santa Fe County. To permanently incorporate the county information into the attribute table of airports, we can assign the combined table back to the attribute table slot of airports, with an expression such as airports@ data=cbind(airports@data,over(airports,nm)).

Examining the opposite relation (when nm is x and airports is y), we can, for example, subset those counties that intersect with at least one airport using the expression nm[airports,]. As noted earlier, using [with two vector layers is in fact a shortcut used to retain those features of x that intersect with y. In this case, an equivalent over expression would be nm[!is.na(over(nm,airports)$name),], but using nm[airports,] is obviously more convenient.

We can plot the nm[airports,] subset to demonstrate the behavior:

```
> plot(nm[airports, ])
> plot(airports, add = TRUE, col = "red", pch = 16, cex = 1.5)
> text(airports, airports$name, pos = 1)
```

The additional `pos` parameter of the `text` function controls the position of the text with respect to the point coordinates (the default behavior we previously witnessed is to place the text centered on the coordinates point itself, with `pos=1` the text is placed below the point; see `?text` for all options). The following screenshot shows the graphical output that is produced as a result of the three function calls:

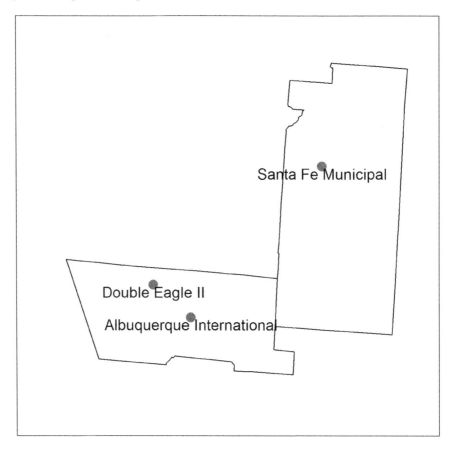

We can see that `nm[airports,]` indeed consists of only those `nm` features that intersect airports.

If we try to match the airports attribute table entries to nm (with over(nm,airports)), only the first airport that intersects each county will be returned in cases where there are multiple matches. If we wish to preserve all matches, we need to specify returnList=TRUE in the over function call. However, the returned object will be a list object since holding sets of elements with variable lengths requires a list rather than a data.frame object. Many of the more advanced uses of R that require such flexibility involve list objects. However, the subject is beyond the scope of this book. More information on lists can be found in the official R's introduction document at http://cran.r-project.org/doc/manuals/r-release/R-intro.pdf and in most introductory books on R.

As an example of querying polygon-polygon relations, we will use another example involving three polygonal Shapefiles:

- Administrative areas of England and Wales (CTYUA_DEC_2013_EW_BFE.shp)
- Buildings in Greater London (london_buildings.shp)
- Natural areas in Greater London (london_natural.shp)

The datasets were downloaded from freely accessible online resources, either from the Office of National Statistics at https://geoportal.statistics.gov.uk/ (administrative areas) or OpenStreetMap (buildings and natural areas).

First, we will read the files into R and bring them to a common CRS. We will begin with the administrative areas layer, reading it from the disk and naming it boundary:

```
> boundary = readOGR("C:\\Data", "CTYUA_DEC_2013_EW_BFE")
```

Using the proj4string function reveals the CRS of boundary—the British National Grid. Note that the resulting string is abbreviated in the following output since it does not fit in a single line:

```
> proj4string(boundary)
[1] "+proj=tmerc +lat_0=49 +lon_0=-2 +k=0.9996012717 +x_0=400000 $
```

Next, we will read the two OpenStreetMap layers:

```
> buildings = readOGR("C:\\Data", "london_buildings")
> natural = readOGR("C:\\Data", "london_natural")
```

Both these layers are defined in a geographical CRS, as the following output demonstrates:

```
> proj4string(buildings)
[1] "+proj=longlat +datum=WGS84 +no_defs +ellps=WGS84 +towgs84=0,$
> proj4string(natural)
[1] "+proj=longlat +datum=WGS84 +no_defs +ellps=WGS84 +towgs84=0,$
```

We will reproject the `buildings` and `natural` layers to the CRS of `boundary`:

```
> buildings = spTransform(buildings, CRS(proj4string(boundary)))
> natural = spTransform(natural, CRS(proj4string(boundary)))
```

Now that the preliminary preparations are complete, we can continue with the exercise. Our goal will be to assign the distance to the River Thames to each of the buildings within the City of London. For this, we will go through the following intermediate steps:

1. Create a subset of `buildings` with only those in the City of London.

2. Create a subset of `natural` with only the riverbanks.

3. Dissolve the riverbank features into a single one.

4. Calculate the distance between each feature in `buildings` and the riverbank.

The administrative boundaries layer comes with an explanatory file (`Product Specification for CTYUA_2013_EW_BFE.docx`, which is also provided on the book's website), where we can find out that the names of the different administrative areas are defined in the `CTYUA13NM` column of the attribute table of this layer. Using this column, we will create a subset, named `city`, containing only the polygon defining the city of the London administrative area:

```
> city = boundary[boundary$CTYUA13NM == "City of London", ]
```

Using the `city` polygon, we will create a subset of only those buildings that are within the City of London. If we were interested in intersection (in other words, buildings that are completely or incompletely within the `city` polygon), we could use the `[` or `over` methods as already shown earlier. To evaluate other types of relationships, the `rgeos` package provides a dozen additional functions: `gContains`, `gContainsProperly`, `gCovers`, `gCoveredBy`, `gCrosses`, `gDisjoint`, `gEquals`, `gEqualsExact`, `gIntersects`, `gTouches`, `gOverlaps`, and `gWithin`. The names of these functions already provide a clue for the relationship they are used to evaluate; the exact definitions are provided in the respective help page of each function.

Since in our example we are interested in creating a subset of the buildings features that are contained within city, we are going to use the function that evaluates containment—gContains. According to the help page of gContains, the expression gContains(city,buildings) will return TRUE for buildings features that are contained within city. Specifying byid=TRUE is necessary to evaluate the relation separately for each feature:

```
> in_city = gContains(city, buildings, byid = TRUE)
```

The result, in_city, is a two-dimensional matrix with rows corresponding to the buildings features (210,937 buildings in Greater London) and columns corresponding to the city features (there is only one, the City of London; if we had more than one feature in city, we would have had more columns):

```
> class(in_city)
[1] "matrix"
> head(in_city)
      119
0 FALSE
1 FALSE
2 FALSE
3 FALSE
4 FALSE
5 FALSE
```

The first (and only) column of this matrix is a logical vector specifying the containment status of each building within the city polygon. Using this vector as a rows index for buildings creates a subset of only those buildings within city:

```
> buildings = buildings[in_city[, 1], ]
```

The first step is now complete. Returning to the natural layer, we will now subset the polygons of type "riverbank" (which in the vicinity of the City of London corresponds to the River Thames):

```
> river = natural[natural$type == "riverbank", ]
```

As the third step, we will dissolve the separate river segments since we will be interested in the shortest distance to any section of the river, rather than the distances to its specific parts. As previously shown in the county example, dissolving can be achieved with gUnaryUnion. This time, the id parameter is left unspecified so that all geometries will be dissolved into a single one:

```
> river = gUnaryUnion(river)
```

Before continuing with the fourth step (calculating distances, which we'll see later in this chapter), we will visually review the processed `buildings` and `river` layers we have at this point, with respect to the administrative boundaries layer `boundary`:

```
> plot(buildings, col = "sandybrown")
> plot(river, col = "lightblue", add = TRUE)
> plot(boundary, border = "dimgrey", add = TRUE)
```

The resulting graphical output is shown in the following screenshot:

In this preceding screenshot, we see the buildings of the City of London (in brown), the dissolved riverbanks polygon (in blue), and the administrative areas boundaries (in gray).

Creating new geometries

The `rgeos` package provides four functions to create new layers based on a pair of existing ones: `gDifference`, `gIntersection`, `gSymdifference`, and `gUnion`. The usage of these functions is very similar to that of functions to query relationships since their main parameters are also a pair of layers and the `byid` parameter. The difference is that they do not return logical values or matched attribute table entries (based on whether the examined relationship holds), but rather a new layer. The following diagram demonstrates how new geometries are generated in each case:

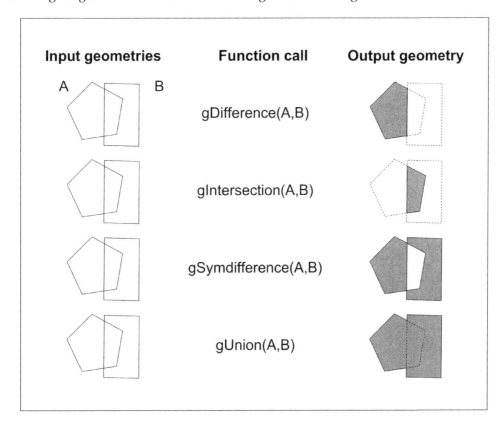

 Note that the `gUnion` function operates in a similar way to `gUnaryUnion`—just that the `gUnioun` function dissolves geometries from two different layers, while the `gUnaryUnion` function operates upon the geometries of a single layer.

Our next example will utilize two of these functions: `gIntersection` and `gDifference`. We will also use three new layers: buildings, natural areas, and administrative borders in Haifa. The buildings and natural areas layers originate from OpenStreetMap data, the same way as in the London example, while the administrative borders of Israel will be downloaded from a global administrative borders dataset directly through R. The buildings and natural areas layers will be named `haifa_buildings` and `haifa_natural` in order to not be confused with the analogous objects `buildings` and `natural` from the London example.

Our goal will be to create a polygon encompassing the natural areas in the vicinity of the buildings in Haifa, excluding those natural areas that are within 50 meters of the nearest building. We will follow four intermediate steps:

1. Read the layers into R and bring them to a common CRS.
2. Create a bounding polygon (convex hull) encompassing the buildings.
3. Clip the natural areas according to the bounding polygon.
4. Remove the natural areas that are 50 meters away from buildings.

As a first step, we will read the Haifa buildings and natural areas layers:

```
> haifa_buildings = readOGR("C:\\Data", "haifa_buildings")
> haifa_natural = readOGR("C:\\Data", "haifa_natural")
```

The third layer involved, the administrative boundaries, will be downloaded from the GADM database of Global Administrative Areas at `http://www.gadm.org/`, which is accessible using the `getData` function from the `raster` package:

```
> israel_adm = getData("GADM", country = "ISR", level = 1)
```

The hereby used arguments of `getData` are as follows:

- `name`: The dataset name (for example, `"GADM"`, which stands for the GADM dataset; using another dataset, `"SRTM"`, will be demonstrated in the next chapter)
- `country` (relevant for the `name="GADM"` option): The country ISO3 code (a list of country codes can be obtained with `getData("ISO3")`)
- `level` (relevant for the `name="GADM"` option): The level of administrative subdivision (`0`: country, `1`: first subdivision, and so on)

In fact, the `county` layer we used earlier comes from the GADM dataset as well (only that FIPS codes have been added to its attribute table). The reason GADM was not used in the London example is that it is less accurate than the Office of National Statistics layer.

We will not need the whole `israel_adm` layer, but only a subset consisting of the Haifa administrative area, which includes the city of Haifa:

```
> haifa_adm = israel_adm[israel_adm$NAME_1 == "Haifa", ]
```

Before proceeding with geometrical calculations, as usual, all three layers (`haifa_adm`, `haifa_buildings`, and `haifa_natural`) will be reprojected to the same CRS. In this case, we are going to use the UTM Zone 36N CRS. We can obtain its parameters from the Landsat image object `l_03` we read into R in one of the previous examples:

```
> haifa_adm =
+spTransform(haifa_adm, CRS(proj4string(l_03)))
> haifa_buildings =
+ spTransform(haifa_buildings, CRS(proj4string(l_03)))
> haifa_natural =
+ spTransform(haifa_natural, CRS(proj4string(l_03)))
```

Having completed the first step, we will take a moment to plot the three layers and see what they look like:

```
> plot(haifa_natural, col = "lightgreen")
> plot(haifa_buildings, add = TRUE)
> plot(haifa_adm, add = TRUE)
```

The resulting graphical output (in the following screenshot) shows the Haifa administrative area border (haifa_adm, in this case marking the Mediterranean sea coastline), the Haifa buildings (haifa_buildings), and the natural areas (haifa_natural, shown in green):

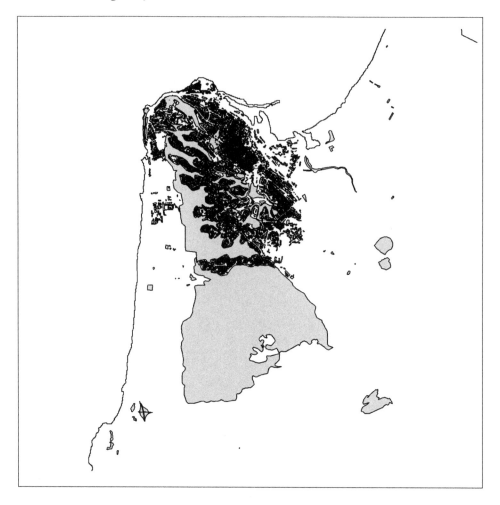

Proceeding with the second step, we will create a convex hull polygon, assigned to buildings_ch, in order to define our area of interest surrounding the buildings. A convex hull is the smallest convex polygon encompassing a certain set of features (see the gray polygon in the next screenshot). A convex hull can be created using the gConvexHull function:

```
> buildings_ch = gConvexHull(haifa_buildings)
```

The convex hull crosses the Mediterranean sea. We would like to, however, retain only those areas of buildings_ch that are within haifa_adm (in other words, on land). This can be achieved by using the gIntersection function on buildings_ch and haifa_adm:

```
> buildings_ch = gIntersection(buildings_ch, haifa_adm)
```

Now that the bounding polygon buildings_ch is set, we proceed to our third step. Turning to the haifa_natural layer, we will merge all of its polygons into one polygon (since we are not interested in discerning different types of natural areas) using gUnaryUnion, similarly to what we did in the London example:

```
> haifa_natural = gUnaryUnion(haifa_natural)
```

Then, we will use buildings_ch to retain only those natural areas that are within our area of interest, using another gIntersection function call:

```
> haifa_natural = gIntersection(haifa_natural, buildings_ch)
```

What remains to be done is our fourth step, which is removing the areas in haifa_natural that are within 50 meters of the nearest building. To do this, we will first create a 50 meter buffer polygon surrounding haifa_buildings, using the gBuffer function (specifying the buffer size with width):

```
> buildings_50m = gBuffer(haifa_buildings, width = 50)
```

Then, using the gDifference function, we will calculate the area in haifa_natural that is not within the 50 meters buffer of haifa_buildings:

```
> haifa_natural = gDifference(haifa_natural, buildings_50m)
```

We are done. To see the resulting layers, we will plot all four of them (buildings_ch, haifa_adm, haifa_natural, and haifa_buildings) together, with the following series of plot function calls:

```
> plot(buildings_ch, col = "lightgrey", border = "lightgrey")
> plot(haifa_adm, add = TRUE)
> plot(haifa_natural, col = "lightgreen", add = TRUE)
> plot(haifa_buildings, add = TRUE)
```

The resulting graphical output is shown in the following screenshot:

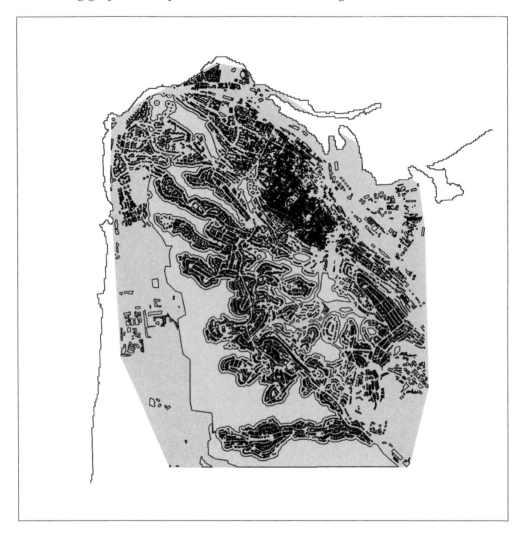

In the preceding screenshot, we can see the bounding polygon `buildings_ch` in gray, the administrative borders, as well as the buildings, in black, and natural areas (those within the bounding polygon and excluding areas within 50 meters of buildings) in green. We will continue working with the Haifa layers we have hereby created in several additional examples in subsequent chapters.

Calculating distances between geometries

Let's now return to the London example, to complete its fourth step (which is distance calculation). Distances between each feature from one layer to each feature in a second layer can be calculated with the gDistance function, setting byid to TRUE. The following expression calculates the distance from each feature in buildings to each feature in river:

```
> dist = gDistance(buildings, river, byid = TRUE)
```

As seen in the gContains example, the result is a matrix:

```
> class(dist)
[1] "matrix"
```

The matrix rows correspond to river features, whereas its columns correspond to buildings features. As the following output of dim demonstrates, we have 1,583 buildings features in the City of London and one river feature (remember that we dissolved the separate riverbank parts into one):

```
> dim(dist)
[1]    1 1583
```

Selecting the first (and only) row of dist will yield a numeric vector with the distances of each building to the nearest riverbank. With the following expression, we can assign the distances to a new column, named dist_river, in the attribute table of buildings:

```
> buildings$dist_river = dist[1, ]
```

Examining the attribute table will demonstrate that, indeed, we now have a distance-to-river entry for each of the buildings in the City of London:

```
> head(buildings@data)
      osm_id                   name               type dist_river
16   4076420              St Brides  place_of_worship   313.1239
56   4364085 Sainsbury's Head Office             block   683.5640
137  4959489          30 St Mary Axe        attraction   653.4159
138  4959510         Bank of England            office   503.7244
139  4959544      St Paul's Cathedral         cathedral   287.7122
140  4959629        Liverpool Street     train_station  1009.8070
```

We are going to wait until *Chapter 9, Advanced Visualization of Spatial Data*, to graphically display this result while learning some additional visualization methods.

Joining geometries with tabular data

In this section, we are going to join an attribute table of a spatial vector layer with plain tabular data (as opposed to joining with the attribute table of another layer based on spatial location). In spatial analysis practice, we often have, at hand, a spatial layer and supplementary tabular data as separate objects, while we would like to work with them in combination. For instance, in the present example, USA Census data regarding county population sizes (a CSV file) will be linked to the county layer defining county geometries, in order to calculate county population densities. To do the latter, we need to know both the population size (from the census table) and area size (from the vector layer) for each county, and the only way to do that is to join both datasets.

The intermediate steps we will perform are as follows:

1. Read the USA Census data.
2. Subset the portion of the data we are interested in.
3. Prepare a common key to join the census data with the county layer.
4. Join!
5. Calculate the population density.

Our first step is to read the USA Census data into R.

 The USA Census data was downloaded from the United States Census Bureau available at https://www.census.gov/popest/data/counties/totals/2012/CO-EST2012-alldata.html.

The CSV file, CO-EST2012-Alldata.csv, is provided on the book's website in its original form. The following expression reads its contents and assigns it to a data.frame object named dat:

```
> dat = read.csv("C:\\Data\\CO-EST2012-Alldata.csv")
```

The expression colnames(dat) reveals that we have as many as 52 variables in this table. To save space, only the first 15 values are printed here:

```
> colnames(dat)[1:15]
 [1] "SUMLEV"            "REGION"           "DIVISION"
 [4] "STATE"             "COUNTY"           "STNAME"
 [7] "CTYNAME"           "CENSUS2010POP"    "ESTIMATESBASE2010"
[10] "POPESTIMATE2010"   "POPESTIMATE2011"  "POPESTIMATE2012"
[13] "NPOPCHG_2010"      "NPOPCHG_2011"     "NPOPCHG_2012"
```

As the accompanying file CO-EST2012-alldata.pdf informs, the first seven variables are geographical identifiers such as STATE (state FIPS code) or CTYNAME (county name), while the other 45 are measured variables related to demography, such as CENSUS2010POP (April 4, 2010 resident Census 2010 population) or BIRTHS2011 (births between July 1, 2010 to June 30, 2011). For our example, we will use only one of the measured variables (CENSUS2010POP), which is found in the 8th column. When joining the data with the county layer, however, we will also require the STATE column (the fourth column) and COUNTY column (the fifth column). Using the latter two columns, we will create a FIPS code column in dat that we will use to join dat to the attribute table of county.

We could subset the three columns of interest by simply using the expression dat[,c(4,5,8)]. However, it is recommended you refer to the column names themselves rather than to their numeric indices, to make the code more general (so that it will still work if the column order is altered):

```
> selected_cols = c("STATE", "COUNTY", "CENSUS2010POP")
> dat = dat[, colnames(dat) %in% selected_cols]
```

Note that here, we first created a vector with the column names of interest (selected_cols), used it to create a logical vector pointing to the indices of the respective columns (colnames(dat) %in% selected_cols), and finally used this logical vector as the column index of dat to create the subset.

The first few rows of dat now appear as follows:

```
> head(dat)
  STATE COUNTY CENSUS2010POP
1     1      0       4779736
2     1      1         54571
3     1      3        182265
4     1      5         27457
5     1      7         22915
6     1      9         57322
```

For convenience, we can convert the column names to lowercase using the tolower function:

```
> colnames(dat) = tolower(colnames(dat))
> colnames(dat)
[1] "state"        "county"         "census2010pop"
```

Examining the table will also reveal that it contains subtotal entries, for entire states, in addition to the county entries. These entries are marked with the value 0 in the county column. Since we are interested in counties, not states, these entries need to be removed:

```
> dat = dat[dat$county != 0, ]
```

With the first and second steps now complete, we are going to create a key with which the county layer and the dat table will be joined. The least problematic option is to use the FIPS codes as a key since county names may be slightly different among datasets.

We already have a FIPS column in the county layer. For example, the FIPS codes of the first 10 features are as follows:

```
> county$FIPS[1:10]
 [1] "09005" "09003" "09013" "09015" "06093" "06015" "06049"
 [8] "09011" "09001" "09007"
```

These five-digit codes encompass the state code (digits 1 to 2) and county code (digits 3 to 5). As we can see, when the state or county code is fewer than two or three digits, it is preceded by zeros. For example, the first county polygon has the FIPS code 09005, which means its state code is 9 (state of Connecticut) and county code is 5 (Litchfield County). However, in the dat table, the state and county FIPS codes are kept as separate numeric values without leading zeros (9 and 5). In order to get matching values with the county layer, we need to perform the following steps:

1. Add leading zeros in the state column to get uniform two-digit codes.
2. Add leading zeros in the county column to get uniform three-digit codes.
3. Paste the state and county columns together to get the FIPS codes.

The first two steps can be performed using the formatC function. This function can deal with several formatting tasks including the one we need — padding the values of a vector with leading zeros, to obtain a common character length. In this particular case, we need to specify three arguments: the vector to work upon, the required final character count (the width parameter), and the format modifier "0" (the flag parameter, where "0" marks the *pad with leading zeros* scenario; see ?formatC):

```
> dat$state = formatC(dat$state, width = 2, flag = "0")
> dat$county = formatC(dat$county, width = 3, flag = "0")
```

We can examine the first few values of the modified `state` and `county` columns to make sure the expected outcome was obtained:

```
> dat$state[1:10]
 [1] "01" "01" "01" "01" "01" "01" "01" "01" "01" "01"
> dat$county[1:10]
 [1] "001" "003" "005" "007" "009" "011" "013" "015" "017" "019"
```

Note that the numeric values have been automatically converted to characters since a numeric value cannot have leading zeros.

Finally, we will paste the state and county codes into county FIPS codes and assign them to a new column called `FIPS`:

```
> dat$FIPS = paste0(dat$state, dat$county)
```

Now, we have in `dat$FIPS` an identical format as seen in `county$FIPS`:

```
> dat$FIPS[1:10]
 [1] "01001" "01003" "01005" "01007" "01009" "01011" "01013"
 [8] "01015" "01017" "01019"
```

We are ready to move on to the fourth step—joining the attribute table of `county` with the `dat` table. In fact, we are going to use a subset of `dat`, containing only two columns: FIPS (since the join will be based upon it) and `census2010pop` (since these are the data we are interested in) because the `state` and `county` columns are of no use to us at this stage. The join operation is done using the `join` function from the `plyr` package (see *Chapter 3, Working with Tables*):

```
> library(plyr)
> county@data = join(county@data,
+ dat[, colnames(dat) %in% c("FIPS", "census2010pop")],
+ by = "FIPS")
```

Using `county@data` as the first argument in `join` and the type of join that is being used (`"left"`, by default), ensures that all entries in `county@data` are preserved in their original order (regardless of whether they have a match in `dat`). This is extremely important since the rows of `county@data` correspond to the county polygons. Thus, changing the order of rows would result in a discrepancy between the attribute table and the spatial features. Concerning vector layers, operations such as `join(county@data, x, type="left")` are safe to perform, while manual modification of the `@data` component involving altering the row order (for example, deleting a single row) should be generally avoided.

As a result, we now have the matching `census2010pop` entries in the attribute table of `county`:

```
> head(county@data)
      NAME_1       NAME_2 TYPE_2   FIPS      area census2010pop
1 Connecticut Litchfield County 09005  2451.876        189927
2 Connecticut    Hartford County 09003  1941.110        894014
3 Connecticut     Tolland County 09013  1077.789        152691
4 Connecticut     Windham County 09015  1350.476        118428
5  California    Siskiyou County 06093 16416.572         44900
6  California   Del Norte County 06015  2626.707         28610
```

We can check and see that only one entry in the `county` layer could not be matched with a `census2010pop` entry from `dat` (and thus, has `NA` in the `census2010pop` column). This entry corresponds to Clifton Forge City, Virginia:

```
> county@data[is.na(county$census2010pop),
+ c("NAME_1", "NAME_2")]
        NAME_1            NAME_2
2591 Virginia Clifton Forge City
```

Our fifth and final step will be to calculate population densities for each county, by dividing the population size (the `census2010pop` column) by county area (the `area` column). The result can be assigned to a new column, named `density`, in the attribute table of `county`:

```
> county$density = county$census2010pop / county$area
```

Examining the attribute table shows that the new column, holding average population density per km^2, has indeed been added to the `county` layer:

```
> head(county@data)
      NAME_1       NAME_2 TYPE_2   FIPS      area census2010pop
1 Connecticut Litchfield County 09005  2451.876        189927
2 Connecticut    Hartford County 09003  1941.110        894014
3 Connecticut     Tolland County 09013  1077.789        152691
4 Connecticut     Windham County 09015  1350.476        118428
5  California    Siskiyou County 06093 16416.572         44900
6  California   Del Norte County 06015  2626.707         28610
     density
1  77.461920
2 460.568482
3 141.670638
4  87.693548
5   2.735041
6  10.891965
```

Preparing a map of population densities per county is postponed until we reach *Chapter 9, Advanced Visualization of Spatial Data*.

Summary

In this chapter, we covered the basic operations involved in working with vector layers in R. First, we reviewed the classes used to represent spatial vector layers in R, and explored two ways to bring spatial vector data into R (geocoding and reading from a file). Second, we discussed how to examine and modify the attribute tables of vector layers, how to create subsets of layers according to their attribute tables, and how to join new data to an attribute table (either from a separate table or from another vector layer). Third, the major types of geometry-related operations with vector layers, including the calculation of geometrical properties, evaluation of relations between layers, and the creation of new layers based on the existing ones, were presented.

In the next chapter, we will delve into rasters in more detail, examining geometry-related modification of rasters (such as reprojection), utilizing elevation rasters (such as DEMs), and working with spatio-temporal raster data (such as time series data from satellite images). Later, in *Chapter 7, Combining Vector and Raster Datasets*, we are going to discuss several common procedures associated with interrelations between raster and vector data.

6
Modifying Rasters and Analyzing Raster Time Series

In this chapter, we will continue with the material presented in *Chapter 4, Working with Rasters*, moving on to more advanced operations. These involve either the modification of the geometric properties of a raster or direction- and distance-related calculations on rasters; mostly using additional functions in the `raster` package. Examples related to the analysis of spatio-temporal remote sensing data will be presented in the last section of this chapter, to demonstrate how more complex, custom-made procedures of raster processing can be constructed.

In this chapter, we will use objects that we previously created in *Chapter 3, Working with Tables*, and *Chapter 4, Working with Rasters*.

In this chapter, we'll cover the following topics:

- Modifying the geometry of raster layers
- Applying focal filters
- Clumping patches of connected cells
- Resampling and reprojection of rasters
- Performing topography-related calculations on elevation data
- Aggregating spatio-temporal raster data

Changing the spatial extent or resolution of rasters

With reference to raster geometry, so far we have only dealt with operations where the raster extent is manually reduced by selecting a certain combination of rows and columns to retain (refer to *Chapter 4, Working with Rasters*). In this chapter, we will review more operations that provide us with the freedom to modify the raster geometry of datasets according to our specific requirements.

In this section, we will see how we can change the extent or resolution of rasters without modifying the underlying grid arrangement. This category includes operations such as merging rasters, cropping, or aggregating/disaggregating raster cells. In the next section, we will see how the underlying grid (and possibly the CRS) can be modified through resampling and reprojection.

In the first few examples of this chapter, we will work with a DEM of the area surrounding Haifa, and experiment with the modification of raster extent and resolution. A DEM is a raster holding elevation values, thus representing the topography of the specific area that it covers. There are many ways of creating a DEM, including interpolation from a limited set of elevation measurements (such as points or contours) or conducting continuous measurements of the surface (with instruments such as **Light Detection and Ranging (LIDAR)** or stereoscopy). Here, we will use a part of the near-global DEM created in 2000, in an effort called the **Shuttle Radar Topography Mission (SRTM)**. In this mission, elevation data has been collected using an instrument on board the Space Shuttle Endeavour, covering the Earth's surface up to 60 degrees latitude, north and south.

SRTM data is available online for free (visit `http://srtm.csi.cgiar.org/`). It is also directly accessible through R, using the `getData` function of the `raster` package (we already used this function in the previous chapter to obtain the Haifa administrative borders layer). The SRTM DEM is divided into tiles of 5 x 5 degrees of longitude/latitude that can be downloaded separately. With `getData`, we need to set the dataset name to `"SRTM"` and specify geographic coordinates of interest (longitude and latitude). The returned object is a `RasterLayer` covering the corresponding tile.

Incidentally, the longitude of Haifa is 34.99 degrees (you can check this quickly with `geocode("Haifa")`; refer to the previous chapter), and thus it is located at the intersection of two 5 x 5 degrees tiles. To cover Haifa, we will download both tiles:

- longitude 30-35, latitude 30-35
- longitude 35-40, latitude 30-35

As mentioned earlier, we can specify a given tile by entering any point that falls in it, for example, (33,33) for the first tile and (38,33) for the second. The following code downloads the two tiles and assigns them to the `RasterLayer` objects named `dem1` and `dem2`, respectively:

```
> library(raster)
> dem1 = getData("SRTM", lon=33, lat=33)
> dem2 = getData("SRTM", lon=38, lat=33)
```

> Note that `rgdal` is automatically loaded (if it hasn't been already) since it is necessary to execute `getData`.

We now have two DEMs covering adjacent areas, which we will use to demonstrate several operations involving the modification of raster spatial extent or resolution.

Merging rasters

Separate rasters can be merged into a single one using the `merge` or `mosaic` functions. Both accept two (or more) rasters and return a merged raster.

> The difference between `merge` and `mosaic` is in the way they deal with overlaps of input rasters. The `merge` function assigns the values of the first raster in cases of overlap, whereas in `mosaic`, we supply a function (such as `mean`, `min`, or `max`) to calculate the values in areas of overlap based on all input layers.

With both `merge` and `mosaic`, the rasters must have the same resolution, origin, and CRS; in other words, they need to constitute parts of the same grid. When rasters that do not belong to the same grid need to be combined, resampling is a necessary preliminary step to bring them to a single grid before employing `merge` or `mosaic`.

Our rasters `dem1` and `dem2` do not overlap at all, so we do not need to worry about ways to resolve assignment of values in areas of overlap. Therefore, we can use the `merge` function to combine `dem1` and `dem2` and create a single raster named `dem`:

```
> dem = merge(dem1, dem2)
```

Certain operations with rasters (such as merging or reprojection) can be time-consuming. A useful additional parameter to the `merge` function, and many other functions in the `raster` package, is `progress`. Setting `progress="text"` or `progress="window"` will show a progress bar (in the textual output or in a separate window) while the function code runs. This way, the user can assess how much time a given operation will take (and perhaps modify the code to bypass extremely time-consuming steps). The `rasterOptions(progress="text")` expression sets the `progress` parameter to `"text"` globally for the current R session.

We now have a DEM of the whole area of longitude 30-40 and latitude 30-35 (as shown in the following screenshot). Our next step will be to isolate the area of interest surrounding Haifa. We will define the area as the bounding box of `haifa_buildings` (refer to the previous chapter), supplemented with 0.25 degrees on all four sides. For this purpose, we will calculate the bounding box of `haifa_buildings` (using the `extent` function) and then add 0.25 degrees to it, as follows. Beforehand, we will read the `haifa_buildings` layer once again to have it in a geographic CRS:

```
> haifa_buildings = readOGR("C:\\Data", "haifa_buildings")
> haifa_surrounding = extent(haifa_buildings) + 0.25
```

The created object `haifa_surrounding` is an `Extent` object defining our rectangular area of interest. Let's plot `dem` and the `Extent` object using a pair of `plot` function calls:

```
> plot(dem)
> plot(haifa_surrounding, add = TRUE)
```

The graphical output is shown in the following screenshot:

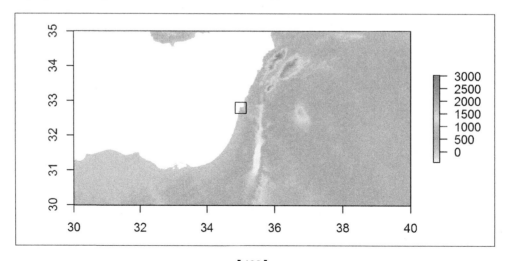

The two merged tiles seem in perfect alignment, which is expected as they originate from the same (larger) DEM. The black rectangle delineates our areas of interest centered on Haifa, which indeed intersects the 35 degrees meridian.

Cropping and trimming

Cropping is the production of a smaller raster from an existing one by selecting a certain range of rows and columns. While the manual subset methods we used in *Chapter 4, Working with Rasters*, are also considered cropping, in practice we usually would like to select the required range of rows and columns by overlaying the raster with another spatial layer, rather than by manually entering row and column indices.

The `crop` function, given a raster and an `Extent` object, returns a smaller raster with the required extent. Instead of an `Extent` object, a raster or a vector layer can also be provided, in which case their extent is extracted and used in cropping. For example, the following expression crops `dem` according to `haifa_surrounding`:

```
> dem = crop(dem, haifa_surrounding)
```

To examine the effect, we can visualize the raster once again using the `plot(dem)` expression. The following screenshot shows the graphical output that is produced as a result:

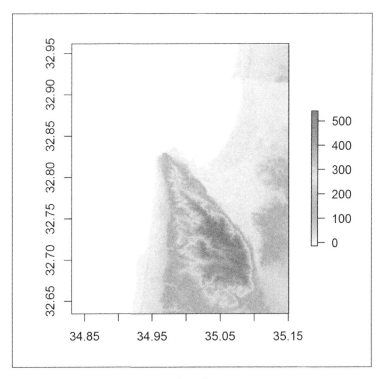

The high-elevation area in the lower half of the preceding screenshot is Mount Carmel. The city of Haifa is located on its northern slopes.

Another useful function within the context of raster cropping is trim. This function removes the outer rows and columns of a raster that all have the same value. For example, using trim(x), we can automatically remove unnecessary NA margins from the raster x.

> A raster (in R, and in general) is by definition rectangular; rasters where values cover a non-rectangular area are obtained by surrounding the area of interest with NA values (such as the Mediterranean sea area in the preceding screenshot). Both crop and trim are used to carve smaller rectangular extents from existing rasters by removing whole rows and columns from their margins. When we are interested in carving non-rectangular shapes, we need, in fact, to fill the unnecessary areas with NA, which is made possible with the mask function (we'll see this in the next chapter).

Aggregating and disaggregating

Aggregation is the creation of a lower-resolution raster by grouping rectangular sets of cells in the original raster into individual, larger cells in the new raster. Aggregation might be necessary when we are ready to lose detail to gain processing efficiency or noise reduction. For example, MODIS satellite data products are distributed in several spatial (and temporal) resolutions, from 250 to 5600 m, with the lower-resolution products usually being the results of aggregation from the original higher-resolution data. The lower-resolution images are useful since as we increase the spatial and temporal extent that is being analyzed, it becomes increasingly unfeasible (and unnecessary) to work with high resolutions. For example, an analysis of NDVI trends over time at a 250 meter resolution on a global scale would involve huge amounts of data; a 5,600 meter resolution is more reasonable for such a task (it would reduce the amount of data 500-fold!). In addition, lower-resolution products are typically associated with greater confidence since noisy pixels are averaged out during aggregation.

The `aggregate` function performs aggregation by grouping adjacent pixels into new ones, given an input raster and the aggregation factor `fact`. The aggregation factor controls the size of the new raster cells in units of the original cells. It can either be a single integer (in which case, aggregation is equal on both axes) or a vector of length 2 (in which case, different levels of aggregation are applied on the x and y axes). For example, using `fact=8` means that each set of 8*8 cells in the original raster becomes a single cell in the new raster. Using `fact=c(5,10)` means that each rectangle of 5*10 cells (5 along the x axis, 10 along the y axis) becomes a single cell. In addition, the `fun` parameter specifies which function will be used to calculate the new values based on existing ones (the default is `mean`), and the `na.rm` parameter specifies whether `NA` values are removed from each set prior to calculation (the default is `TRUE`). To demonstrate the behavior of `aggregate`, we will apply it on our `dem` raster, aggregating 8*8 and 16*16 sets of cells:

```
> dem_agg8 = aggregate(dem, fact = 8)
> dem_agg16 = aggregate(dem, fact = 16)
```

The following expressions sequentially plot the original `dem`, and the aggregation results `dem_agg8` and `dem_agg16`, along with the appropriate plot titles specified using the `main` parameter:

```
> plot(dem, main = "Original image")
> plot(dem_agg8, main = "8x8 aggregated")
> plot(dem_agg16, main = "16x16 aggregated")
```

The following screenshot shows the resulting individual plots from left to right:

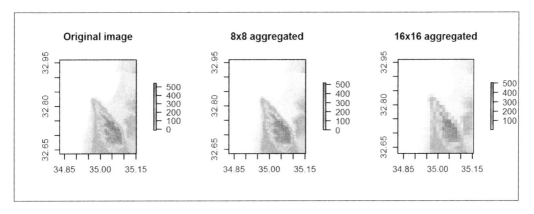

We can see that the preceding screenshot becomes increasingly blurred as the degree of aggregation increases.

The opposite operation from aggregation is disaggregation; it can be performed with the disaggregate function. For example, the disaggregate(dem_agg8,fact=8) expression would yield back a higher-resolution raster with the same resolution of dem. However, the information that has been lost in aggregation is not recovered (each set of 8*8 adjacent cells would have the same value) and the disaggregated raster will visually appear identical to dem_agg8.

Raster resampling and reprojection

In this section, we are going to transfer the values of a given raster from its own grid to a different grid. This operation is known as resampling. Raster reprojection is a closely related operation; it is basically resampling to a grid having a different CRS than that of the original raster.

Raster resampling

Raster resampling can be performed using the resample function. The required parameters of this function are as follows:

- The raster whose values are to be resampled (x)
- A raster that defines the grid to which the values will be transferred (y)
- The resampling method (method)

The resample function currently provides two resampling methods. The method that we use determines the way in which a cell in the new raster gets its value, based on the old raster's values:

- "ngb": Nearest-neighbor; assigns the value of the nearest cell
- "bilinear": Bilinear interpolation; assigns a weighted average of the four nearest cells (the default)

 Other resampling methods exist. For instance, in the bicubic interpolation a weighted average of the nearest 16 cells is assigned in each cell.

The nearest-neighbor interpolation retains the original values, only transferring them to the new grid according to proximity, while resampling methods that use weighted averages from several cells (such as bilinear interpolation) inevitably involve modification of the original values thus producing a smoother image. Therefore, in cases where the original values should be preserved, the nearest-neighbor resampling method is recommended. In categorical rasters with integers representing different cover types, for example, it would make no sense to calculate a weighted average of categories. For instance, in a raster with two categories, say 1 for forest and 2 for pasture, the average of the four cell values is frequently not going to be equal to either 1 or 2, making the resulting image meaningless. On the other hand, when visual appearance is the primary consideration, bilinear interpolation and similar weighted-average methods are recommended.

For our resampling examples, we will use two NDVI images: one from Landsat and one from MODIS. As the Landsat and MODIS images are defined in the same CRS and they overlap (the MODIS image extent encompasses the Landsat image extent) — although they have very different resolutions (the Landsat image resolution is 30 m while the MODIS resolution is 500 m) — we can resample each one with the other. In the following three examples, we will perform these steps:

1. Compare the original Landsat image with the one resampled according to the MODIS grid.

2. Compare the original MODIS image with the one resampled according to the Landsat grid.

3. Compare the MODIS image resampling results using two methods: nearest-neighbor and bilinear interpolation.

For a Landsat NDVI image, we will use the `ndvi_00` raster that we previously calculated based on an image obtained on October 4, 2000. As for MODIS, the raster `r` contains 280 NDVI images for the period between February 18, 2000 and April 6, 2012 (refer to *Chapter 4*, *Working with Rasters*). To make the comparison more interesting, we will select the date of acquisition closest to October 4, 2000. Using the `dates$date` vector of MODIS acquisition dates (as we saw in *Chapter 3*, *Working with Tables*), we can find out the index of the date closest to October 4, 2000 by performing the following steps:

1. Find the vector of differences between each date in `dates$date` and October 4, 2000.

2. Calculate absolute differences using the `abs` function.

3. Find the index of the minimal difference value using `which.min`.

These three steps can be accomplished with a single line of code, as follows:

```
> l_date = which.min(abs(dates$date - as.Date("2000-10-04")))
```

The result, assigned to `l_date`, is the index of the MODIS image closest in its acquisition date to October 4, 2000. It is equal to `15`:

```
> l_date
[1]  15
```

Thus, for the examples, we will use `r[[l_date]]`, the fifteenth layer of the multiband raster `r` (the corresponding date of acquisition is September 29, 2000, as `dates$date[l_date]` will show).

In our first example, we will resample the Landsat image `ndvi_00` to the MODIS grid of the `r[[l_date]]` image using the nearest-neighbor method as follows:

```
> l_resample = resample(ndvi_00, r[[l_date]], method = "ngb")
```

Let's compare the original Landsat image `ndvi_00` and the resampled image `l_resample` by plotting both as follows:

```
> plot(ndvi_00, main = "Original Landsat image")
> plot(l_resample, ext = extent(ndvi_00),
+ main = "Resampled to MODIS")
```

Note that when plotting `l_resample`, we supply the `ext` parameter with the extent of the original Landsat image `ndvi_00` to zoom in on the area of overlap. The `l_resample` image is, in fact, larger than `ndvi_00` (it has the same extent as `r[[l_date]]`) but all cells that do not overlap with `ndvi_00` are assigned with `NA`.

The resulting two images are shown in the following screenshot:

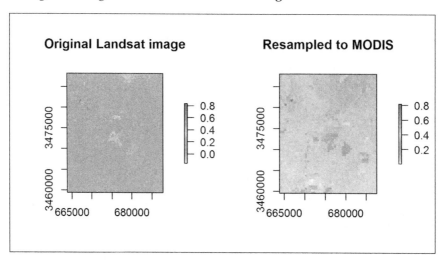

On the left, we can see the detailed 30 meter resolution `ndvi_00` image and on the right we see the rough 500 meter resolution image where the values of the nearest pixels of `ndvi_00` were assigned to each of the pixels in `r[[l_date]]`.

> When the original raster is much more detailed than the resampled result (such as in the previous example), considerable data loss takes place. This happens due to the fact that the value of only a single (in nearest-neighbor) or a few (in bilinear interpolation) 30 meter pixel(s) determines the value of a much larger 500 meter pixel in the new image, in our particular example for instance. Aggregation and zonal extraction according to polygons (as we will see in the next chapter) are more desired solutions when raster resolution is greatly reduced as part of resampling.

The opposite operation is to resample the MODIS NDVI values from `r[[l_date]]` to the Landsat grid of the `ndvi_00`, again using the nearest-neighbor method:

```
> r_resample = resample(r[[l_date]], ndvi_00, method = "ngb")
```

In this case, the result `r_resample` is smaller in its extent than the original MODIS image `r[[l_date]]`; it has the same extent as `ndvi_00`. To show them side-by-side more conveniently, we will first extend `r_resample` to match the extent of `r[[l_date]]`. This can be done using the `extend` function that extends the raster according to and an `Extent` object (or an object from which an `Extent` object can be derived, such as a `RasterLayer`). The `extend` function adds `NA` rows and columns as necessary to increase the raster extent; it is therefore, in a way, the opposite of `trim`:

```
> r_resample = extend(r_resample, r[[l_date]])
```

We will now plot the results of our second resampling example: the original MODIS image `r[[l_date]]` and the resampled image `r_resample`. While plotting `r[[l_date]]`, we will add a rectangle surrounding the extent of `ndvi_00` to aid in the comparison:

```
> plot(r[[l_date]], main = "Original MODIS image")
> plot(extent(ndvi_00), add = TRUE)
> plot(r_resample, main = "Resampled to Landsat")
```

The two resulting images are shown in the following screenshot:

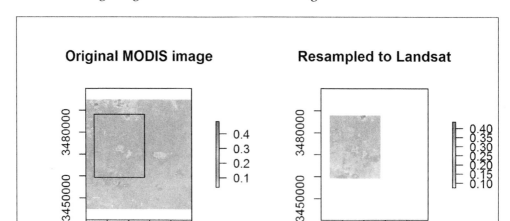

As we can see, the resampled image is identical in its appearance to the respective portion of the original image, although it has a 30 meter resolution unlike the original image that has a 500 meter resolution. The reason is that each set of 30 m Landsat pixels that coincides with a single 500 meter pixel in the MODIS image gets the value of that single pixel. Thus, it appears as if we have 500 meter pixels even if the underlying resolution is much higher.

What if we want to make the image look smoother? In such a case, we can use the bilinear interpolation method instead of the nearest-neighbor method. Let's perform the resampling operation from the last example twice, using the nearest-neighbor method (the same way we just did, assigning the result to r_resample_ngb this time) and the bilinear interpolation method (assigning the result to r_resample_bil). The results will then be combined in a two-band raster with layer names specifying resampling method:

```
> r_resample_ngb = resample(r[[1_date]], ndvi_00, method = "ngb")
> r_resample_bil = resample(r[[1_date]], ndvi_00,
+ method = "bilinear")
> resample_results = stack(r_resample_ngb, r_resample_bil)
> names(resample_results) = c("Nearest neighbor",
+ "Bilinear interpolation")
```

We will plot the results using the `levelplot` function of the `rasterVis` package. Contours are enabled with `contour=TRUE` to highlight the differences between methods:

```
> library(rasterVis)
> levelplot(resample_results,
+ par.settings = RdBuTheme,
+ contour = TRUE)
```

The following screenshot shows the graphical output:

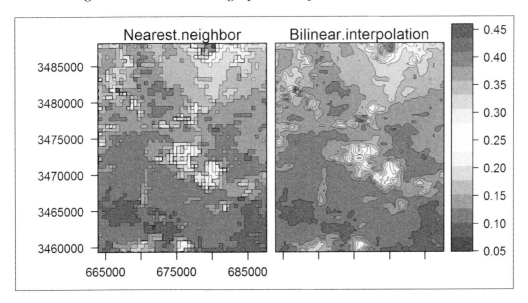

As we saw in the previous example with nearest-neighbor resampling (the left image), sets of adjacent cells that overlap with a single 500 meter pixel get the same value, and thus the contours follow the coarse-grained pattern of MODIS pixels. With bilinear interpolation (the right image), on the other hand, each 30 m cell gets the average of four MODIS pixels closest to it, weighted according to their respective distances; thus, most (if not all) cell values are unique and the image is much smoother.

Raster reprojection

As mentioned earlier, raster reprojection—unlike vector layers reprojection—involves resampling. Unlike vector layers, where all points are independent and thus their coordinates can be individually transformed to a new CRS (refer to the previous chapter), raster pixel coordinates that are transformed to a different CRS will not form a legitimate grid on that CRS (that is, a grid with equal distances between all adjacent pixels and parallel to the CRS x and y axes); rasters therefore require resampling. Thus, raster reprojection consists of two steps: reprojection of the raster pixel coordinates to the new CRS (analogous to reprojecting a vector layer) and resampling of the pixel values to a grid defined in the new CRS.

There are two main ways of defining the new grid in raster reprojection: we can either provide only the new CRS definition and let the grid be generated automatically, or we can provide a specific grid of our own. In the latter case, the process is very similar to resampling; the only change is that the new grid has a different CRS from that of the original raster.

In R, the `projectRaster` function provides raster reprojection functionality and supports both previously mentioned ways of defining a new grid. In the first case, when we want the grid to be automatically generated, we need to supply:

- The raster to be reprojected (`from`)
- The target CRS, as a PROJ.4 string (`crs`)
- Optionally, the required resolution (`res`)

In the second case, when we want to define the grid ourselves, we need to supply:

- The raster to be reprojected (`from`)
- The raster defining the target grid (`to`)

In both scenarios, we also need to specify the resampling method, either `"ngb"` or `"bilinear"` (the default).

As an example, we will reproject `dem` from its geographic CRS to the UTM Zone 36N projection. The corresponding PROJ.4 string, as we have already done in the previous chapters, will be obtained from another raster (`r`). Prior to reprojection, let's print out the current properties of `dem` in order to compare them later with the properties of the reprojection result:

```
> dem
class      : RasterLayer
dimensions : 390, 384, 149760  (nrow, ncol, ncell)
resolution : 0.0008333333, 0.0008333333  (x, y)
```

```
extent       : 34.83083, 35.15083, 32.63583, 32.96083   (xmin, xmax$
coord. ref. : +proj=longlat +datum=WGS84 +ellps=WGS84 +towgs84=0,$
data source : in memory
names        : layer
values       : -14, 541   (min, max)
```

We see that, indeed, dem is defined in a geographic CRS, and has a resolution of
0.0008333333 degrees, longitude and latitude.

In case we do not have any special requirements for the projected dem to align with
an existing layer, we can follow the first reprojection approach, supplying only the
CRS and letting the grid be generated automatically. We can also supply the optional
res argument, primarily to make sure the x and y axes resolution will be equal (90 m,
for example). You can try and execute the following expression without specifying
res, to verify that the default grid generated in this case will have a resolution of
78 m and 92.4 m on the x and y axes respectively:

```
> dem = projectRaster(from = dem,
+ crs = proj4string(r),
+ method = "ngb",
+ res = 90)
```

Printing the properties of the reprojected dem reveals several differences:

```
> dem
class        : RasterLayer
dimensions  : 417, 351, 146367   (nrow, ncol, ncell)
resolution  : 90, 90   (x, y)
extent       : 670666.3, 702256.3, 3611918, 3649448   (xmin, xmax, $
coord. ref. : +proj=utm +zone=36 +datum=WGS84 +units=m +no_defs +$
data source : in memory
names        : layer
values       : -14, 541   (min, max)
```

We can see that the CRS definition has changed to UTM Zone 36N. Also, the extent,
resolution, and dimensions are now different and characterize the new grid that has
been generated.

Plotting the new raster with `plot(dem)` produces the following graphical output:

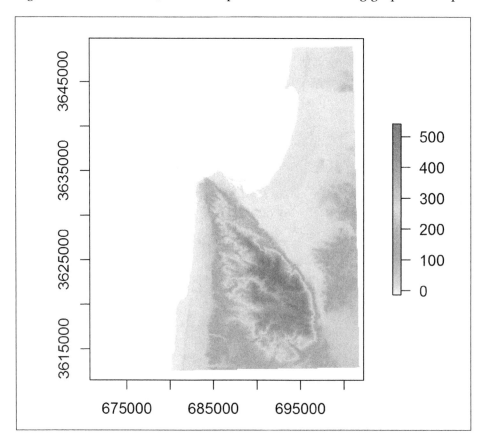

UTM Zone 36N coordinates are now shown along the axes. In addition, you may have noticed that the projected dem image is not exactly parallel to the axes, as the UTM grid was not strictly parallel to the geographic one. Since a raster must be rectangular (refer to the preceding screenshot), empty areas around image margins, consisting of NA values, have been generated.

Filtering and clumping

In this section, and the following one, we move on from the subject of changing raster geometry to the subject of relations between neighboring raster cell values. These relations can be summarized in the form of a new raster using a variety of methods. In this section, we will introduce two such methods: focal filtering and clumping.

Focal filtering involves assigning in each cell of a raster (the focal cell) the result of a function, whose input is the set of values from a neighborhood of cells surrounding the focal one (including itself). The neighborhood size is predetermined (for example, a neighborhood of 3*3 cells is commonly used), and the input raster is scanned in a moving window manner until complete coverage has been reached. There are many appropriate functions that can be implemented in filters for various purposes. For example, using the mean function (also known as a low-pass filter) makes an image look smoother, while using a function that finds the most common value (also known as a majority filter) is useful for reducing noise in a categorical raster.

The focal function is used to apply a focal filter on a RasterLayer object. The three major parameters of this function are as follows:

- The RasterLayer object to be filtered (x)
- A matrix defining the neighborhood and the cell weights (w)
- A function to be applied on the neighborhood (fun)

The w argument should be a matrix defining the neighborhood. It should have odd dimensions (such as a 3*3 or 7*5), since its center defines the focal cell position. The matrix values define the weights that are applied on cell values before these are transferred to the focal function. However, using weights is optional—a matrix where all values are equal to 1 would imply having no weights. Weights of 0 can also be used to create a non-symmetric and/or non-rectangular window. The fun argument should be a function to be applied on the neighborhood values (the default is sum).

For the filtering example, we will return to l_rec, a reclassified NDVI raster (0 for NDVI≤0.2 and 1 for NDVI>0.2) based on the Landsat image obtained on October 4, 2000 (refer to *Chapter 4*, *Working with Rasters*, for more information). This raster shows the locations of the more densely vegetated areas (such as planted pine forests); however, the image is quite grained, with 0 values appearing within the otherwise continuous high-vegetation (1) zones.

To increase continuity, we will buffer the NDVI>0.2 zone by converting all cells having at least one immediate 1 neighbor to 1, thus reducing gaps of 0s between or within vegetated areas. This operation can be carried out by applying a focal filter with a 3*3 window and the max function with no weights. With max, each cell gets the maximal value of its 3*3 neighborhood. Thus, a 0 cell either retains its value (if all nine neighbors are 0) or converts to 1 (in case at least one of its neighbors is 1). All 1 cells retain their value, since they have at least one 1 neighbor (the cell itself). Since we do not need weights, we will use a 3*3 matrix consisting of plain 1s for the w argument. This can be created as follows:

```
> matrix(1, nrow = 3, ncol = 3)
     [,1] [,2] [,3]
[1,]    1    1    1
[2,]    1    1    1
[3,]    1    1    1
```

Therefore, the complete expression that applies the filter on l_rec is as follows:

```
> l_rec_focal = focal(l_rec,
+ w = matrix(1, nrow = 3, ncol = 3),
+ fun = max)
```

The result is assigned to l_rec_focal; comparing it with the original l_rec raster shows the buffering of vegetated areas that took place (refer to the next screenshot).

Our second example of an operation concerning cell neighbors is clumping. In clumping, we are interested in the detection of cell patches that have the same value. For example, you may wish to learn how many patches there are, what their size distribution is, what properties they have with respect to the values of other rasters, and so on. Clumping can be performed with function clump, which returns a new raster where a unique ID is assigned to every connected patch of cells that have the same value in the input raster (except for values of 0 or NA, which are ignored and used as background). The operation is only useful with categorical rasters—in continuous rasters, all (or most) cells usually have unique values. Thus, no patches larger than one cell can be formed.

The clump function accepts a RasterLayer object and returns a raster where each patch of similar-valued cells has a unique ID. Specifying gaps=FALSE will force these IDs to be consecutive integers, starting with 1 and going to *n* (where *n* is the total number of patches). For example, let's clump the l_rec_focal regions of 1:

```
> l_rec_focal_clump = clump(l_rec_focal, gaps = FALSE)
```

The result `l_rec_focal_clump` is a raster where `0` regions were converted to `NA` (and used as background), while all cells that are part of a continuous patch of 1s received a unique ID. Checking out how many unique non-`NA` values `l_rec_focal_clump` contains (for example, with the expression `max(l_rec_focal_clump[],na.rm=TRUE)`) will show that we have 507 separate NDVI>0.2 patches. Had we skipped the filtering step and performed the clumping on `l_rec`, we would have got 1,258 patches.

 The `igraph` package is required for running `clump`, so make sure it is installed.

Let's visualize the filtering and clumping results along with the original raster:

```
> plot(l_rec, main = "Original image")
> plot(l_rec_focal, main = "Filtered")
> plot(l_rec_focal_clump, main = "Clumped")
```

The following screenshot shows the plots of `l_rec`, `l_rec_focal`, and `l_rec_focal_clump`, respectively from left to right:

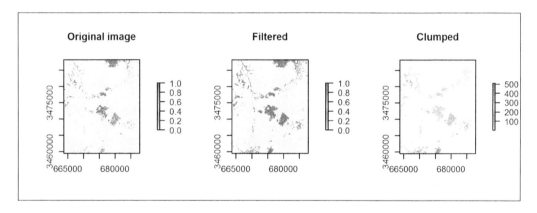

We can see that filtering has thickened the NDVI>0.2 areas, while clumping has assigned IDs (going from `1` to `507`) in each patch. In the next chapter, we will continue working with `l_rec_focal_clump` to see how these patches can be converted to polygons and how patches of interest can be isolated.

Topography-related calculations with elevation data

Deriving topography-related variables from a DEM is a central task in terrain analysis. Many functions and algorithms have been developed for this purpose, and different GIS software packages include different sets of such tools. The `raster` package currently provides several basic terrain analysis functions (of which three examples will be shown in this section).

 A variety of terrain analysis (and other) algorithms are available in R through interfacing with open source GIS software, such as SAGA GIS (using the `RSAGA` package) and GRASS GIS (using the `spgrass6` package). To use these, you will require to download and install the (freely available) respective software, but the subject is beyond the scope of the present book, which focuses on standalone R functionality.

Slope and aspect calculation

Calculation of topographic slope and aspect is among the most basic DEM analysis procedures. These two variables have many uses in their own right (for example, aspect is an important environmental measure due to its association with solar radiation load), and as inputs for subsequent calculations (for example, slope is one of the parameters in the calculation of Topographic Wetness Index). Both are calculated for each cell in an elevation raster by comparing focal cell elevation with the elevations of its eight neighbors (in a 3*3 neighborhood).

The `terrain` function can calculate slope and aspect (and several other terrain characteristics), when provided with a DEM raster and the respective option (`"slope"` or `"aspect"`). Let's take a look at the following example:

```
> slope = terrain(dem, "slope")
> aspect = terrain(dem, "aspect")
```

We now have slope and aspect rasters, by default in radians (using `units="degrees"` will give results in degrees instead). We can check what the results look like using the following expression:

```
> plot(stack(slope, aspect))
```

The following screenshot shows the graphical output:

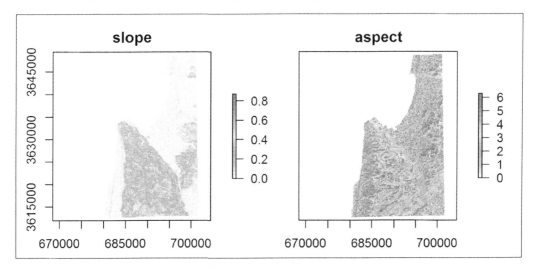

As expected, `slope` shows higher values across Mount Carmel and moderate values in the lowlands on both of its sides. The most prominent features in the `aspect` raster are the opposing aspects of the east-facing and west-facing slopes of Mount Carmel.

Hillshade

A hillshade layer is a hypothetical illumination appearance, as viewed from above, based on topography and the sun's position. Shaded relief maps, used to display topography in an intuitive manner, were traditionally prepared with manual shading (by an artist or a cartographer). Today, such maps can be generated by calculating a hillshade layer based on a DEM; this will be demonstrated in the following example.

The `hillShade` function can calculate a hillshade layer based on four parameters (the first two characterizing the topography and the last two characterizing the sun's position):

- `slope`: Slope (in radians)
- `aspect`: Aspect (in radians)
- `angle`: The sun's elevation angle (in degrees)
- `direction`: The sun's direction (in degrees)

For example, using the slope and aspect layers that we previously calculated, the following expression creates a hillshade layer according to the sun's elevation of 20 degrees and the sun's direction of 235 degrees:

```
> hill = hillShade(slope, aspect, 20, 235)
```

Now, with the following expression, we will plot the resulting `hill` raster using grayscale (as indicated by the `par.settings` argument `GrTheme`):

```
> levelplot(hill, par.settings = GrTheme, margin = FALSE)
```

The following screenshot shows the graphical output:

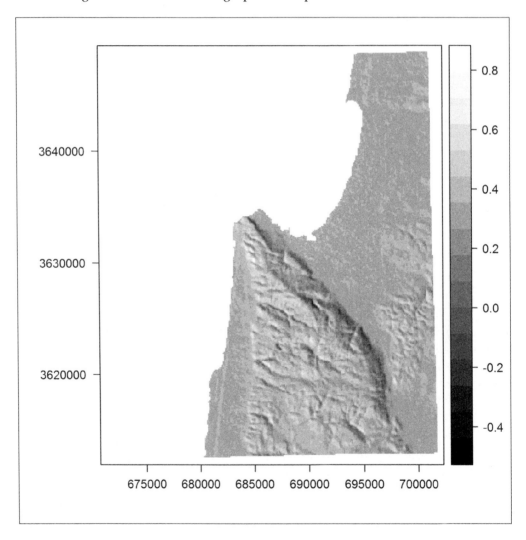

This image clearly shows the relief of Mount Carmel. Since the light source is located in the South-west (sun direction: 235°) and at quite a low angle above the horizon (sun elevation: 20°), the north-eastern slopes of the mountain are in shade while the western slopes are lighted.

Aggregating spatio-temporal raster data

Spatio-temporal data, such as MODIS images, time series, or meteorological records from several stations (see *Chapter 3, Working with Tables*) pose a challenge for analysis and visualization due to their three-dimensional nature. One approach to simplify such data is to perform aggregation in spatial and/or temporal dimensions (another approach to simplify spatio-temporal data is, for example, cluster analysis).

In this section, we will experiment with two approaches to aggregate the data held in the multiband raster r in order to get additional perspectives on the spatio-temporal behavior of NDVI within the geographic area this raster covers.

 More specialized classes and methods (including aggregation) for various types of spatio-temporal data are defined in the spacetime package. An overview of this package can be found in the introductory paper *"spacetime: Spatio-Temporal Data in R"* by its creator Pebesma E. 2012.

The time dimension

In our first example, we will aggregate r along the temporal dimension (that is, the layers). In fact, the previous example where we mapped the minimum and maximum values for each pixel in r using overlay with the range function (see *Chapter 4, Working with Rasters*, for more information) is also an example of aggregation. However, instead of aggregating all layers, what if you want to learn the properties of different time series portions? In such cases, you have to perform several overlay operations, and then combine the results into a multiband raster. That is exactly what we are going to do next.

Let's say we are interested in examining the seasonal NDVI averages across the studied area. In such cases, we need to perform an overlay of all layers for each season using the mean function, and then combine the results into a four-band raster (where each layer corresponds to one of the four seasons). Conceptually, the simplest way of doing this is with a for loop that goes through the four seasons, selecting the appropriate layers of r each time, applying overlay on those layers, and keeping the result to form a final multiband raster in the end.

As a preliminary step to construct the loop, we will define a character vector with season names (seasons) and an empty RasterStack object (season_means). The seasons vector will define loop iterations, while season_means will be used to hold the results:

```
> seasons = c("winter", "spring", "summer", "fall")
> season_means = stack()
```

Now, we are ready to execute the for loop:

```
> for(i in seasons) {
+ season_means = stack(season_means,
+ overlay(r[[which(dates$season == i)]],
+ fun = function(x) mean(x, na.rm = TRUE)))
+ }
```

The loop code section is executed four times (since the number of elements in seasons is four), each time assigning the next season name into i. The code adds the mean of the relevant layers in r (selected using the dates$season vector that we previously created; refer to *Chapter 3, Working with Tables*) to season_means. Therefore, in the first loop iteration, the mean of the "winter" layers in r is added to the empty season_means; in the second iteration, the mean of "spring" is added to season_means (which already has one layer), and so on until all four seasons are covered.

Now that the result season_means is ready, we can add season names to the respective layers for convenience:

```
> names(season_means) = seasons
```

We will view the result using the levelplot function:

```
> levelplot(season_means, par.settings=RdBuTheme, contour=TRUE)
```

The following screenshot shows the graphical output:

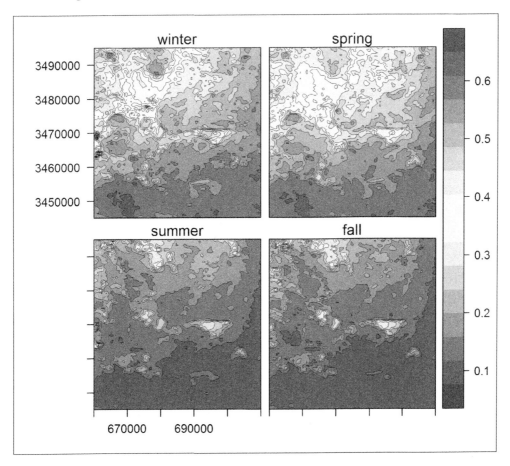

The preceding screenshot shows average NDVI for each season. We can see that NDVI is generally high during winter and spring and low during summer and fall. The image also shows that certain areas (such as the north-west corner of the image) have much higher NDVI in the wet season than in the dry one, while other areas (such as the three patches in the center of the image) maintain relatively high NDVI values in the summer months as well. The former are, in fact, areas where agricultural crops and natural herbaceous vegetation proliferate due to the relatively more abundant rainfall in the wet season, while the latter are planted evergreen pine forests where vegetation activity is maintained even in the dry season.

Another way of aggregating raster layers, bypassing the necessity to construct a loop, is with the stackApply function. Similar to the way in which tapply can be used to apply a function on different portions of a vector (as we discussed in *Chapter 3, Working with Tables*), the function stackApply has been defined to apply a function on different portions of layers in a multiband raster. Analogous to tapply, the main three parameters of stackApply are as follows:

- The input multiband raster (x)
- A vector of indices defining the layers grouping (indices)
- The function to be applied on each group (fun)

Unlike tapply, the indices vector must be composed of consecutive integers, starting with 1. An additional parameter of stackApply is na.rm, which controls whether NA values are removed from calculations.

For example, we can calculate the monthly NDVI means as follows:

```
> month_means = stackApply(r,
+ indices = dates$month,
+ fun = mean,
+ na.rm = TRUE)
```

As in the previous example, we will name the layers of the result month_means:

```
> names(month_means) = month.abb
```

 The character vector month.abb is a predefined one in R; it holds the three-letter abbreviated month names: "Jan", "Feb", "Mar", and so on.

We can visualize the result with levelplot:

```
> levelplot(month_means, par.settings = RdBuTheme, contour = TRUE)
```

The following screenshot shows the graphical output:

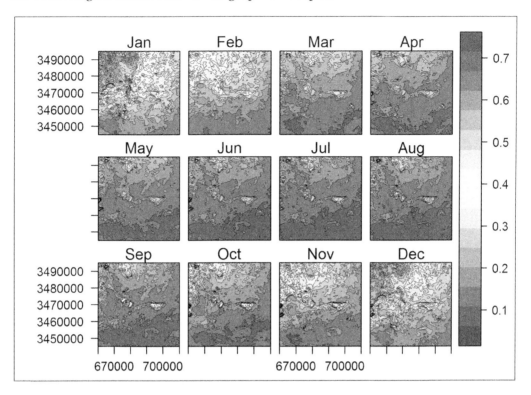

The preceding screenshot shows NDVI dynamics with greater detail on a monthly scale rather than a seasonal scale. We can see that NDVI starts to increase around October-November and declines around February-March. During April-September (the dry season), NDVI is just about constant.

Using the monthly averages, we can derive other informative products. For example, with the following `overlay` function call, we can create a raster that shows the month in which the lowest NDVI value is observed at each location:

```
> min_month = overlay(month_means, fun = which.min)
```

To save space, we will not plot the result here.

As mentioned earlier, the `indices` parameter in `stackApply` accepts a vector of integers starting with `1`, which the `dates$months` vector conveniently was. However, how should we deal with other grouping vectors—character vectors or numeric vectors—that are not consecutive or that do not start with `1`? We must first encode these as consecutive integer vectors, for example, by converting them to a factor (with the `factor` function) and then extracting the factor level indices (with the `as.numeric` function). Let's take a look at the following example:

```
> dates$year[1:30]
 [1]  2000 2000 2000 2000 2000 2000 2000 2000 2000 2000 2000 2000
[13]  2000 2000 2000 2000 2000 2000 2000 2000 2001 2001 2001 2001
[25]  2001 2001 2001 2001 2001 2001
> as.numeric(factor(dates$year))[1:30]
 [1]  1 1 1 1 1 1 1 1 1 1 1 1 1 1 1 1 1 1 1 1 1 2 2 2 2 2 2 2 2 2
```

Here, we reclassified the `dates$year` vector (which contains 13 unique years) to a vector of integers from 1 to 13 (only the first 30 values were printed to save space).

Spatial dimensions

In our second example, we will aggregate `r` along the `y` axis spatial dimension. Doing this will allow us to observe the average NDVI at a given position on the north-south axis over time. In other words, we will reduce the number of dimensions from three to two by averaging all values of a given `y` axis/date position into a single value. The following schematic diagram describes our action plan:

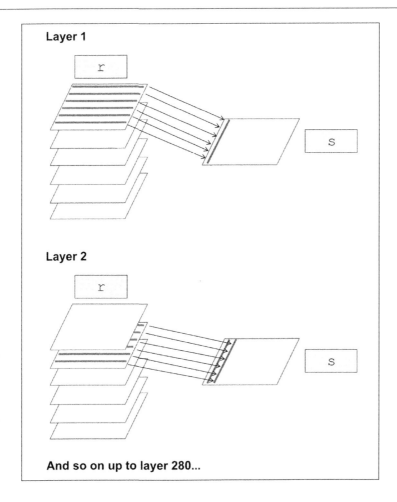

Layer 1

Layer 2

And so on up to layer 280...

As we can see in the preceding diagram, our goal is to create a new raster s, where each column holds the vector of row averages from r. In other words, each s row is going to represent an r row (or *y* axis positions in space), while each s column is going to represent an r layer (or positions in time). We will perform the operation in two steps: first, creating an empty raster s (with the required dimensions) and second, populating it with values. We will also see two different ways of accomplishing the task: using a `for` loop and using `apply`.

As we can see in the preceding diagram, the number of rows in s should be equal to the number of rows in r, while the number of columns in s should be equal to the number of layers in r. In addition to setting row and column numbers, using parameters xmn, xmx, ymn, and ymx, we will set the minimum and maximum coordinates on the *x* and *y* axes (to avoid the default, where the extent is -180 to 180 on the *x* axis and -90 to 90 on the *y* axis). The coordinate ranges on the *x* and *y* axes are going to be 0 to 280 and 0 to 100, respectively; moreover, since the number of columns and rows is accordingly 280 and 100, the raster resolution will be 1 (an arbitrary unit) on both axes:

```
> s = raster(nrows = nrow(r), ncols = nlayers(r),
+ xmn = 0, xmx = nlayers(r), ymn = 0, ymx = nrow(r))
```

Now that raster s is ready, we need to populate it with values. Following our first for loop method, we will define a new function called raster_rowMeans that, when provided with a raster (x) and the layer index (layer), returns a vector of row means in that layer. This function actually consists of a single expression as it simply applies the base function rowMeans on the matrix of values from a given layer, obtained with as.matrix:

```
> raster_rowMeans = function(x, layer) {
+ rowMeans(as.matrix(x[[layer]]),
+ na.rm = TRUE)
+ }
```

Now, all is left to be done is to go over the layers of r, each time calculating the row means in the current layer (with the raster_rowMeans function) and assigning the resulting vector to the appropriate column of s (exactly as depicted in the preceding diagram):

```
> for(i in 1:nlayers(r)) {
+ s[ ,i] = raster_rowMeans(r, i)
+ }
```

Now s is filled with the appropriate values, and we can use the levelplot function to display it. The additional at parameter of the levelplot function sets the breaks between color levels and contours. We use it to slightly reduce the quantity of contours and make the image clearer:

```
> levelplot(s,
+ par.settings = RdBuTheme,
+ contour = TRUE,
+ margin = FALSE,
+ at = seq(0,0.6,0.05))
```

The graphical output is shown in the following screenshot:

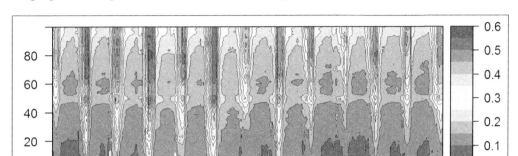

The preceding screenshot shows the average NDVI at each point in time (x axis) and north-south position in space (y axis). Two main patterns are evident: first, along the x axis (time) we can see the periodical behavior of NDVI between the interchanging wet and dry seasons. However, there are also inter-annual differences—in certain years, NDVI is higher or lower than average—due to variation in climatic conditions and therefore in vegetation activity. Second, along the y axis (the north-south position), we can see the NDVI gradient from the relatively wet conditions, and thus a higher NDVI to the north, compared to drier conditions; consequently, we can also see a lower and more stable NDVI to the south.

The second method of obtaining the same result will be defined with less code, although it might be conceptually more difficult to grasp. The first step of the task, defining the empty raster s, is identical:

```
> s = raster(nrows = nrow(r), ncols = nlayers(r),
+ xmn = 0, xmx =  nlayers(r), ymn = 0, ymx = nrow(r))
```

However, the second step is different. Instead of going over the layers of r with a for loop, we will convert r to a three-dimensional array and utilize the apply function. The former is accomplished with the as.array function:

```
> r_array = as.array(r)
```

The result, r_array, is an array object where the first dimension corresponds to r rows, the second dimension to r columns, and the third dimension to r layers. We can therefore use apply to utilize rowMeans on the third dimension, obtaining the vector of row means for each third-dimension element (layer), which is exactly what we need. The values of the resulting matrix can be directly transferred to s:

```
> s[] = apply(r_array, 3, rowMeans, na.rm = TRUE)
```

The raster s we just created is identical to the one created (and plotted) earlier. Although the same results were produced, an important difference between the two methods is in the speed of execution. Accessing one raster layer at a time using a loop is slow compared to an apply operation on an array, which is generally very fast. For example, on the computer this book is written on, calculating the values of s using the first method is performed in about 1.8 minutes as compared to 2.6 seconds using the second method (that is ~40 times faster!). It is therefore often useful to transform a raster into a simpler object (matrix or array) before doing intensive calculations.

Summary

In this chapter, you learned additional methods and procedures for working with raster layers in R. We now know how to crop, aggregate, or reproject a raster to bring it to the desired extent, resolution, and CRS. We discussed how focal filtering and clumping can be applied to highlight patterns of interest in a raster. We also discussed how topography-related variables can be derived from a DEM, and how spatio-temporal raster data can be aggregated.

In the next chapter, you will learn about the interface between rasters and vector layers, and the different ways in which both can be combined in a spatial analysis.

7
Combining Vector and Raster Datasets

Generating new insight by overlaying several layers of spatial information, one on top of the other, constitutes one of the main concepts of spatial data analysis, as we have already seen in the previous chapters. So far, however, we have only used operations involving either rasters alone or vector layers alone, but not a combination of both. Although the two types of spatial layers have their characteristic uses (such as rasters for DEMs and vector layers for administrative borders), combining them in a single analysis is often desired. As we shall see, this is a less straightforward task, characterized by specific procedures and decisions.

In this chapter, we are going to explore the interplay between vector and raster layers, and the way it is implemented in the `raster` package. The way rasters and vector layers can be interchanged and queried, one according to the other, will be demonstrated through examples.

In this chapter, we are going to use objects that were created in the previous chapters and the packages we used to do that (`plyr`, `raster`, and `rgeos`). Make sure these are loaded before running the code sections in this chapter. For convenience, this chapter's code file on the book's website repeats the relevant code sections from the previous chapters.

In this chapter, we'll cover the following topics:

- Creating rasters from vector layers and vice versa
- Masking rasters with vector layers
- Extracting raster values according to vector layers

Creating rasters from vector layers

One of the main reasons to convert a vector layer to a raster is that we are interested in employing raster analysis tools or procedures on data that is currently held in vector form (and vice versa). For example, when preparing a multiband raster with various environmental characteristics of a given area, such as slope or NDVI, we may wish to add layers that are commonly given in the vector format, such as built area polygons or road lines. To do this, we first need to convert these vector layers to rasters, and then supplement the multiband raster with the additional layers.

The process of converting a vector layer to a raster is called rasterizing, in the `raster` package terminology, and it is performed with the `rasterize` function. In this section, we will see an example of how to rasterize a point vector layer, while keeping in mind that the procedures to rasterize lines and polygons are analogous. You will also learn the related operations of raster masking using a vector layer, which conceptually is a special case of rasterizing and overlay.

Rasterizing vector layers

Creating a raster out of a vector layer is quite simple in concept. Given a vector layer and a raster grid, the new raster cells get filled with values in places where the raster overlaps with the vector layer. The rest of the raster cells (those that are not in contact with the vector layer) are left with NA. Those raster cells that overlap with an individual feature in the vector layer are assigned unique values. These values can simply be consecutive integers, or they can come from any vector corresponding to the number of features (such as an attribute table column). The procedure will be made clearer with the following example.

In our first example, we will use a simple point layer with the locations of two towns: Lahav Kibbutz and Lehavim. We will first create a layer named `towns`, using geocoding as follows (see *Chapter 5, Working with Points, Lines, and Polygons,* for more information):

```
> library(ggmap)
> towns_names = c("Lahav Kibbutz", "Lehavim")
> towns = geocode(towns_names)
> coordinates(towns) = ~ lon + lat
> proj4string(towns) = CRS("+proj=longlat +datum=WGS84")
> towns = spTransform(towns, CRS(proj4string(l_00)))
```

Note that in the last expression, the layer is transformed to the CRS of the Landsat image 1_00, which we assume is in memory (see *Chapter 4, Working with Rasters*, for more information). Let's visualize the towns layer using the 1_00 image as the background:

```
> plotRGB(l_00, r = 3, g = 2, b = 1, stretch = "lin")
> plot(towns, col = "red", pch = 16, add = TRUE)
> text(coordinates(towns), towns_names, pos = 3, col = "white")
```

The resulting graphical output is shown in the following screenshot:

Note that the dark patch of green vegetation neighboring Lahav Kibbutz to the west is Lahav forest. Another forest, Kramim, can be seen to the South-East of the Kibbutz. We will return to these two forests in the examples later.

Now let's see how the vector layer `towns` can be converted to a raster. Since we have two points, our result is going to be a raster with two cells having a non-NA value, no matter which grid we use, as long as both points are within its extent and the cell size is not large enough to encompass both points within a single cell. The `rasterize` function, to convert a vector to a raster, requires two main arguments:

- The vector layer to rasterize (x)
- The raster defining the grid (y)

Note that the role of y is only to provide a raster grid definition; its values do not participate in the operation in any way (similar to the role of the `to` parameter in raster reprojection; see the previous chapter). In this example, we will use the MODIS raster r (see *Chapter 4, Working with Rasters*) to transfer `towns` onto its 500 meter grid, as follows:

```
> towns_r = rasterize(towns, r)
```

The result, `towns_r`, is a `RasterLayer` object with two non-NA values, 1 and 2, since the raster values are defined as the feature indices (numbers from 1 to n, where n is the total number of features) by default:

```
> towns_r[!is.na(towns_r)]
[1] 1 2
```

In our case, the 1 cell corresponds to the first feature in `towns` (Lahav Kibbutz) and the 2 cell corresponds to the second one (Lehavim).

To display `towns_r`, we will first crop it according to the extent of `towns` plus a 3-kilometer buffer:

```
> towns_r = crop(towns_r, extent(towns) + 3000)
```

Let's plot the resulting raster, and the original vector layer on top of it, including the relevant labels. We will use the `col` parameter of `plot` to specify a two-color scale with `"lightblue"` (this color will be used for 1) and `"brown"` (this color will be used for 2):

```
> plot(towns_r, col = c("lightblue", "brown"))
> plot(towns, add = TRUE)
> text(coordinates(towns), towns_names, pos = 3)
```

The resulting graphical output is shown in the following screenshot:

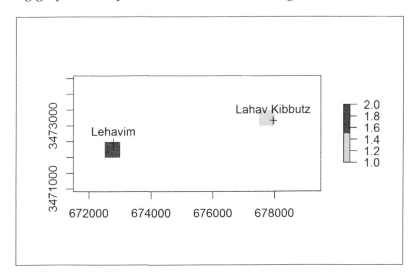

The white background we see corresponds to the NA-filled area in towns_r. These are the raster cells where no point in towns falls. The two colored pixels are the two cells that have been assigned with values. The light blue pixel is the one assigned with the value of 1 (corresponding to Lahav Kibbutz), while the brown pixel is the one assigned with 2 (Lehavim).

Two other useful parameters of rasterize are field and fun.

Using field, we can override the default assignment of raster values and provide a single number, vector, or the name of an attribute table column determining the values (see *Chapter 8, Spatial Interpolation of Point Data*, for an example of the latter). For example, using the rasterize(towns,r,field=c(3,4)) expression will yield a raster with the value of 3 for Lahav Kibbutz and 4 for Lehavim.

The fun parameter determines the method to assign the raster values, and is only relevant when some raster cells overlap with more than one feature. It can be provided either with a function or one of the predefined character values: "first", "last", "count", "sum", "min", or "max" (the default value is "last"). For example, the rasterize(towns,r,fun="count") expression yields a raster stating how many towns are in each of the 500 meter cells (in our case, this is not very instructive—the raster will have two 1 values because there is only one town in each of the two individual cells).

Masking values in a raster

As mentioned in the previous chapter, a raster is always rectangular. However, in raster subsetting, we are often interested in going beyond the selection of rectangular extents. Non-rectangular rasters can be created by assigning all cells, excluding those we are interested in, with NA. This operation is called masking, again in the `raster` package terminology.

Masking is most often performed using a polygonal layer defining an area of interest. Therefore, conceptually, masking can be viewed as a two-step operation. The first step consists of a vector-to-raster conversion, where the area of interest is rasterized according to the raster we would like to mask. The second step consists of an overlay to construct the masked raster, with NA in those cells where the area-of-interest raster has NA or the original value otherwise. In practice, the operation may be performed with a single step, using the `mask` function.

In the following example, we will mask the Haifa `slope` raster from the previous chapter to create two new rasters—first masking all areas other than those coinciding with buildings (the `haifa_buildings` polygonal layer), and then all areas other than natural areas (the `haifa_natural` polygonal layer). The latter two layers should be in the same CRS of `slope`; see *Chapters 5, Working with Points, Lines, and Polygons,* and *Chapter 6, Modifying Rasters and Analyzing Raster Time Series,* to learn how they were created.

Since we would like to focus on the Haifa area, we will first create an `Extent` object encompassing `haifa_buildings` and a 2-kilometer buffer. Later, we will use this object (named `haifa_ext`) to clip our results and display them more conveniently:

```
> haifa_ext = extent(haifa_buildings) + 2000
```

Before proceeding, let's review the layers involved—`slope`, `haifa_buildings`, and `haifa_natural`—by plotting them as follows (zooming in to `haifa_ext`):

```
> plot(slope, ext = haifa_ext)
> plot(haifa_buildings, add = TRUE)
> plot(haifa_natural, col = "lightgreen", add = TRUE)
```

The resulting graphical output is shown in the following screenshot:

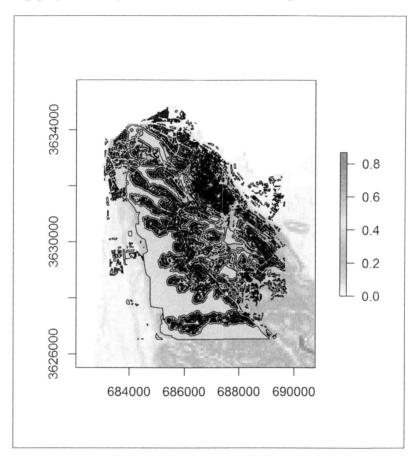

The preceding graphical output is familiar from *Chapter 5, Working with Points, Lines, and Polygons* (see the last screenshot in that chapter); the only difference is that now the `slope` raster appears in the background. The area appears to be characterized by variable topography. Are the natural and built areas characterized by different topographic slopes? This question motivates our next task—subsetting the `slope` pixels covered by natural areas and buildings, separately, to compare their value distributions.

The `mask` function that we will use to do this task expects two main arguments:

- The raster to be masked (`x`)
- The object determining which values to mask (`mask`)

The `mask` argument can either be an overlapping raster (in which case the values in x corresponding to NA in `mask` are assigned with NA) or a vector layer (in which case the values in x not coinciding with any feature in `mask` are assigned with NA). Therefore, the following expression yields a new raster based on `slope` where all pixels not covered by `haifa_natural` are masked (that is, assigned with NA):

```
> natural_mask = mask(slope, haifa_natural)
```

 The previous expression is analogous to the following expression:
```
> natural_mask = mask(slope,
+ rasterize(haifa_natural, slope))
```

For convenience, we will crop the result, `natural_mask`, using `haifa_ext`:

```
> natural_mask = crop(natural_mask, haifa_ext)
```

We will repeat the exact same procedure with `haifa_buildings` to get the `buildings_mask` raster as well:

```
> buildings_mask = mask(slope, haifa_buildings)
> buildings_mask = crop(buildings_mask, haifa_ext)
```

Now let's plot both `natural_mask` and `buildings_mask`, side-by-side, to observe how masking has been carried out:

```
> plot(stack(natural_mask, buildings_mask))
```

The resulting graphical output is shown in the following screenshot:

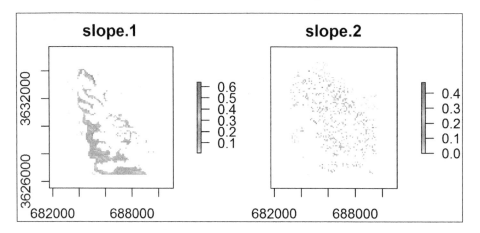

After observing the two results, we can see that while `natural_mask` (the left panel) mostly consists of continuous patches of non-NA areas, `buildings_mask` (the right panel) is composed of very small non-NA patches containing a few pixels. The reason for such behavior is that masking with a polygonal layer retains the values of only those cells whose cell center falls within a polygon. This behavior is appropriate for `haifa_natural`, which is mainly composed of large polygons, each one encompassing many cells. However, for `haifa_buildings`, the pixels that are retained are only those whose center falls within either one of the building polygons in `haifa_buildings`. This clearly underestimates the built area. A simple solution would be to mask using building centroids instead, in which case those pixels where a centroid of `haifa_buildings` falls will be retained. For this purpose, we will create a point layer to build centroids named `buildings_ctr`:

```
> buildings_ctr = gCentroid(haifa_buildings, byid = TRUE)
```

Now, we will repeat the masking procedure using this layer:

```
> buildings_mask = mask(slope, buildings_ctr)
> buildings_mask = crop(buildings_mask, haifa_ext)
```

Let's plot the result once again to see the difference:

```
> plot(stack(natural_mask, buildings_mask))
```

The graphical output is shown in the following screenshot:

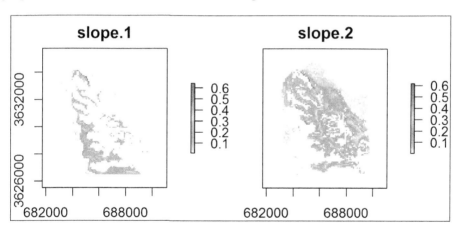

This time, many more pixels remained unmasked in `buildings_mask` since all pixels coinciding with a centroid of at least one building were retained (as in the previous example of `towns` rasterization).

We will proceed with this example in *Chapter 9, Advanced Visualization of Spatial Data*, displaying the value distribution of both rasters with histograms.

Creating vector layers from a raster

The opposite operation to rasterization, which has been presented in the previous section, is the creation of vector layers from raster data. The procedure of extracting features of interest out of rasters, in the form of vector layers, is often necessary for analogous reasons underlying rasterization—when the data held in a raster is better represented using a vector layer, within the context of specific subsequent analysis or visualization tasks. Scenarios where we need to create points, lines, and polygons from a raster can all be encountered. In this section, we are going to see an example of each.

Raster-to-points conversion

In raster-to-points conversion conversion, each raster cell center (excluding NA cells) is converted to a point. The resulting point layer has an attribute table with the values of the respective raster cells in it.

Conversion to points can be done with the `rasterToPoints` function. This function has a parameter named `spatial` that determines whether the returned object is going to be `SpatialPointsDataFrame` or simply a `matrix` holding the coordinates and the respective cell values (`spatial=FALSE`, the default value). For our purposes, it is thus important to remember to specify `spatial=TRUE`.

As an example of a raster, let's create a subset of the raster `r`, with only layers 1-2, rows 1-3, and columns 1-3:

```
> u = r[[1:2]][1:3, 1:3, drop = FALSE]
```

To make the example more instructive, we will place NA in some of the cells and see how this affects the raster-to-point conversion:

```
> u[2, 3] = NA
> u[[1]][3, 2] = NA
```

Now, we will apply `rasterToPoints` to create a `SpatialPointsDataFrame` object named u_pnt out of u:

```
> u_pnt = rasterToPoints(u, spatial = TRUE)
```

Let's visually examine the result we got with the first layer of u serving as the background:

```
> plot(u[[1]])
> plot(u_pnt, add = TRUE)
```

The graphical output is shown in the following screenshot:

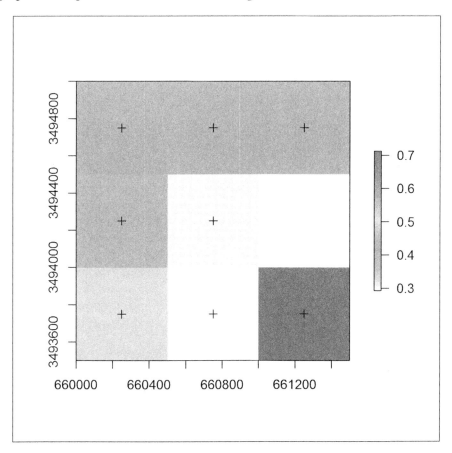

We can see that a point has been produced at the center of each raster cell, except for the cell at position (2,3), where we assigned NA to both layers. However, at the (3,2) position, NA has been assigned to only one of the layers (the first one); therefore, a point feature has been generated there nevertheless.

The attribute table of u_pnt has eight rows (since there are eight points) and two columns (corresponding to the raster layers).

```
> u_pnt@data
  layer.1 layer.2
1  0.4242  0.4518
2  0.3995  0.3334
3  0.4190  0.3430
4  0.4495  0.4846
```

```
5   0.2925   0.3223
6   0.4998   0.5841
7      NA   0.5841
8   0.7126   0.5086
```

We can see that the seventh point feature, the one corresponding to the (3,2) raster position, indeed contains an NA value corresponding to layer 1.

Raster-to-contours conversion

Creating points (see the previous section) and polygons (see the next section) from a raster is relatively straightforward. In the former case, points are generated at cell centroids, while in the latter, rectangular polygons are drawn according to cell boundaries. On the other hand, lines can be created from a raster using various different algorithms designed for more specific purposes. Two common procedures where lines are generated based on a raster are constructing contours (lines connecting locations of equal value on the raster) and finding least-cost paths (lines going from one location to another along the easiest route when cost of passage is defined by raster values). In this section, we will see an example of how to create contours (readers interested in least-cost path calculation can refer to the gdistance package, which provides this capability in R).

As an example, we will create contours from the DEM of Haifa (dem; see the previous chapter). Creating contours can be done using the rasterToContour function. This function accepts a RasterLayer object and returns a SpatialLinesDataFrame object with the contour lines. The rasterToContour function internally uses the base function contourLines, and arguments can be passed to the latter as part of the rasterToContour function call. For example, using the levels parameter, we can specify the breaks where contours will be generated (rather than letting them be determined automatically).

The raster dem consists of elevation values ranging between -14 meters and 541 meters:

```
> range(dem[], na.rm = TRUE)
[1] -14 541
```

Therefore, we may choose to generate six contour lines, at 0, 100, 200, …, 500 meter levels:

```
> dem_contour = rasterToContour(dem, levels = seq(0, 500, 100))
```

Now, we will plot the resulting `SpatialLinesDataFrame` object on top of the dem raster:

```
> plot(dem)
> plot(dem_contour, add = TRUE)
```

The graphical output is shown in the following screenshot:

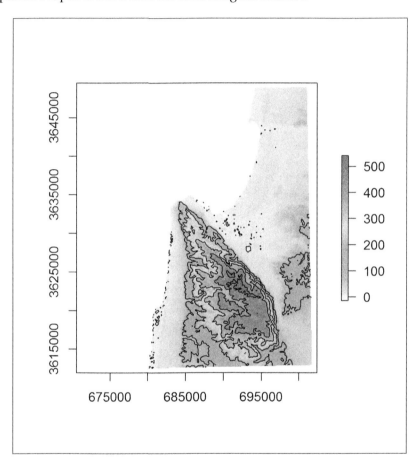

Mount Carmel is densely covered with elevation contours compared to the plains surrounding it, which are mostly within the 0-100 meter elevation range and thus have only few a contour lines.

Let's take a look at the attribute table of `dem_contour`:

```
> dem_contour@data
    level
C_1    0
C_2   100
C_3   200
C_4   300
C_5   400
C_6   500
```

Indeed, the layer consists of six line features—one for each break we specified with the `levels` argument.

Raster-to-polygons conversion

As mentioned previously, raster to polygon conversion involves the generation of rectangular polygons in the place of each raster cell (once again, excluding NA cells). Similar to the raster-to-point conversion, the resulting attribute table contains the respective raster values for each polygon created. The conversion to polygons is most useful with categorical rasters when we would like to generate polygons defining certain areas in order to exploit the analysis tools this type of data is associated with (such as extraction of values from other rasters, geometry editing, and overlay).

Creation of polygons from a raster can be performed with a function whose name the reader may have already guessed, `rasterToPolygons`. A useful option in this function is to immediately dissolve the resulting polygons according to their attribute table values; that is, all polygons having the same value are dissolved into a single feature. This functionality internally utilizes the `rgeos` package and it can be triggered by specifying `dissolve=TRUE`.

In the previous chapter, we prepared a raster named `l_rec_focal_clump`, a categorical raster with consecutively numbered NDVI>0.2 patches. In our next example, which we will begin in this chapter and finish in *Chapter 9, Advanced Visualization of Spatial Data*, we will visually compare the average NDVI time series of Lahav and Kramim forests (see earlier), based on all of our Landsat (three dates) and MODIS (280 dates) satellite images. In this chapter, we will only prepare the necessary data by going through the following intermediate steps:

1. Creating the Lahav and Kramim forests polygonal layer.
2. Extracting NDVI values from the satellite images.
3. Creating a `data.frame` object that can be passed to graphical functions later.

Commencing with the first step, using `l_rec_focal_clump`, we will first create a polygonal layer holding all NDVI>0.2 patches, then subset only those two polygons corresponding to Lahav and Kramim forests. The former is achieved using `rasterToPolygons` with `dissolve=TRUE`, converting the patches in `l_rec_focal_clump` to 507 individual polygons in a new `SpatialPolygonsDataFrame` that we hereby name `pol`:

```
> pol = rasterToPolygons(l_rec_focal_clump, dissolve = TRUE)
```

Plotting `pol` will show that we have quite a few large patches and many small ones. Since the Lahav and Kramim forests are relatively large, to make things easier we can omit all polygons with `area` less than or equal to 1 km²:

```
> pol$area = gArea(pol, byid = TRUE) / 1000^2
> pol = pol[pol$area > 1, ]
```

The attribute table shows that we are left with eight polygons, with area sizes of 1-10 km². The `clumps` column, by the way, is where the original `l_rec_focal_clump` raster value (the clump ID) has been kept (`"clumps"` is the name of the `l_rec_focal_clump` raster layer from which the values came).

```
> pol@data
      clumps     area
112        2   1.2231
114      200   1.3284
137      221   1.9314
203      281   9.5274
240      314   6.7842
371      432   2.0007
445        5  10.2159
460       56   1.0998
```

Let's make a map of `pol`:

```
> plotRGB(l_00, r = 3, g = 2, b = 1, stretch = "lin")
> plot(pol, border = "yellow", lty = "dotted", add = TRUE)
```

The graphical output is shown in the following screenshot:

The preceding screenshot shows the continuous NDVI>0.2 patches, which are 1 km² or larger, within the studied area. Two of these, as expected, are the forests we would like to examine. How can we select them? Obviously, we could export `pol` to a Shapefile and select the features of interest interactively in a GIS software (such as QGIS), then import the result back into R to continue our analysis. The `raster` package also offers some capabilities for interactive selection (that we do not cover here); for example, a function named `click` can be used to obtain the properties of the `pol` features we click in a graphical window such as the one shown in the preceding screenshot. However, given the purpose of this book, we will try to write a code to make the selection automatically without further user input.

To write a code that makes the selection, we must choose a certain criterion (either spatial or nonspatial), that separates the features of interest. In this case, for example, we can see that the `pol` features we wish to select are those closest to Lahav Kibbutz. Therefore, we can utilize the `towns` point layer (see earlier) to find the distance of each polygon from Lahav Kibbutz, and select the two most proximate ones.

Using the `gDistance` function (see *Chapter 5*, *Working with Points, Lines, and Polygons*), we will first find out the distances between each polygon in `pol` and each point in `towns`:

```
> dist_towns = gDistance(towns, pol, byid = TRUE)
> dist_towns
              1          2
112 14524.94060 12697.151
114  5484.66695  7529.195
137  3863.12168  5308.062
203    29.48651  1119.090
240  1910.61525  6372.634
371 11687.63594 11276.683
445 12751.21123 14371.268
460 14860.25487 12300.319
```

The returned matrix, named `dist_towns`, contains the pairwise distances, with rows corresponding to the `pol` feature and columns corresponding to the `towns` feature. Since Lahav Kibbutz corresponds to the first `towns` feature (column `"1"`), we can already see that the fourth and fifth `pol` features (rows `"203"` and `"240"`) are the most proximate ones, thus corresponding to the Lahav and Kramim forests. We could subset both forests by simply using their IDs—`pol[c("203","240"),]`. However, as always, we are looking for general code that will select, in this case, the two closest features irrespective of the specific IDs or row indices. For this purpose, we can use the `order` function, which we have not encountered so far. This function, given a numeric vector, returns the element indices in an increasing order according to element values. For example, applying `order` to the first column of `dist_towns`, we can see that the smallest element in this column is in the fourth row, the second smallest is in the fifth row, the third smallest is in the third row, and so on:

```
> dist_order = order(dist_towns[, 1])
> dist_order
[1] 4 5 3 2 6 7 1 8
```

We can use this result to select the relevant features of `pol` as follows:

```
> forests = pol[dist_order[1:2], ]
```

The subset `SpatialPolygonsDataFrame`, named `forests`, now contains only the two features from `pol` corresponding to the Lahav and Kramim forests.

```
> forests@data
     clumps    area
203     281  9.5274
240     314  6.7842
```

Let's visualize `forests` within the context of the other data we have by now. We will plot, once again, `l_00` as the RGB background and `pol` on top of it. In addition, we will plot `forests` (in red) and the location of Lahav Kibbutz (as a red point). We will also add labels for each feature in `pol`, corresponding to its distance (in meters) from Lahav Kibbutz:

```
> plotRGB(l_00, r = 3, g = 2, b = 1, stretch = "lin")
> plot(towns[1, ], col = "red", pch = 16, add = TRUE)
> plot(pol, border = "yellow", lty = "dotted", add = TRUE)
> plot(forests, border = "red", lty = "dotted", add = TRUE)
> text(gCentroid(pol, byid = TRUE),
+ round(dist_towns[,1]),
+ col = "White")
```

The graphical output is shown in the following screenshot:

The preceding screenshot demonstrates that we did indeed correctly select the features of interest.

We can also assign the forest names to the attribute table of forests, relying on our knowledge that the first feature of forests (ID "203") is larger and more proximate to Lahav Kibbutz and corresponds to the Lahav forest, while the second feature (ID "240") corresponds to Kramim.

```
> forests$name = c("Lahav", "Kramim")
> forests@data
     clumps    area     name
203     281  9.5274    Lahav
240     314  6.7842   Kramim
```

We now have a polygonal layer named `forests`, with two features delineating the Lahav and Kramim forests, named accordingly in the attribute table. In the next section, we will proceed with extracting the NDVI data for these forests.

Extracting raster values based on vector layers

So far, we have covered operations to transform a vector layer to a raster and vice versa. The third operation involving vector layers and rasters, and the focus of this final section, is the extraction of raster values according to vector layers. We are often interested in reducing or summarizing raster data using point, line, or polygon features, which is when this operation comes in handy. For example, we may wish to calculate the elevation profile covered by a GPS track (raster-to-line extraction) or the average NDVI of a given forest (raster to polygon extraction). In this section, we will see two examples involving extraction by points and extraction by polygons.

Extracting by points

Extraction of raster values, according to a vector layer of any kind, can be done with the `extract` function. The first two parameters of this function are as follows:

- The raster whose values are to be extracted (x)
- The object (usually a vector layer) defining the locations to extract values (y) from

When extracting values according to points, which is the simplest extract scenario, the returned object may be either of the following:

- *Vector* — when extracting values from a single band raster
- *Matrix* — when extracting values from a multiband raster

As an example of extracting single band raster values to points, we will use the `spain_stations.csv` file we previously created (see *Chapter 3, Working with Tables*), which contains a table with the spatial location records of 96 meteorological stations in Spain. We will create a `SpatialPointsDataFrame` object based on this table, and then use it to extract elevation values from a DEM of Spain. The DEM will be obtained from a file (available on the book's website) named `spain_elev.tif`.

First, we will read the DEM file into R. This file, by the way, was created by merging SRTM tiles downloaded with `getData`—exactly as we did to create the Haifa DEM in the previous chapter—followed by reprojection, masking, and aggregation to a 900 meter resolution.

```
> dem_spain = raster("C:\\Data\\spain_elev.tif")
```

Now, we will read the station records from `spain_stations.csv`:

```
> stations = read.csv("C:\\Data\\spain_stations.csv",
+ stringsAsFactors = FALSE)
```

As you remember, the station locations are stored in the `longitude` and `latitude` columns; therefore, the `data.frame` object can be promoted to a `SpatialPointsDataFrame` object as follows:

```
> coordinates(stations) = ~ longitude + latitude
```

The station coordinates are given in degrees according to a geographic CRS. Therefore, we will define this CRS, and then reproject `stations` to match the CRS of `dem_spain` (UTM zone 30N) as follows:

```
> proj4string(stations) = CRS("+proj=longlat +datum=WGS84")
> stations = spTransform(stations, CRS(proj4string(dem_spain)))
```

Let's plot `stations` on top of `dem_spain` to see that they indeed match in location:

```
> plot(dem_spain)
> plot(stations, add = TRUE)
```

The graphical output is shown in the following screenshot:

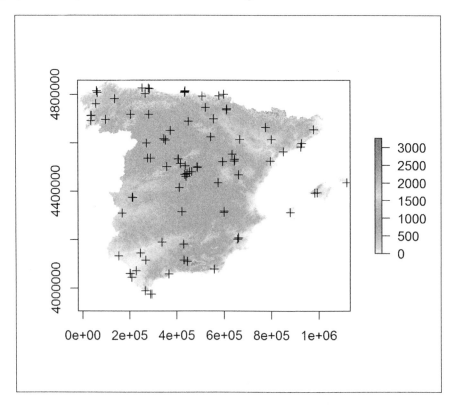

What we see here is the elevation map of Spain (the dem_spain raster), with station locations on top (stations point layer). The stations seem to cover the whole area of the country, more or less evenly. Note that some of the stations are not shown since they are located on the Canary Islands and thus they are beyond the scope of the dem_spain raster.

To extract the elevation values underlying each station, we employ the extract function with the raster and the points as the first two arguments, respectively. Since the returned object is going to be a numeric vector with the respective elevation values for each station, we can directly assign it to a new column in stations named elev_dem:

```
> stations$elev_dem = extract(dem_spain, stations)
```

Examining the attribute table of `stations` shows that now we have two elevation entries per station. These are the elevation values originally provided along with the meteorological records (the `elevation` column) and the elevation values we just obtained from the DEM (the `elev_dem` column):

```
> head(stations@data)
           station elevation elev_dem
1 GHCND:SP000003195       667   651.96
2 GHCND:SP000004452       185   184.24
3 GHCND:SP000006155         7     5.80
4 GHCND:SP000008027       251   212.44
5 GHCND:SP000008181         4     3.55
6 GHCND:SP000008202       790   787.28
```

Examining this table more closely will show that some of the stations were assigned with `NA` in the `elev_dem` column either since they are located near Spain's border (and incidentally outside the DEM scope) or since they are located in the Canary Islands (which the `dem_spain` raster does not cover at all).

It would be interesting to see the degree of agreement between the two sources of information by plotting one vector as a function of the other:

```
> plot(elev_dem ~ elevation, stations,
+ xlim = c(0, 2000),
+ ylim = c(0, 2000),
+ xlab = "Elevation from station record (m)",
+ ylab = "Elevation from DEM (m)")
```

Note that the `plot(elev_dem~elevation,stations)` expression is analogous to `plot(stations$elev_dem~stations$elevation)`. In the latter syntax, the vector names are provided explicitly; while in the former (often more convenient), the formula addresses columns from a `data.frame` object, provided as a second argument.

To make the assessment more convenient, we will also use the `abline` function that can add a straight line to an existing plot. One way of specifying the line's location is providing its intercept (a) and slope (b). We are going to add a *1:1* line (that is, a line with an intercept of 0 and a slope of 1), in order to see how well the `elevation` and `elev_dem` records match:

```
> abline(a = 0, b = 1, lty = "dotted")
```

The graphical output is shown in the following screenshot:

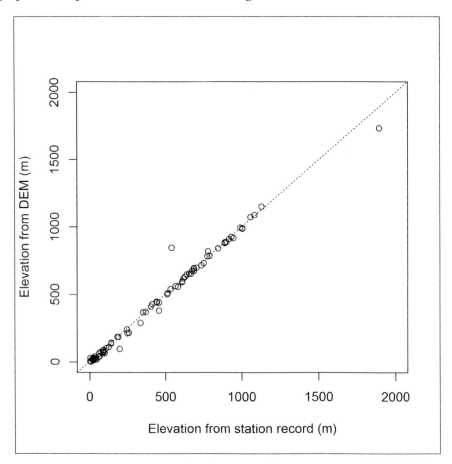

Each point corresponds to a single station, and we can see the respective `elevation` and `elev_dem` values on the *x* and *y* axes, respectively. The agreement between the two sources of information is, unsurprisingly, very good, except for a few stations that lie slightly farther from the 1:1 line.

Extracting by polygons

When extracting raster values using line or polygon layers, each feature may correspond to more than one value in each raster layer (unlike with points, where each feature always corresponds to a single value). In fact, a variable number of values may be extracted for each feature, depending upon its shape. For example, the polygon delineating the Lahav forest, which we created earlier, covers 10,586 Landsat pixels and 38 MODIS pixels, while the Kramim polygon covers 7,538 Landsat pixels and 28 MODIS pixels. We have two ways to deal with this variation:

- Reducing the vector of values from each feature into a single value (specifying a function to do that, with the `fun` parameter), in which case the returned object may be, just as with point layers:
    - A *vector* — when extracting from a single-band raster
    - A *matrix* — when extracting from a multiband raster

- Keeping all values (specifying no function with `fun=NULL`, the default value), in which case the returned object will be a `list` (with `df=FALSE`, the default value) or a `data.frame` object (with `df=TRUE`)

When a function is provided with the `fun` parameter, the additional parameter `na.rm` determines whether `NA` cells are included in the calculation.

Proceeding with the `forest` example, we will now complete the two remaining steps: extracting the NDVI data and arranging it in a table. We are going to extract NDVI values according to the `forests` layer with the first alternative — summarizing the values (specifically with `fun=mean`, giving a mean NDVI per forest). Our ultimate goal is to have, by the end of this chapter, a table with three ID columns (`date`, `sat` – satellite, and `forest`) and a fourth column (`ndvi`) holding the measured average NDVI values.

Starting with the assembly of NDVI images (`ndvi_98`, `ndvi_00`, `ndvi_03`, and `r`), we will read the Landsat images from 1998 and 2003 and calculate NDVI (assuming that `r` and `ndvi_00` are already in memory, as is our custom-made `ndvi` function; see *Chapter 4, Working with Rasters*).

```
> l_98 = brick("C:\\Data\\landsat_15_10_1998.tif")
> l_03 = brick("C:\\Data\\landsat_11_09_2003.tif")
> ndvi_98 = calc(l_98, fun = ndvi)
> ndvi_03 = calc(l_03, fun = ndvi)
```

Next, we will create a `Date` object, named `l_dates`, holding the Landsat image dates (see the filenames). We will use this object later when creating a table of results.

```
> l_dates = as.Date(c("1998-10-15", "2000-10-04", "2003-09-11"))
```

We are ready to proceed with the extraction—employing the `extract` function on the three Landsat NDVI images to obtain the mean NDVI values per forest, per date:

```
> l_forests = extract(stack(ndvi_98, ndvi_00, ndvi_03),
+ forests,
+ fun = mean,
+ na.rm = TRUE)
```

 Note that to make things clearer, we first apply `extract` on a `RasterStack` object of the three Landsat images. The MODIS data will be extracted from `r` in a separate step.

Since we are extracting values from a multiband raster, yet employing a function (`mean`) to summarize those values; the returned object, assigned to `l_forests`, is a `matrix`. Its two rows correspond to the `forests` features, while its three columns correspond to the layers of `stack(ndvi_98,ndvi_00,ndvi_03)`. For example, we can see that the average NDVI observed by Landsat on October 15, 1998 in the Lahav forest was `0.3053538`:

```
> l_forests
        layer.1    layer.2   layer.3
[1,] 0.3053538 0.2487563 0.284487
[2,] 0.2840073 0.2190098 0.243326
```

Right now we can already tell that, in both forests, NDVI decreased between 1998-2000 and then (incompletely) recovered between 2000-2003.

By repeating the same procedure with `r`, we will create the analogous `r_forests` matrix:

```
> r_forests = extract(r,
+ forests,
+ fun = mean,
+ na.rm = TRUE)
```

This time the matrix has 280 columns since `r` has 280 layers:

```
> dim(r_forests)
[1]   2 280
```

Proceeding with the third step, we would like to have the information from `l_forests` and `r_forests` in a single `data.frame` object with all NDVI values in a single column, and additional columns characterizing the measurements (`date`, `sat`, and `forest`). Starting with the `l_forests` matrix, we will first transpose it (using the `t` function) and convert it to a `data.frame` object (using the `as.data.frame` function):

```
> l_forests = as.data.frame(t(l_forests))
> l_forests
                V1          V2
layer.1 0.3053538 0.2840073
layer.2 0.2487563 0.2190098
layer.3 0.2844870 0.2433260
```

Now, we can set the appropriate column names (the forest names) and create new columns for dates (obtained from `l_date`) and satellite (`"Landsat"`) as follows:

```
> colnames(l_forests) = forests$name
> l_forests$date = l_dates
> l_forests$sat = "Landsat"
```

The new `l_forests` matrix looks as follows:

```
> l_forests
             Lahav     Kramim       date      sat
layer.1 0.3053538 0.2840073 1998-10-15 Landsat
layer.2 0.2487563 0.2190098 2000-10-04 Landsat
layer.3 0.2844870 0.2433260 2003-09-11 Landsat
```

Exactly the same procedure is repeated for `r_forests` (with acquisition dates taken from `dates$date` and the satellite name set to `"MODIS"`):

```
> r_forests = as.data.frame(t(r_forests))
> colnames(r_forests) = forests$name
> r_forests$date = dates$date
> r_forests$sat = "MODIS"
```

Now, we can combine the two `data.frame` objects using `rbind`:

```
> forests_ndvi = rbind(l_forests, r_forests)
```

The combined `data.frame` object, which we named `forests_ndvi`, contains all average NDVI records for the two forests from the two satellites, collectively for 283 dates (three dates from Landsat and 280 dates from MODIS). Its first few rows are printed as follows:

```
> head(forests_ndvi)
            Lahav    Kramim       date      sat
layer.1 0.3053538 0.2840073 1998-10-15 Landsat
layer.2 0.2487563 0.2190098 2000-10-04 Landsat
layer.3 0.2844870 0.2433260 2003-09-11 Landsat
modis.1 0.3725111 0.3416607 2000-02-18   MODIS
modis.2 0.3959158 0.3850857 2000-03-05   MODIS
modis.3 0.4102210 0.3956179 2000-03-21   MODIS
```

What is left to be done is transform the `data.frame` object to a longer form (see *Chapter 3, Working with Tables*), creating another column for forest identity and to transfer the NDVI values to a designated values column. This can be performed with the `melt` function from the `reshape2` package:

```
> library(reshape2)
> forests_ndvi = melt(forests_ndvi,
+ measure.vars = forests$name,
+ variable.name = "forest",
+ value.name = "ndvi")
```

Note that the measured variables here are `"Lahav"` and `"Kramim"`, while the rest are treated as ID variables. Instead of typing the measure variable column names, we passed the `forests$name` vector, which already contains the necessary names:

```
> forests$name
[1] "Lahav"   "Kramim"
```

The additional parameters `variable.name` and `value.name` in the `melt` function call are used to specify the names of the newly created variable and value columns (to replace the default names `"variable"` and `"value"`, respectively). The final table looks as follows:

```
> head(forests_ndvi)
        date      sat forest       ndvi
1 1998-10-15 Landsat  Lahav 0.3053538
2 2000-10-04 Landsat  Lahav 0.2487563
3 2003-09-11 Landsat  Lahav 0.2844870
4 2000-02-18   MODIS  Lahav 0.3725111
5 2000-03-05   MODIS  Lahav 0.3959158
6 2000-03-21   MODIS  Lahav 0.4102210
```

In *Chapter 9, Advanced Visualization of Spatial Data*, we are going to use this table to create a plot of the NDVI evolution over time in these two forests. A table of this form, where:

- Each variable forms a column
- Each observation forms a row
- There is only one type of observational unit

constitutes a so-called *tidy data* table (see the paper by Hadley Wickham on this subject, 2014). As we shall see, bringing our data to such a form is often required to use more sophisticated graphical functions such as those in the `ggplot2` package.

Summary

In this chapter, we closed the gap between the two main spatial data types (rasters and vector layers) that we dealt with separately in the previous three chapters. We now know how to make the conversion from a vector layer to raster and vice versa, and we can transfer the geometry and data components from one data model to another when the need arises. We also saw how raster values can be extracted from a raster according to a vector layer, a fundamental step in many analysis tasks involving raster data.

At this point, we conclude the review of basic spatial data analysis tool implementation in R. We now know how to work with—including import, transform, and combine in various ways—rasters and vector layers in R. In the next two chapters, examples of more specialized applications of R for spatial data analysis are going to be presented; specifically, spatial interpolation and visualization of spatial data.

8
Spatial Interpolation of Point Data

Spatial interpolation is an example of a geostatistical analysis technique with a wide range of applications. In this chapter, we are going to learn how spatial interpolation can be carried out in R through examples of interpolating meteorological point measurements to create annual temperature maps of Spain.

The purpose of this exercise is two-fold. First, we will see how several common interpolation methods are applied in practice in R. We will see, for instance, that specialized classes are used to represent the input data and/or the results of statistical analyses in R, and witness the advantages of such an approach. Second, we will see how, through the use of loops, we can automate complex tasks such as spatial interpolation, and perform them repeatedly in order to accomplish otherwise unfeasible tasks.

 In this chapter, we are going to use objects previously created in *Chapter 3, Working with Tables*.

In this chapter, we'll cover the following topics:

- Spatially interpolating point data
- Calculating an empirical variogram
- Automatically fitting variogram models
- Calculating the **root mean square error (RMSE)** of prediction

Spatially interpolating point data

Spatial interpolation is the procedure by which the behavior of a certain phenomenon of interest is predicted in locations where it has not been measured. For this purpose, we need a spatial prediction model—a set of procedures to obtain the predicted values given the calibration data. The two types of calibration data usually encountered are:

- **Field measurements**: Available for a limited set of locations (usually points), for example, meteorological data from stations in Spain
- **Covariates**: Available for each location within the area of interest, for example, elevation data from Spain's DEM

The spatial prediction model of our choice is calibrated using the calibration data. This model can then be used to calculate the predicted level of the phenomenon of interest in any location (usually points). The two main types of spatial interpolation methods recognized are:

- **Deterministic model**: In this model, model parameter values are arbitrarily determined
- **Statistical model**: In this model, model parameter values are objectively estimated from specific calibration data

Simply put, while both types of models use the calibration data to make predictions, deterministic models are predefined using fixed formulas to calculate predicted values given the calibration data; on the other hand, statistical models use the calibration data twice, first to fine-tune the model itself and then (as in the deterministic models) to calculate the predicted values. Examples of deterministic models are **inverse distance weighted** (**IDW**) interpolation and splines. Examples of statistical models are kriging and ordinary regression.

Our purpose in this chapter is to present spatial interpolation from a practical point of view. Comprehensively covering the statistical theory and equations behind spatial interpolation techniques is well beyond the scope of this book. Readers familiar with the subject of spatial interpolation will, hopefully, get a perspective from this chapter on the way statistical tools such as these are applied in R. Readers unfamiliar with the subject of spatial interpolation are referred to the not-too-technical overview in the first two chapters of Tomislav Hengl's book *A Practical Guide to Geostatistical Mapping*, published in 2009 (available online), for supplementary reference. Those uninterested in this particular subject may skip to the last image in this chapter, and the few paragraphs that follow, where a dataset that we are going to use in the next chapter is described.

Two different approaches, or point of views, in selecting the appropriate spatial prediction model are also worth mentioning:

- If we wish to prepare the most accurate predictions of a certain phenomenon (for example, to produce a map), we will be mainly interested in selecting the model that minimizes prediction error (and may not care very much what kind of model that is)

- If we are interested in better understanding the phenomenon itself, we will seek to find the best model characterizing the observed pattern and estimating its parameters and our confidence in them (while prediction error will be of secondary interest)

Here, we strictly follow the first approach; we will test several commonly used models to see which one produces the least number of prediction errors, and then use it to produce continuous maps of temperature in Spain. However, we should remember that we are not investigating the mechanisms underlying the behavior of temperature in space, which would suggest the second approach. Diggle and Ribeiro's book *Model-based Geostatistics* (2007) is a good example that focuses on the latter approach utilizing another R package (geoR) for geostatistical analysis, which we do not cover here.

In the examples in this chapter, we will be working with three data sources: the spain_stations.csv and spain_annual.csv tables that hold the annual climatic data from Spain (see *Chapter 3, Working with Tables*), and the spain_elev.tif raster with Spain's DEM (see the previous chapter). The first thing we will do is assemble these objects into memory. We will also perform a four-fold aggregation of the DEM, from a 900 meter resolution to a 3,600 meter resolution, in order to make subsequent calculations faster:

```
> library(raster)
> dem_spain = raster("C:\\Data\\spain_elev.tif")
> dem_spain = aggregate(dem_spain, 4)
> spain_stations = read.csv("C:\\Data\\spain_stations.csv",
+ stringsAsFactors = FALSE)
> spain_annual = read.csv("C:\\Data\\spain_annual.csv",
+ stringsAsFactors = FALSE)
```

As we have already seen in previous chapters, spain_stations holds spatial location information for the 96 meteorological stations of Spain, while spain_annual holds the meteorological data itself. The tables can be joined by the common station column. The meteorological data consists of average measurements of three variables (precipitation, minimum temperature, and maximum temperature) obtained in different years (1984-2013). We are going to interpolate measurements for different year/variable combinations.

Therefore, it will be useful to write a function that accepts the variable and year we are currently interested in, and returns a point layer with the required data. The code for such a function consists of procedures already familiar to the reader from the previous chapters, so we will review its contents briefly. The function accepts five arguments:

- `stations`: A `data.frame` object with location data for stations (in our case, `spain_stations`)

- `annual`: A `data.frame` object with the annual meteorological data (in our case, `spain_annual`)

- `year`: The year we would like to get meteorological data for

- `variable`: The meteorological variable we would like to get data for

- `new_proj`: The CRS for the output `SpatialPointsDataFrame` object as a PROJ.4 string

Utilizing these arguments, the function performs the following steps:

1. Takes the `stations` table and converts it to a `SpatialPointsDataFrame` object.
2. Defines the CRS of `stations` (geographical CRS).
3. Removes Canary Islands stations (retaining stations eastwards to the 20°W meridian, that is, stations with *x* coordinate > `-10`; see the map of Spain's mainland and the Canary Islands to understand why).
4. Subsets the meteorological `variable` and the required `year`.
5. Joins the meteorological data with the attribute table of `stations`.
6. Removes stations with `NA` for the respective year/variable combination.
7. Transforms stations to the CRS defined by `new_proj` and returns the resulting object.

The function code is as follows:

```
> create_pnt = function(stations,annual,year,variable,new_proj) {
+ library(plyr)
+ # (1) Promoting stations to SpatialPointsDataFrame
+ coordinates(stations) = ~ longitude + latitude
+ # (2) Defining geographic CRS
+ proj4string(stations) = CRS("+proj=longlat +datum=WGS84")
+ # (3) Removing Canary Islands stations
+ stations = stations[coordinates(stations)[, 1] > -10, ]
+ # (4) Subsetting climatic data
+ annual = annual[
+ annual$year == year &
+ annual$variable == variable, ]
+ # (5) Joining meteorological data with stations layer
```

```
+ stations@data = join(stations@data, annual, by = "station")
+ # (6) Removing incomplete records
+ stations = stations[complete.cases(stations@data), ]
+ # (7) transforming to the required CRS
+ spTransform(stations, CRS(new_proj))
+ }
```

 Note that the `stations` and `annual` arguments are local objects that exist only when the function code is executed; they are not related to the `spain_annual` and `spain_stations` objects of the global environment, which are left unaltered (see *Chapter 2, Working with Vectors and Time Series*).

After reading the function into memory, let's give it a try. The following function call creates, for example, a `SpatialPointsDataFrame` object containing average annual minimum temperature for 2002 defined in the CRS of `dem_spain`:

```
> dat = create_pnt(stations = spain_stations,
+ annual = spain_annual,
+ year = 2002,
+ variable = "mmnt",
+ new_proj = proj4string(dem_spain))
```

We can examine the first few rows of the attribute table of the resulting object `dat` to see that it, indeed, contains minimum temperature values ("`mmnt`") from the year `2002`:

```
> head(dat@data)
           station elevation variable year      value
1 GHCND:SP000003195       667     mmnt 2002 10.475000
2 GHCND:SP000004452       185     mmnt 2002 10.775000
3 GHCND:SP000006155         7     mmnt 2002 14.491667
4 GHCND:SP000008027       251     mmnt 2002 11.100000
5 GHCND:SP000008181         4     mmnt 2002 11.608333
6 GHCND:SP000008202       790     mmnt 2002  5.983333
```

Since the Canary Island stations were removed altogether (see step 3), and stations that do not have a minimum temperature record for 2002 were subsequently filtered out (see step 6), the number of features in the point layer is always smaller than 96 and differs between year/variable combinations. For example, `dat` consists of 75 points:

```
> nrow(dat)
[1] 75
```

In the following sections, you are going to learn how to interpolate the dat temperature records using different methods. Afterwards, we are going to write code to automatically evaluate the prediction error for each model. Finally, we will interpolate data for several years and variables at once using a loop.

Nearest-neighbor interpolation

Before we begin our journey through the three main interpolation methods featured in this chapter (see the next three sections), it is worth pointing out the principle common to most spatial interpolation methods: that the states of the phenomenon of interest are more similar among locations nearer to each other than among locations further apart. In other words, the phenomenon is autocorrelated in space (otherwise predictions should simply be reduced to a global mean, or calculated based on a nonspatial prediction model, such as ordinary regression). With spatial autocorrelation present, it makes sense for predicted values to be more similar to measured values that are nearest to them, and less similar to measured values further apart. For example, if we have a temperature measurement of 20°C at location A, it would be reasonable to assume that the temperature in location B, which is, say, 100 meters away from A, will be fairly similar to 20°C since the air temperature is a spatially autocorrelated phenomenon. The way and the degree to which measured values affect predictions as a function of distance is the main feature that differentiates the various interpolation methods.

The simplest interpolation method based on spatial autocorrelation is nearest-neighbor interpolation. However, it is rarely used in practice in the context of mapping for reasons that will become apparent shortly. It is hereby presented only to demonstrate the concept of spatial interpolation in its simplest form.

In nearest-neighbor interpolation, each predicted location simply takes the value of the nearest measured location. For instance, returning to the previous temperature example, location B will receive a predicted value of exactly 20°C unless there is another measured point within fewer than 100 meters from B (and then it will determine B's predicted value instead of A). We will now perform nearest-neighbor interpolation of the temperature data in dat to understand this point more clearly. We will hereby write code that performs nearest-neighbor interpolation. It is going to consist of the following steps:

1. Creating a set of points for which we would like to make predictions (grid).
2. Finding out which point in dat is the one closest to each point in grid.
3. Assigning nearest-neighbor values of dat to the grid points.

As for the first step, prediction points are most commonly determined using a regular grid (that is, a raster) so that as a result of interpolation we would get a continuous predicted surface. Following this approach, we will use dem_spain for our grid of prediction points. However, since we are going to calculate distances between pairs of points using the gDistance function (which operates on vector layers; see *Chapter 5, Working with Points, Lines, and Polygons*), the raster cells should first be converted to points with rasterToPoints (see the previous chapter) as follows:

```
> grid = rasterToPoints(dem_spain, spatial = TRUE)
```

Moving on to the second step, now we can calculate the distance matrix between each point in dat and each point in grid:

```
> library(rgeos)
> dist = gDistance(dat, grid, byid = TRUE)
```

The resulting object, dist, is a matrix with 39,250 rows (corresponding to the grid features, that is, the number of cells of dem_spain that are not NA) and 75 columns (corresponding to the dat features):

```
> dim(dist)
[1] 39250    75
```

The values of this matrix are the pairwise distances, in meters, between the dat and grid features. In order to assign the value of the nearest points in dat to grid, we need to find out which point is the nearest neighbor in each case. This can be achieved with apply and which.min. The following expression yields a vector of indices indicating the minimal element in each row of dist:

```
> nearest_dat = apply(dist, 1, which.min)
```

Since nearest_dat now holds the indices of the dat features from which we need to obtain the temperature value for each predicted point in grid, the following expression assigns those values to a new column, named nn, in the attribute table of grid:

```
> grid$nn = dat$value[nearest_dat]
```

We have now completed the third step. What is left is to convert grid back to a raster, that is, to rasterize it (see the previous chapter) for easier visualization. The following expression rasterizes grid, with the field parameter set to the "nn" attribute table column, thus transferring its values to the dem_spain raster:

```
> grid = rasterize(grid, dem_spain, "nn")
```

The result is a nearest-neighbor predicted surface with the value of each pixel being the predicted temperature at the respective location. Let's see what it looks like using the following expressions:

```
> plot(grid)
> plot(dat, add = TRUE)
```

The graphical output is shown in the following screenshot:

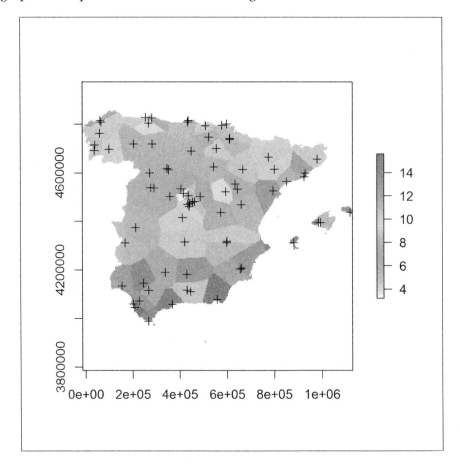

The preceding screenshot clearly shows that the nearest-neighbor interpolation method has, in practice, divided the area of interest into discrete subareas. Each subarea includes all the locations that are more proximate to a given measured point (that is, a given meteorological station) than to any other. In fact, we could have also carried out nearest-neighbor interpolation by creating polygons defining such subareas and rasterized them, to produce the same result. Within the context of GIS, such polygons are known as **Thiessen** or **Voronoi** polygons (interested readers will find at least one way to create them in R; for example, using the `dirichlet` function of the `spatstat` package).

As mentioned earlier, nearest-neighbor interpolation is rarely useful to predict the behavior of natural phenomena in space. For example, it is clearly unrealistic to assume that discrete polygonal areas surrounding each meteorological station have uniform temperatures, with a sharp increase or decrease in temperature, along the borders between them (as the previous screenshot suggests). In reality, the temperature changes more or less gradually from place to place. To describe such gradual transitions, we need to use more elaborate methods, such as those described in the upcoming sections.

IDW interpolation

The three interpolation methods we will employ next—IDW, **Ordinary Kriging (OK)**, and **Universal Kriging (UK)**—all utilize the same principal procedure, where the predicted value of a given point is determined as a weighted average of the values from the measured points. Moreover, the weight of each measured value is always a function of its distance from the point we are trying to predict (a nearby point usually having a higher weight, or influence, on the predicted value than a point further away). Within this framework, nearest-neighbor interpolation is, in fact, an extreme private case, where the weight of the nearest point is 1 while the weights of all other points are 0.

To better understand the subsequent material in this chapter, we can already state that the differences between the three methods concern two properties: the trend and the weights definition. The trend is basically an additional function, independent of the measured points values, added to the weighted average of the latter. In IDW, the trend is 0 and in OK it is a constant value, thus having no effect on the predicted pattern in either case. However, in UK, the trend is a function of additional covariates. Regarding the weights, in IDW they are arbitrarily determined (thus the method is considered deterministic); in OK and UK, conversely, they are estimated from the data itself (thus the methods are considered statistical).

As noted earlier, the predicted values in all three methods are the weighted averages of measured points:

$$\hat{z}(x_0) = \sum_{i=1}^{n} \lambda_i(x_0) z(x_i) \qquad (1)$$

Here, $\hat{z}(x_0)$ is the predicted value at location 0, $z(x_i)$ is the measured value i, and $\lambda_i(x_0)$ is the weight for the measured value i, while n is the total number of measured points.

In IDW, the weight $\lambda_i(x_0)$ is a function of the inverse distance, shown as follows:

$$\lambda_i(x_0) = \frac{d^{-\beta}(x_0, x_i)}{\sum_{i=0}^{n} d^{-\beta}(x_0, x_i)} \qquad (2)$$

Here, $d^{-\beta}(x_0, x_i)$ is the geographic distance between the measured point i and the predicted point at location 0 to the power $-\beta$, and n is the total number of measured points. The default value for β is 2. This means that the importance of each measured point in determining a predicted value diminishes as a function of squared distance. When β is smaller, the predicted surface will be smoother; when β is larger, the predicted surface will be less smooth, giving more emphasis to the nearest neighbor.

We will now interpolate the temperature data in dat using the IDW method. To apply this method, and subsequent ones later in this chapter, we will use functions in the gstat package. This package provides extensive capability for univariate and multivariate geostatistical analysis, of which we will see a few examples.

 For an overview of gstat, see the official introductory document at http://cran.r-project.org/web/packages/gstat/vignettes/gstat.pdf.

The core of the gstat package is a function named gstat, which is used to produce objects (of a class also named gstat) that hold all necessary information to perform spatial interpolation (as well as other operations such as cross-validation). Among the numerous parameters that the gstat function accepts, there is, in fact, no parameter where we can specify the desired interpolation method. Instead, when interpolation is triggered on a gstat object, the method is determined based on the input data the object contains. In this chapter, we are going to explore only a portion of the functionality of gstat, utilizing three of its parameters:

- formula: The formula that defines the dependent and independent variables (an object of the formula class)
- data: The measured point data (a SpatialPointsDataFrame object; it can also be a data.frame object but we will not use this option)
- model: The variogram model (an object of the variogramModel class)

These three parameters determine whether IDW, OK, or UK is used based on the following decision tree:

- If there is no variogram model (model=NULL, the default), IDW is used
- If a variogram model is passed to model, and the formula:
    ◦ contains no independent variables, OK is used
    ◦ contains at least one independent variable, UK is used

Our dependent variable column is value and an *intercept-only* model (that is, a model with no independent variables) formula in R is, by convention, specified by ~1. Therefore, the following expression creates a gstat object (named g) that holds the necessary information to predict the minimum temperature based on the measured data in dat using IDW:

```
> library(gstat)
> g = gstat(formula = value ~ 1, data = dat)
```

Printing g shows a summary of the information it contains as follows:

```
> print(g)
data:
var1 : formula = value`~`1 ; data dim = 75 x 5
```

Note that this is just a summary; g, in fact, also contains the dat object itself, with the measured values and independent variables (if any), since it serves as the calibration data necessary to actually perform the interpolation.

To interpolate, what we now need is to provide the points for which we would like to make predictions. Conveniently, the `raster` function includes a function named `interpolate` that, given a raster (the `object` parameter) and a spatial prediction model (the `model` parameter), yields a new raster with predicted values. This way, we do not need to make the manual conversions to and from a raster, as we did in nearest-neighbor interpolation. For example, the following expression uses the model and calibration data held in `g` to make temperature predictions for the grid defined by `dem_spain`:

```
> z = interpolate(dem_spain, g)
```

There are two things to note here:

- First, as you remember, text messages are omitted in this book to save space. However, readers who run the preceding expression in R will see the message [inverse distance weighted interpolation] appearing on the screen. This reassures the user that indeed the expected type of model has been chosen by `gstat`.

- Second, it is important to understand that, if we do not use covariates (that is, independent variables in the model formula), the `dem_spain` raster serves only as a grid pointing to the locations where we would like to calculate predicted values (the raster values play no role in the interpolation). This is opposed to UK interpolation, where the raster serves both to point at predicted locations and provide covariate values for each location.

Plotting the predicted surface `z` will show that predicted values were generated for all raster cells (including NA cells). It is usually reasonable to make predictions for a more specific extent, such as the land area of Spain. We can use `mask` to remove the unnecessary predictions:

```
> z = mask(z, dem_spain)
```

Now let's plot the predicted value raster, and the station locations on top of it, with the following pair of expressions:

```
> plot(z)
> plot(dat, add = TRUE)
```

The graphical output is shown in the following screenshot:

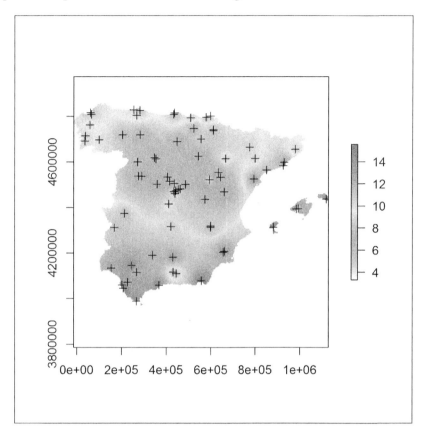

In the preceding screenshot, we see the predicted average minimum temperature for 2002 in Spain. It seems the central-northern parts of the country were generally colder, while the south was warmer (this general pattern was also evident in the nearest-neighbor interpolation image). The effect of the station locations on the predicted surface is also notable. As you remember, the weight of a given station increases as the predicted point is nearer. Therefore, each point generates a sort of circular zone of influence around itself, especially if its value markedly differs from the values of its proximate neighbors.

To understand the role of the β parameter (see equation (2)) more vividly, let's produce two more IDW-predicted surfaces: one with β set to a very small value (say, `0.3`) and one with β set to a very large value (say, `30`). Then, we will compare the results with the preceding graphical output (where β was set to `2`, which is the default value). The following code generates the two additional predicted surfaces and assigns them to objects `z1` and `z2`, respectively:

```
> g1 = gstat(formula = value ~ 1, data = dat, set = list(idp=0.3))
> g2 = gstat(formula = value ~ 1, data = dat, set = list(idp=30))
> z1 = interpolate(dem_spain, g1)
> z2 = interpolate(dem_spain, g2)
> z1 = mask(z1, dem_spain)
> z2 = mask(z2, dem_spain)
```

Note that the `set=list(idp=0.3)` part determines the value of β in `gstat`. Using the following expression, we can visualize the three rasters: `z1`, `z`, and `z2` (the `pch` and `cex` parameters are used to control the symbol type and size, respectively, when drawing the `dat` points):

```
> plot(z1, main = c("beta = 0.3"))
> plot(dat, add = TRUE, pch = 20, cex = 0.5)
> plot(z, main = c("beta = 2"))
> plot(dat, add = TRUE, pch = 20, cex = 0.5)
> plot(z2, main = c("beta = 30"))
> plot(dat, add = TRUE, pch = 20, cex = 0.5)
```

The graphical outputs shown here, side by side, are produced as a result. The respective values of β are stated above each output:

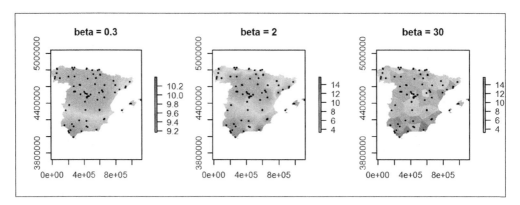

These images demonstrate the previously stated expectations. Decreasing β (the leftmost image) results in a smoother surface due to more homogeneous weight distribution among the measured points. On the other hand, increasing β (the rightmost image), results in sharper boundaries between the zones of influence of each point, resembling nearest-neighbor interpolation results in appearance.

Now that we have produced several interpolation results, how can we assess the predictive ability of this (or any other) interpolation method? The obvious way is to compare predicted values to observed ones, preferably when the validation points come from an independent dataset—one that did not participate in model calibration. Since measurements are usually scarce and valuable (we do not have an infinite number of meteorological stations), however, we would like to include each and every measurement in the model calibration, leaving no measurements for validation. The compromise approach to this problem is the process of cross-validation, where we set aside some of the observed points for validation. In the process of cross-validation, we then try to predict their values using the remaining points and compare the predicted values to the observed ones. A special case of cross-validation is **leave-one-out cross-validation (LOOCV)**, where every observed point is removed in turn, its value being predicted based on the remaining points to obtain a table with observed and predicted values for all observations. Assessing the differences between observed and predicted values based on such a table gives us a measure of the accuracy of our prediction model.

The `gstat.cv` function can automatically perform cross-validation given an object of the `gstat` class. The default method is LOOCV; therefore, in the following expression, all we need to do is perform LOOCV on the IDW interpolation of temperature data:

```
> cv = gstat.cv(g)
```

This expression, in practice, triggers the execution of 75 spatial interpolation operations, each time leaving out one meteorological station and trying to predict its temperature value using the 74 remaining ones. The result is a `SpatialPointsDataFrame` object with the same number of features as `dat` and with the same spatial locations. Only the attribute table is different, now containing the cross-validation results:

```
> head(cv@data)
  var1.pred var1.var  observed    residual zscore fold
1  8.971923       NA 10.475000  1.5030771     NA    1
2 10.244447       NA 10.775000  0.5305532     NA    2
3 10.914591       NA 14.491667  3.5770756     NA    3
4  9.992180       NA 11.100000  1.1078202     NA    4
5 12.024766       NA 11.608333 -0.4164331     NA    5
6  7.435642       NA  5.983333 -1.4523087     NA    6
```

The attribute table columns of the cross-validation result refer to the following information:

- `var1.pred`: Predicted value
- `var1.var`: Variance (only for kriging)
- `observed`: Observed value
- `residual`: Residual, the difference between observed and predicted values
- `zscore`: Z-score (only for kriging)
- `fold`: Cross-validation count

The important column, for our purpose here, is `residual` — the difference between the observed and predicted values. Based on the residuals, we can assess how far predicted values are from the observed ones, or in other words, prediction accuracy. One of the simplest and most common metrics of agreement between observed and predicted values is the RMSE. Given a set of predicted-observed value pairs, the RMSE is calculated as follows:

$$RMSE = \sqrt{\frac{\sum_{i=1}^{n}\left(pred_i - obs_i\right)^2}{n}} \qquad (3)$$

Here, *RMSE* is the root mean square error, *n* is the overall number of points, and *pred_i* and *obs_i* are the predicted and observed values at point *i*, respectively. As the difference between predicted and observed values is smaller, the RMSE will be lower, indicating that the model is more accurate. Given the same input data, we can compare the RMSE values among different models to select the most accurate one. Translating equation (3) to the R syntax, we can calculate RMSE based on the attribute table of `cv` as follows:

```
> sqrt(sum((-cv$residual)^2)/nrow(cv))
[1] 1.88049
```

The RMSE in this case is equal to `1.88049`. Note that the expression consists of the `-cv$residual` vector (equivalent to `cv$var1.pred-cv$observed`) squared, then summed, and divided by the total number of points. Finally, the square root of the result is extracted.

For convenience, we can wrap this expression into our own function, which calculates RMSE, given a `gstat.cv` output:

```
> rmse = function(x) sqrt(sum((-x$residual)^2)/nrow(x))
> rmse(cv)
[1] 1.88049
```

We will use this function later.

You may have noticed that the `gstat` object we initially defined (`g`) was hereby used for two distinct and independent purposes. First, to calculate predicted values (using the `interpolate` function), then to perform cross-validation (using the `gstat.cv` function). This is not incidental, but rather a characteristic object-oriented behavior common to all, or most, of R's statistical procedures. This approach is advantageous over the menu-based approach commonly encountered in statistical or GIS software, where we carry out a given analysis by making selections in a set of dialog boxes, and receive a set of results (some of which we do not need, while others are lacking since the tool's creator did not include them). Conversely, when a statistical function is applied in R, we usually get an object that holds all the data that is necessary to carry out the analysis (such as `g`) or an object that holds a comprehensive set of results (such as `cv`). From such objects, we can then derive the results we are interested in by applying specific functions. Moreover, we can create functions of our own to carry out calculations or extract meaningful data, for which no built-in methods have been defined (such as the `rmse` function we defined earlier). Readers who are interested in using R as a general statistical analysis toolbox will repeatedly encounter this approach. For example, the `lm` function is used to perform ordinary linear regression in R; on its returned object, of class `lm`, numerous functions (such as `summary`, `residuals`, and `plot`) may be applied to derive the information we are interested in.

Interpolation using Ordinary Kriging

In kriging, as mentioned earlier, the weight $\lambda_i(x_0)$ given to each measurement when calculating a predicted value (see equation (1)) is determined statistically, rather than arbitrarily (such as by choosing the value of β ourselves in equation (2)). The function determining weights in kriging is called a variogram model. The variogram model is a function fitted to the empirical variogram, which in turn describes the spatial autocorrelation structure of the observed pattern. What is important to understand is that the empirical variogram describes the average degree of autocorrelation between observed values, and the variogram model is a continuous function fitted to these data. The variogram model determines, in plain terms, the importance of points nearby and further away in the calculation of predicted values. For example, if autocorrelation is high over short distances, it would make sense to let nearby points largely determine the predicted value, making the predicted surface rougher; when autocorrelation is low, the weight distribution over distance may be more uniform and the predicted surface smoother. Elaborating on the subject of variogram modeling is beyond the scope of this book; interested readers can find more information in *A practical guide to geostatistical mapping of environmental variables*, Hengle, T. (2007) or in any textbook on geostatistics.

An empirical variogram can be calculated using the `variogram` function, once again based on a `gstat` object. Let's take a look at the following example:

```
> ev = variogram(g)
```

The returned object of the `gstatVariogram` class contains semivariance values (expressing the degree of correlation) for different distance bins. Note that there are numerous optional parameters controlling the way a variogram is computed, that we will not go into, such as the way the latter bins are determined (see `?variogram`). The `plot` method for a `gstatVariogram` object plots the empirical variogram as follows:

```
> plot(ev)
```

The following screenshot shows how the plot appears in our case:

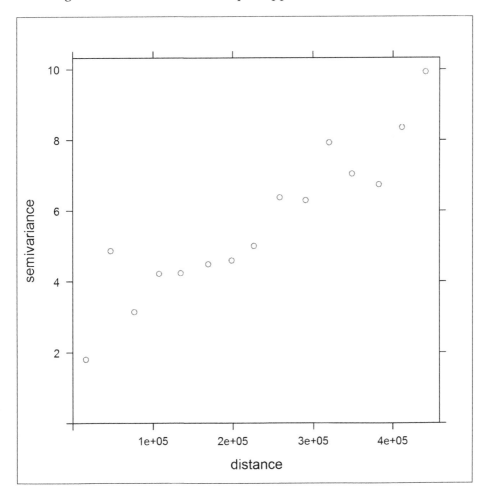

We can see that semivariance increases with distance. This means that temperature values are more diverse when considering stations further apart. In other words, temperature is spatially autocorrelated.

As mentioned earlier, a variogram model is a function fitted to the empirical variogram. There are several specific functions that are adequate to describe the characteristic behavior of an empirical variogram (increasing semivariance with distance, usually reaching saturation at some point). These functions, such as the spherical and exponential functions, are generally used for a variogram model (type vgm() for a list of the functions implemented in gstat or show.vgms() for a visual). In addition to choosing one of these functions, we need to decide on its specific parameters. There are three main approaches, not mutually exclusive, to select a variogram model: a function plus its set of parameters (based on an empirical variogram):

- Setting the function and its parameters by hand (for example, using the vgm function from the gstat package)
- Visually fitting a function to the empirical variogram by interactively varying the function type and its parameters and seeing how its appearance changes (for example, using the eyefit function from the geoR package)
- Statistically selecting the function and parameters that minimize some goodness-of-fit criterion (for example, using the fit.variogram function from the gstat package, the variofit function from the geoR package, or the autofitVariogram function from the automap package)

Since we are hereby taking a simple, practical approach, we will use the third option of letting the computer select the function that follows the empirical variogram most closely. Moreover, we are going to bypass the requirement to supply the function type and initial parameter estimates (as required, for example, in fit.variogram) and use a wrapper function named autofitVariogram that automatically optimizes this decision for us.

The autofitVariogram function is defined in the automap package. It accepts the formula and data arguments (named input_data) analogously for gstat. The following expression, therefore, fits a variogram model to our data:

```
> library(automap)
> v = autofitVariogram(formula = value ~ 1, input_data = dat)
```

Plotting the returned object of the autofitVariogram class generates a plot with an empirical variogram and the fitted variogram model on top of it:

```
> plot(v)
```

The resulting output is shown in the following screenshot:

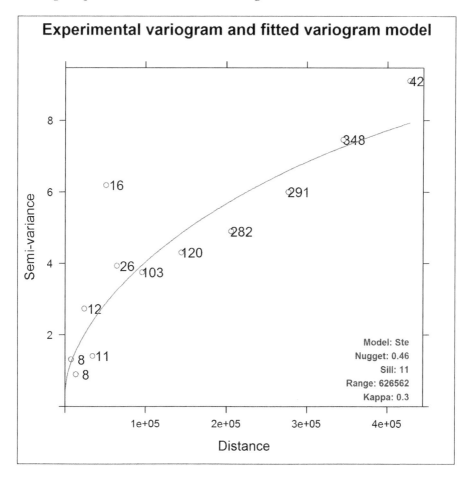

The points, once again, show an empirical variogram, while the continuous line is the fitted variogram model. In this case, for instance, the selected model was "Matern, M. Stein's parameterization" (code name `"Ste"`), with the four parameter values stated in the bottom-right corner of the image. The object v contains several components, such as the empirical variogram data points and the sums of squares between the sample variogram and the fitted variogram model. The component we are interested in is the fitted variogram model. This components' name is `var_model`, and it can be accessed with the $ operator, using the expression v$var_model (this behavior stems from the fact that an `autofitVariogram` class is built upon a `list`, and list elements can be accessed the same way as `data.frame` columns with $).

The important point here is that the v$var_model component of v is an object of class variogramModel, containing the function type and parameters defining a variogram model. A variogramModel object can be passed to the gstat function to indicate a variogram model. Therefore, we can create an object containing all the necessary information to perform the OK interpolation as follows:

```
> g = gstat(formula = value ~ 1, data = dat, model = v$var_model)
> g
data:
var1 : formula = value`~`1 ; data dim = 75 x 5
variograms:
        model       psill   range kappa
var1[1]   Nug  0.4594258      0.0   0.0
var1[2]   Ste 10.9549186 626562.4   0.3
```

The printed output shows that the object indeed contains a variogram model. We can now use the interpolate function to produce the predicted OK surface, and the mask function to clip the area of interest, exactly the same way we did in IDW interpolation:

```
> z = interpolate(dem_spain, g)
> z = mask(z, dem_spain)
```

Those readers who execute the above expression in R should see, this time, the message [using ordinary kriging] on screen.

Let's plot the interpolation result with the following expressions:

```
> plot(z)
> plot(dat, add = TRUE)
```

The graphical output is shown in the following screenshot:

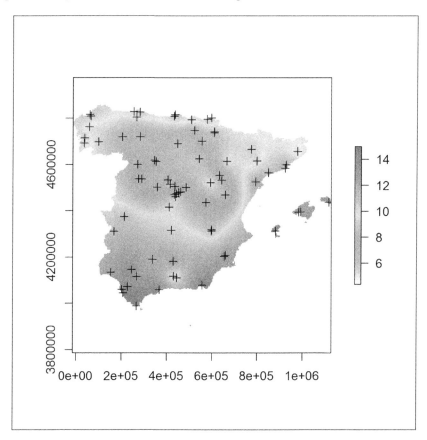

One of the notable visual differences in predicted rasters between IDW and kriging, in general, is that the weight of a given measured point always approaches 1 in IDW as we get nearer. Therefore, the values around each measurement point tend to approach the measured value itself (see the previous screenshot); in kriging, however, this is not necessarily so.

We can now perform LOOCV of the OK prediction model in order to compare the resulting RMSE with that of IDW:

```
> cv = gstat.cv(g)
> rmse(cv)
[1] 1.680153
```

The RMSE is smaller in this case, which suggests that OK produces more accurate prediction than IDW interpolation.

Using covariates in Universal Kriging interpolation

Universal Kriging (also referred to as Kriging with External Drift or Regression Kriging) is, in fact, a general model of which OK is a special case. While both methods involve spatial autocorrelation modeling, they differ in the definition of the trend. In OK, the trend is a constant value, while the trend is a linear function of one or more covariates in UK. In other words, in OK the predicted value is some constant plus a weighted function of neighboring measurements, while it is a predicted value based on covariates plus a weighted function of neighboring measurements in UK.

For instance, it is well known that temperature is negatively correlated with elevation (it gets colder as we climb to a higher altitude). Using a simple scatterplot, we can see that this rule holds true in the present case as well:

```
> plot(value ~ elevation, dat@data,
+ xlab = "Elevation (m)",
+ ylab = "Temperature (degrees Celsius)")
```

The resulting plot clearly shows the negative relationship between elevation and temperature, although the relation is not perfect:

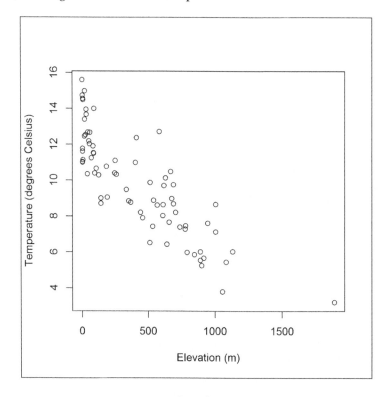

Sometimes the temperature for a given altitude is lower than usual and sometimes higher. Can we create a model where the temperature is predicted using elevation and then fine-tuned using nearby meteorological measurements? UK does exactly this by adding a weighted average of stations values (as OK does) to a general trend surface defined by a linear function based on covariates (in this case, elevation).

To interpolate the temperature data using UK with elevation as a covariate, we need to make two principal alterations compared to the OK procedure:

- The variogram model is constructed according to the so-called residual variogram, which portrays the spatial autocorrelation of the residuals from the chosen trend

- The predicted values are calculated based on both the neighboring measured values (as in OK) and the covariates; thus, each point we would like to predict must be accompanied by its respective set of covariate values

Starting with the variogram model, as opposed to OK, our formula now contains elevation as an independent variable:

```
> v = autofitVariogram(formula = value ~ elevation,
+ input_data = dat)
```

Plotting the new v object will show that both the empirical variogram and the variogram model are different from what we previously had since they now concern the residuals from the elevation trend. Next, we need to create the gstat object, which contains the information to perform UK interpolation, supplying value~elevation as the formula and v$var_model as the variogram model:

```
> g = gstat(formula = value ~ elevation,
+ data = dat,
+ model = v$var_model)
> g
data:
var1 : formula = value`~`elevation ; data dim = 75 x 5
variograms:
        model     psill    range kappa
var1[1]   Nug 0.7410872     0.00   0.0
var1[2]   Ste 0.9696567 35781.93   0.2
```

By supplying the appropriate formula in the variogram fitting stage and in the `gstat` function call, we dealt with the first issue. As for the second issue, it is necessary for us to provide an elevation value for each point where we try to predict the temperature (otherwise the trend cannot be calculated). Since the points are specified in the form of a raster, it is only natural that the covariate values will come from the raster values themselves. This is exactly what the `interpolate` function expects, but in order for this function to correctly identify which raster layers contain the values of the covariates, the respective layers must be named exactly the same way as the covariates are (in the `formula` passed to `autofitVariogram` and `gstat`, as well as in the measurements point layer). In our case, there is only one covariate (`elevation`) and one layer in the `dem_spain` raster. Therefore, we just need to make sure that layer is named `"elevation"`:

```
> names(dem_spain)
[1] "spain_elev"
> names(dem_spain) = "elevation"
> names(dem_spain)
[1] "elevation"
```

In addition, we need to make one final adjustment to the `interpolate` function call—setting `xyOnly=FALSE`, which instructs the `interpolate` function to consider the raster values as covariates (rather than just coordinates of prediction points). The option `xyOnly=FALSE` should be specified whenever we have a model with covariates:

```
> z = interpolate(dem_spain, g, xyOnly = FALSE)
```

When running the previous expression, you should see the [using universal kriging] message on screen. Let's plot the UK predictions:

```
> z = mask(z, dem_spain)
> plot(z)
> plot(dat, add = TRUE)
```

The graphical output is shown in the following screenshot:

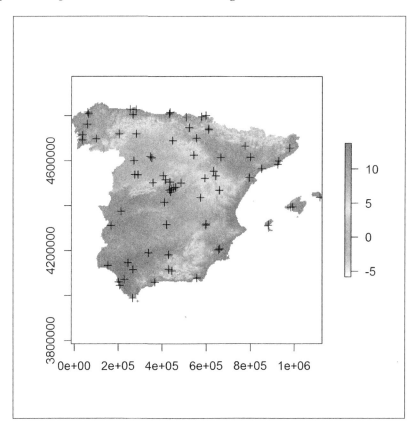

The preceding screenshot quite obviously resembles Spain's DEM. In fact, it shows the elevation profile of Spain transposed to temperature units (using a linear relation based on the data from meteorological stations) and locally calibrated using, once again, the stations data. This is what UK results commonly look like.

Let's examine the RMSE of the UK prediction model as well:

```
> cv = gstat.cv(g)
> rmse(cv)
[1] 1.455196
```

We see that the RMSE of UK, in this case, is even lower than that of OK. This result suggests that utilizing the value~elevation trend has further improved prediction accuracy.

Mapping the annual temperature in Spain

In the previous sections, we saw how to perform spatial interpolation of point data in R using several methods, including IDW, OK, and UK. We also learned that, in the case of minimum temperature in 2002, UK outperformed the other two methods in terms of accuracy, with a LOOCV RMSE value of 1.46, compared to 1.88 and 1.68 for IDW and OK, respectively. In this section, we are going to see how we can automate spatial interpolation in order to produce a set of temperature maps for different years with a single code execution command. For this purpose, we are going to construct two loops:

- The first loop will go through 20 point layers (10 years * 2 variables), each time calculating the RMSE of LOOCV in prediction using each of the three methods (IDW, OK, and UK). Based on the results, we will select the most accurate method (on average) out of these three.

- We will then construct the second loop to produce predicted temperature maps of Spain (for 5 years—2006-2010) using the selected method.

We will begin with the first task of systematically evaluating RMSE among the different years, variables, and methods. A very useful function for such tasks, named expand.grid, will help us keep track of the examination. Given a set of vectors, expand.grid returns a data.frame object with all possible combinations of the elements from each vector. The following expression, for example, creates a data.frame object, named cv_results, with four columns (variable, year, method, and rmse):

```
> cv_results = expand.grid(
+ variable = c("mmnt", "mmxt"),
+ year = 2001:2010,
+ method = c("IDW", "OK", "UK"),
+ rmse = NA)
```

Since only three of the columns have more than one possible element, and there are 2 variables * 10 years * 3 methods = 60 unique ways to combine them, cv_results has 60 rows. The first few rows of this data.frame object look as follows:

```
> head(cv_results)
  variable year method rmse
1     mmnt 2001    IDW   NA
2     mmxt 2001    IDW   NA
3     mmnt 2002    IDW   NA
4     mmxt 2002    IDW   NA
5     mmnt 2003    IDW   NA
6     mmxt 2003    IDW   NA
```

This table is going to help us in two ways:

- First, we are going to go through its rows, each time performing LOOCV for yet another prediction model defined with the respective values in the `variable`, `year`, and `method` columns. This way, we can be sure that all the possible combinations are covered.

- Second, the resulting RMSE values will be assigned in the respective position in the `rmse` column so that, by the time the loop execution is complete, we will conveniently have a table with all of the results.

The loop will be defined to go through all rows of `cv_results`, with `i` being assigned the current row index each time. The code within the loop will then perform the following operations:

1. Create a point layer named `dat` (using the `create_pnt` function we previously defined) with the variable and year set according to the current row of `cv_results` (rather than at fixed values such as `2002` and `"mmnt"`).

2. Create an object defining the prediction formula (`form`) and variogram model (`v_mod`).

3. Create a `gstat` object based on the appropriate point layer (`dat`), formula (`form`), and variogram model (`v_mod`).

4. Perform LOOCV.

5. Calculate RMSE and assign the result in the appropriate position in the `rmse` column of `cv_results`.

The code snippet, with the code sections for each of the preceding steps marked by a comment, is as follows:

```
> for(i in row(cv_results)) {
+ # (1) Create point layer as required
+ dat = create_pnt(stations = spain_stations,
+ annual = spain_annual,
+ year = cv_results$year[i],
+ variable = cv_results$variable[i],
+ new_proj = proj4string(dem_spain))
+ # (2) Create *form* and *v_mod* objects
+ if(cv_results$method[i] == "IDW") {
+ form = value ~ 1
+ v_mod = NULL} else {
+ if(cv_results$method[i] == "OK") {
+ form = value ~ 1}
+ if(cv_results$method[i] == "UK") {
+ form = value ~ elevation}
```

```
+ v_mod =
+ autofitVariogram(
+ formula = form,
+ input_data = dat)$var_model}
+ # (3) Create gstat object
+ g = gstat(formula = form, data = dat, model = v_mod)
+ # (4) Perform cross-validation
+ cv = gstat.cv(g)
+ # (5) Calculate RMSE and assign to cv_results
+ cv_results$rmse[i] = rmse(cv)
+ }
```

Note that, in step 2, nested conditional statements are used in order to determine form and v_mod according to the interpolation method that is being used. We can write down the procedure this particular code section performs in the form of a decision tree:

- If the method is "IDW", then form is value~1 and v_mod is NULL
- Otherwise:
    ○ If the method is "OK", then form is value~1
    ○ If the method is "UK", then form is value~elevation
    ○ The v_mod is calculated according to form

Once the loop execution is completed (this may take a few moments), the rmse column of cv_results will be filled with the resulting RMSE values instead of NA values:

```
> head(cv_results)
  variable year method     rmse
1     mmnt 2001    IDW 1.942872
2     mmxt 2001    IDW 1.594996
3     mmnt 2002    IDW 1.880490
4     mmxt 2002    IDW 1.570574
5     mmnt 2003    IDW 1.912887
6     mmxt 2003    IDW 1.605938
```

Note that, for instance, the RMSE value at the third row table (1.880490), which corresponds to the IDW interpolation of "mmnt" for 2002 as expected, is identical to the result we have previously obtained manually. Several interesting comparisons can be made using this RMSE table. As previously stated, we are mainly interested in seeing which interpolation method is the most accurate, on average, across 10 years and the two variables. To find out, we can use `tapply`:

```
> tapply(cv_results$rmse, cv_results$method, mean)
     IDW       OK       UK
1.773243 1.908957 1.458997
```

The result shows that, on average, UK yields the lowest prediction error among the three methods. Interestingly, OK is less accurate, on average, than IDW although in the particular example we previously saw it was the other way around. Based on this result, UK is going to be our method of choice to produce annual temperature maps of Spain.

It should be noted that comparing cross-validation RMSE is only meaningful among different spatial prediction models of the same data. Otherwise, RMSE may be higher or lower not only because the prediction error is different but also because the predicted values themselves are on different scales. For example, RMSE of the precipitation amount ("tpcp") prediction would have been much higher than RMSE of temperature prediction in our case (you can try and see this), simply because the generally observed annual precipitation amounts in Spain (in mm) are higher by an order of magnitude than temperatures (in Celsius degrees). However, this does not mean that the prediction models of precipitation are less accurate with respect to the scale of the measured variable itself.

We are ready to move on and produce annual temperature maps using another loop that calculates the predicted values (rather than performing cross-validation, which we just did). Once again, a well-organized way of doing this is to construct a table describing the set of parameters we need for each spatial interpolation, then go through that table and perform the required operations in turn. We will once again use the `expand.grid` function, producing all combinations of just two variables this time: `year` (the 5 years 2006-2010) and `variable` ("mmnt" and "mmxt"). The method will be left unspecified as we have already decided it should be invariably UK.

```
> spainT_tab = expand.grid(
+ year = 2006:2010,
+ variable = c("mmnt", "mmxt"))
```

The resulting table, named `spainT_tab`, looks as follows:

```
> spainT_tab
   year variable
1  2006     mmnt
2  2007     mmnt
3  2008     mmnt
4  2009     mmnt
5  2010     mmnt
6  2006     mmxt
7  2007     mmxt
8  2008     mmxt
9  2009     mmxt
10 2010     mmxt
```

We are ready to create the second loop that will go through the rows of `spainT_tab` and spatially interpolate the respective temperature data. Since our results are going to be rasters (rather than numeric values, as was the case with the cross-validation loop) in this case, they cannot be appended to the table itself. Instead, we are going to stack the results in a multiband raster where each layer is going to correspond to a row in `spainT_tab`. In other words, `spainT_tab` is going to function as a supplementary table for the resulting multiband raster (much as `dates` served the same purpose for the raster `r`; see *Chapter 4, Working with Rasters*). To construct the raster, we will first create an empty `RasterStack` to which the interpolation results will be appended during loop execution:

```
> spainT = stack()
```

The loop will go through the rows of `spainT_tab`, each time performing the following set of operations:

1. Creating a point layer named `dat` with the variable and year set according to the current row of `spainT_tab`.

2. Fitting a variogram model (`v`).

3. Creating a `gstat` object (`g`) according to `dat` and `v`.

4. Calculating the raster of predicted values (`z`) with `interpolate`, based on `g` and `dem_spain`.

5. Masking `z` according to `dem_spain` and attaching the result to `spainT`.

The loop code appears as follows:

```
> for(i in 1:nrow(spainT_tab)) {
+ # (1) Create point layer as required
+ dat = create_pnt(stations = spain_stations,
+ annual = spain_annual,
+ year = spainT_tab$year[i],
+ variable = spainT_tab$variable[i],
+ new_proj = proj4string(dem_spain))
+ # (2) Automatically fit variogram model
+ v = autofitVariogram(formula = value ~ elevation,
+ input_data = dat)
+ # (3) Create gstat object
+ g = gstat(formula = value ~ elevation,
+ model = v$var_model,
+ data = dat)
+ # (4) Interpolate!
+ z = interpolate(dem_spain, g, xyOnly = FALSE)
+ # (5) Mask and add predicted surface to results stack
+ spainT = stack(spainT, mask(z, dem_spain))
+ }
```

Once loop execution is complete, interpolation results are stored as individual layers of the spainT raster. The raster should consist of 10 layers, corresponding to the 10 rows in spainT_tab. Right now, the layer names are not very informative:

```
> names(spainT)
 [1] "var1.pred.1.1.1" "var1.pred.2.1.1" "var1.pred.1.2.1"
 [4] "var1.pred.2.2.1" "var1.pred.1.1.2" "var1.pred.2.1.2"
 [7] "var1.pred.1.2.2" "var1.pred.2.2.2" "var1.pred.1"
[10] "var1.pred.2"
```

However, with spainT_tab at our disposal, we can easily change this as follows:

```
> names(spainT) = paste(spainT_tab$variable,
+ spainT_tab$year,
+ sep = "_")
> names(spainT)
 [1] "mmnt_2006" "mmnt_2007" "mmnt_2008" "mmnt_2009" "mmnt_2010"
 [6] "mmxt_2006" "mmxt_2007" "mmxt_2008" "mmxt_2009" "mmxt_2010"
```

Let's now plot `spainT` using the `levelplot` function. With `layout=c(5,2)`, we make sure that the minimum and maximum temperature maps are plotted in distinct rows:

```
> library(rasterVis)
> levelplot(spainT, par.settings = "BuRdTheme", layout = c(5,2))
```

The graphical output is shown in the following screenshot:

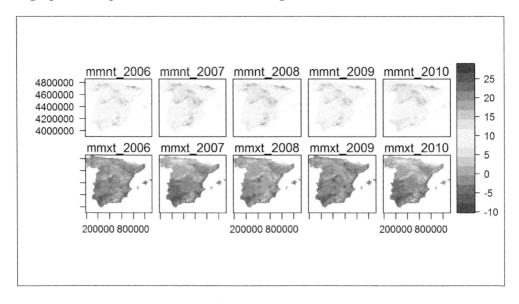

The preceding screenshot shows predicted minimum (top row) and maximum (bottom row) temperatures in Spain for each of the years from 2006 to 2010. As can be expected, maximum temperatures are always higher than minimum temperatures. The predicted spatial pattern of temperature is fairly similar over the years, which also makes sense—colder areas are generally colder repeatedly, in all years, as are warmer areas. However, the latter poses a problem when interpreting this type of result, as the characteristic temperature pattern within each year overwhelms the differences among years and makes it difficult for us to notice the year-to-year variation. This can be partially addressed by plotting minimum and maximum temperature rasters separately (in order to use a wider color scale each time). The interested reader can see for himself that it does little to solve the problem.

When we are interested in interannual differences only, the most reasonable course of action is to find out what is the characteristic annual temperature state, find out the deviation of each individual year's state from the characteristic state, and then compare the deviation images rather than the original ones. Calculating deviations from a general trend is a very common practice to highlight patterns of interest in our data, and there are many ways to find both the general trend and the deviations of each observation from it. Here, we will employ the simplest possible approach—the characteristic temperature in each pixel will be defined as the 5-year average observed in that pixel, and the deviations will be equal to arithmetic differences of each observation from the average.

Since we need to treat the minimum and maximum temperature data separately, we will first create two vectors identifying the relevant `spainT` layers for each case:

```
> mmnt_layers = which(spainT_tab$variable == "mmnt")
> mmnt_layers
[1] 1 2 3 4 5
> mmxt_layers = which(spainT_tab$variable == "mmxt")
> mmxt_layers
[1]  6  7  8  9 10
```

We will also create a new two-band `RasterStack`, named `means`, to hold the minimum and maximum mean temperature pattern in its first and second layers, respectively. The two layers will also be named accordingly (`"mmnt"` and `"mmxt"`):

```
> means = stack(mean(spainT[[mmnt_layers]]),
+ mean(spainT[[mmxt_layers]]))
> names(means) = c("mmnt", "mmxt")
```

Now that we have the means, all we need to do is subtract the appropriate mean from each set of layers in `spainT` (the mean of the minimum temperatures from layers 1-5 and the mean of the maximum temperatures from layers 6-10). There are numerous ways to do this. For example, we can divide the `spainT` raster into two, subtract the respective mean from each substack, and then combine them once again. A more elegant way, extendable to any number of categories, however, is to create a new means raster with the same number of layers as `spainT`, by means of duplication, with the relevant means occupying its layers. In other words, we need a raster with `means[[1]]` duplicated five times (occupying layers 1-5) and `means[[2]]` duplicated five times (occupying layers 6-10). To do this, we can utilize the fact that raster layers can also be selected by their names. The following expression therefore takes the `"mmnt"` and `"mmxt"` layers and duplicates them in agreement with the `spainT_tab$variable` column:

```
> means = means[[spainT_tab$variable]]
```

This gives us the desired result, a 10-band raster with temperature means for either the minimum or maximum temperature, according to `spainT_tab` (and thus matching `spainT`). The layer names reveal that indeed the first five layers correspond to the minimum temperature and the last five layers correspond to the maximum temperature:

```
> names(means)
 [1] "mmnt.1" "mmnt.2" "mmnt.3" "mmnt.4" "mmnt.5" "mmxt.1"
 [7] "mmxt.2" "mmxt.3" "mmxt.4" "mmxt.5"
```

What is left to be done is just to subtract one 10-band raster from the other:

```
> spainT = spainT - means
```

The data we now have in the new `spainT` raster is the temperature deviations from the five-year average pattern of either the minimum or maximum temperature. We can check and see that the deviations are within the range of -4 and +4 degrees Celsius around the respective 5-year mean of 2006-2010:

```
> range(spainT[], na.rm = TRUE)
[1] -4.020094  3.200148
```

Plotting these deviations will help us see more clearly where exactly the temperature was high or low, with respect to the average pattern, and what the magnitude of the departure was. This time, we will also indicate that contours should be drawn at 1°C intervals:

```
> levelplot(spainT,
+ par.settings = "BuRdTheme",
+ layout = c(5,2),
+ contour = TRUE,
+ at = c(-4:-1,1:4))
```

The graphical output is shown in the following screenshot:

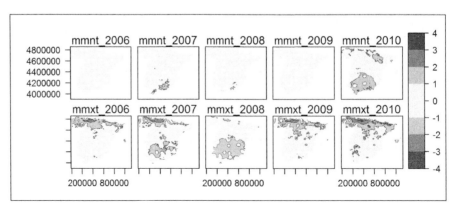

This time, we can easily notice, for example, that the minimum temperatures in 2010 were higher than average in southern Spain while the maximum temperatures were lower than average in the north of the country.

This is the final product we were looking for, according to the goals specified at the beginning of this section. However, we are not done yet. In the next chapter, we will use spainT as one of the sample datasets while discussing how to produce plots with the ggplot2 package. Since ggplot2 is a general-purpose graphical package, the input data must come as a data.frame object. Moreover, the data table should be tidy (see the previous chapter) in order to conveniently exploit all of the possibilities this package offers. What does that mean in the present case? It means that we need to have a data.frame object with all the data currently held in spainT, with each column corresponding to a variable and each row corresponding to an observation. In this case, the variables are as follows:

- x-coordinate
- y-coordinate
- Variable
- Year
- Predicted temperature

Each row in such a data.frame object will correspond to one pixel of an individual layer in spainT.

Luckily, the as.data.frame function (that we encountered in the previous chapter, when converting a matrix to a data.frame) also has a method to convert rasters to the data.frame objects. By setting xy=TRUE, we are specifying that we would like to have a table not only with the raster values (from all of its layers) but also with the respective spatial coordinates:

```
> spainT = as.data.frame(spainT, xy = TRUE)
> head(spainT)
           x       y mmnt_2006 mmnt_2007 mmnt_2008 mmnt_2009
1 -11957.925 4857128        NA        NA        NA        NA
2  -8357.925 4857128        NA        NA        NA        NA
3  -4757.925 4857128        NA        NA        NA        NA
4  -1157.925 4857128        NA        NA        NA        NA
5   2442.075 4857128        NA        NA        NA        NA
6   6042.075 4857128        NA        NA        NA        NA
  mmnt_2010 mmxt_2006 mmxt_2007 mmxt_2008 mmxt_2009 mmxt_2010
1        NA        NA        NA        NA        NA        NA
```

2	NA	NA	NA	NA	NA	NA
3	NA	NA	NA	NA	NA	NA
4	NA	NA	NA	NA	NA	NA
5	NA	NA	NA	NA	NA	NA
6	NA	NA	NA	NA	NA	NA

Each row in this table represents a single pixel, while its spatial coordinates and values in each layer are specified in the respective columns. However, from the first few rows, we can see that NA cells were also included. Since they will not be plotted anyway, we can readily exclude them:

```
> spainT = spainT[complete.cases(spainT), ]
> head(spainT)
            x       y mmnt_2006     mmnt_2007    mmnt_2008 mmnt_2009
33   103242.08 4857128 0.7383187 -0.070727914 0.008270229 0.5218489
34   106842.08 4857128 0.7392765 -0.055515954 0.024604441 0.5227165
38   121242.08 4857128 0.7458803 -0.018719502 0.063198494 0.5252469
39   124842.08 4857128 0.7456079  0.002858330 0.084895939 0.5240072
40   128442.08 4857128 0.7454912  0.023069161 0.105275777 0.5226526
347   92442.08 4853528 0.7061661 -0.006305609 0.051584103 0.5112048
     mmnt_2010 mmxt_2006 mmxt_2007 mmxt_2008 mmxt_2009 mmxt_2010
33   -1.197710  2.012048 -2.361182  1.122896  1.941084 -2.714846
34   -1.231081  1.988164 -2.341944  1.118404  1.918249 -2.682873
38   -1.315606  1.932082 -2.291416  1.103507  1.857861 -2.602034
39   -1.357369  1.894492 -2.252492  1.094646  1.809158 -2.545804
40   -1.396489  1.859306 -2.215895  1.086683  1.763085 -2.493179
347  -1.262649  1.870778 -2.157029  1.059672  1.696265 -2.469685
```

Two things are left to be done to bring this data.frame object to the desired form:

- First, we need to transform the table into a long form, creating a value column and keeping all other variables in separate individual columns. This can be achieved with the melt function (see *Chapter 3, Working with Tables*, for more details), specifying "x" and "y" columns as the ID variables so that the other columns are transferred into a single variable column:

```
> library(reshape2)
> spainT = melt(spainT, id.vars = c("x", "y"))
> head(spainT)
          x       y  variable     value
1 103242.08 4857128 mmnt_2006 0.7383187
2 106842.08 4857128 mmnt_2006 0.7392765
3 121242.08 4857128 mmnt_2006 0.7458803
4 124842.08 4857128 mmnt_2006 0.7456079
5 128442.08 4857128 mmnt_2006 0.7454912
6  92442.08 4853528 mmnt_2006 0.7061661
```

- Second, we need to split the `variable` column into two: the variable itself (`"mmnt"` or `"mmxt"`) and the year (2006, 2007, 2008, 2009, or 2010). Substring extraction with `substr` (see *Chapter 2, Working with Vectors and Time Series*, for more information) comes in handy for this purpose since we can see that characters 1-4 in each element of `spainT$variable` consistently correspond to the variable, and characters 6-9 correspond to the year (to be sure, there are other ways to extract substrings in less convenient scenarios; for instance, the `strsplit` function can be used in the present context). Using the following two expressions, we first create a new (numeric) column holding the year values, and then modify the `variable` column to retain just the variable names:

```
> spainT$year = as.numeric(substr(spainT$variable, 6, 9))
> spainT$variable = substr(spainT$variable, 1, 4)
> head(spainT)
          x        y variable     value year
1 103242.08 4857128     mmnt 0.7383187 2006
2 106842.08 4857128     mmnt 0.7392765 2006
3 121242.08 4857128     mmnt 0.7458803 2006
4 124842.08 4857128     mmnt 0.7456079 2006
5 128442.08 4857128     mmnt 0.7454912 2006
6  92442.08 4853528     mmnt 0.7061661 2006
```

The final `data.frame` object is now complete.

Summary

To summarize, in this chapter you learned how to interpolate point data in space to produce continuous rasters using four different methods. The first of these, nearest-neighbor interpolation, we coded ourselves, while the other three (IDW, OK, and UK) were applied using functions in the `gstat` and `automap` packages. You also learned how to perform LOOCV to calculate RMSE and assess prediction accuracy. Finally, we saw two examples of how to automate a complex procedure to perform it repeatedly over an array of parameter sets.

In the next chapter, you are going to learn how to produce more elaborate plots involving spatial data in R with `ggplot2`.

9
Advanced Visualization of Spatial Data

Visualization of spatial data is vital both during intermediate analysis steps (to examine preliminary results and make sure we are on the right track) and as the final product (to present our results to colleagues or in a publication). In this chapter, we are going to visualize various datasets we created in the previous chapters, bringing closure to the previously presented case studies. While doing this, you will learn how to produce an elaborate and customized graphical output in R.

Most of this chapter is going to concentrate on the popular graphical package `ggplot2`. We will begin by presenting the logic behind the special syntax this package follows. Afterwards, we will review, through examples, the way spatial and nonspatial plots can be produced and customized using this package. The `ggmap` package, which automates downloading static maps from the Web and can be used to complement plots produced with `ggplot2`, will then be presented. Finally, we will experiment a little bit with **three-dimensional** (**3D**) visualization using the `lattice` package.

In this chapter, we'll cover the following topics:

- Using `ggplot2` to produce publication-quality plots
- Using `ggmap` to add static maps as the background
- Using `lattice` to produce 3D plots

 In this chapter, we are going to use objects created in the previous chapters.

Plotting with ggplot2 and ggmap

In this section, you are going to learn how to use `ggplot2` and `ggmap` to visualize spatial data. The section is structured as follows. First, we will review the `ggplot2` framework using a simple example of a time series plot since (as you will see right away) the syntax is quite different from that of other plotting methods we used until now. After that, we will practice a little bit more with producing ordinary, nonspatial plots. Next, we will see how the `ggplot2` plots can be saved for subsequent use, both within the R environment and in external files. Finally, the last two sections will deal with the most important material from this book's perspective. In these two sections, we will see how spatial data can be incorporated into `ggplot2` visualizations to produce maps, and how we can conveniently download reference background images for such maps using `ggmap`.

Before going into the details of `ggplot2`, it is important to state that to use this package, our input data needs to be contained in a `data.frame` object and it needs to be tidy (see *Chapter 7, Combining Vector and Raster Datasets*, for more information). Therefore, in practice, there are two steps when plotting with `ggplot2`:

- Bringing the data to the appropriate form
- Creating the plot

In some of the following examples, when the data is already in the right shape, we will skip the first step and move on to creating the plot right away. Otherwise, we will first have to reshape our data (using methods already familiar to us from the previous chapters) and only then utilize `ggplot2` to create the plot itself.

An overview of ggplot2

The best way to understand the underlying logic of `ggplot2` is through examples. Our first example is going to reproduce the time series plot we created in *Chapter 2, Working with Vectors and Time Series*, when demonstrating the difference between the three graphics systems in R. As you remember, we used the following `data.frame` object (although not knowing that it was a `data.frame` object at the time) that represents a time series of temperature measurements. The `time` column of this `data.frame` object contains dates, while the `tmax` column contains the daily temperature maxima:

```
> head(dat)
       time tmax
1 2006-01-01 13.3
2 2006-01-02 14.4
3 2006-01-03 15.6
```

```
4 2006-01-04 14.4
5 2006-01-05 10.6
6 2006-01-06 12.8
```

We used the following expression to produce the simplest possible line plot of this time series with ggplot2:

```
> library(ggplot2)
> ggplot(dat, aes(x = time, y = tmax)) +
+ geom_line()
```

Although the following screenshot already appeared, in *Chapter 2, Working with Vectors and Time Series*, it is provided again here since we are going to discuss the example for some time now:

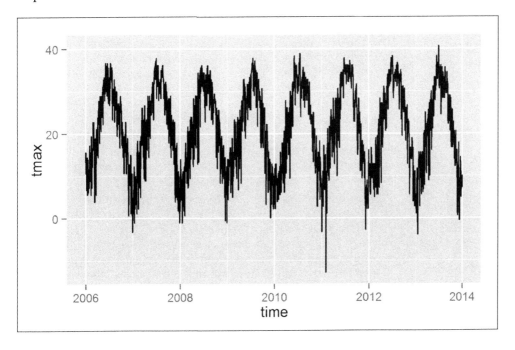

We will now briefly go over the main characteristics of the ggplot2 syntax, referring to the previous example. Later in this chapter, we will produce additional plots using other datasets from the previous chapters. This way, by the end of this chapter, we'll have reviewed the most important concepts and methods of operation for visualization of spatial data with ggplot2.

The ggplot2 package is extremely flexible. Due the abundance of functions and usage options, the variety of plots it is capable of producing is mainly limited by the users' knowledge and expertise. However, this abundance can be overwhelming for beginners. In addition, the ggplot2 syntax is hard to grasp at first, both conceptually and practically. Nevertheless, those who overcome the initial difficulties are greatly rewarded.

The purpose of this chapter is to present, through examples, some of the most important points to note when using ggplot2 to display spatial data. Obviously, we cannot cover all plot types and their optional modifications (even a standalone book cannot accomplish such a task). What we can do is provide the initial knowledge sufficient for orientation. The subsequent usage of ggplot2 will inevitably require trial and error, as well as looking for help online. In addition, the following sources of information on ggplot2 are highly recommended:

- The ggplot2 package is fortunately accompanied by a highly comprehensive collection of help pages (http://docs.ggplot2.org/), where all functions and arguments are reviewed — in most cases with code and graphical output examples.
- Winston Chang's book *R Graphics Cookbook, O'Reilly Media,* which was published in 2012, is notable for providing an extensive coverage in the form of precise recipes for visualization using ggplot2 (although there are relatively few examples involving spatial data).
- Readers interested in more information on the theoretical background of ggplot2 can refer to the absorbing book by the package author Wickham, H. *ggplot2: Elegant Graphics for Data Analysis, Springer, 2009.* Some of the code sections in that book are slightly outdated (the package has evolved since the book was published), but this does not affects the book's utility.

Each expression used to create a plot with ggplot2 is made up of several components as we shall see shortly. It starts with the ggplot function call (such as ggplot(dat, aes (x=time, y=tmax))), followed by additional layers' definitions and settings.

At the core of each plot created with ggplot2 are the *layers*, with each layer necessarily associated with a given *geometry* and the *data* used to draw the layer. A plot with no layers cannot be produced since there will be nothing to show:

```
> ggplot(dat, aes(x = time, y = tmax))
Error: No layers in plot
```

Layers are added to a plot using the + operator, and the data used to create the layer, as well as the *aesthetic mapping* (the link between the data and layers' aesthetic appearance), are specified as arguments either in the `ggplot` function (setting them as *global* arguments for this particular plot) or in the respective layer function (setting them as *local* arguments for the particular layer only).

The most straightforward way to create a layer is to use the `layer` function, where we can (rather verbosely) specify all of the layer characteristics. The preceding plot, for instance, can also be produced with the following expression, which demonstrates that `geom_line` is a layer with a predefined `"line"` geometry and `"identity"` statistical transformation (this means that there is no statistical transformation; the values are taken as is), among other default definitions that remain hidden (such as `colour="black"` for line color):

```
> ggplot(data = dat, aes(x = time, y = tmax)) +
+ layer(geom = "line", stat = "identity")
```

However, in practice, layers are most often specified using predefined layer functions rather than the `layer` function. These functions' names start with `geom` (such as `geom_line`) or `stat` (such as `stat_contour`). There is no conceptual difference between these two types of functions; the difference is just in their defaults — the latter emphasizes statistical transformations while the former does not; therefore, each type of function may be easier to use for a given purpose. However, it should be remembered that the settings of any given layer can be overridden, so in many cases the `geom` and `stat` layers are redundant in terms of the desired result. For example, exactly the same layer of contours can be produced with either `geom_contour` or `stat_contour`.

In general, each layer is composed of the following five components:

- The geometry the layer follows (this is already encompassed in the layer function name, for example, `geom_line`)
- The `data.frame` object where the data come from (for example, `dat`)
- The definition of the link between the data and layer appearance, that is, aesthetic mapping inside the `aes` function (for example, `aes(x=time, y=tmax)`) or the definition of appearance unrelated to the data, that is, aesthetic setting outside the `aes` function
- The statistical transformation that manipulates the data prior to aesthetic mapping (we will not use this here)
- A position adjustment to deal with overlapping graphical objects (we will not use this here)

A function to create a layer (such as `geom_line`) already encompasses defaults for the `geom` (geometry) and `stat` (statistical transformation) parameters; it is rarely necessary to override these in practice. For our purposes in this chapter, we will also not have to deal with position adjustments; these are most useful in nonspatial plots such as histograms and boxplots. Therefore, there are just two parameters we will usually modify in the `ggplot2` layers — the data and aesthetic mappings (and, optionally, aesthetic settings). For example, the previous plot of `tmax` as a function of `time` has only one layer and the geometry type of that layer is `"line"`. The function used to create the layer is named `geom_line`, accordingly. The `data.frame` object from where the `time` and `tmax` values come is `dat`, with `time` mapped to `x` (the *x* axis aesthetic) and `tmax` mapped to `y` (the *y* axis aesthetic).

The following table lists the specific layer functions we will use in this chapter in order to produce several common types of layers. The table also shows the set of required and optional parameters of each function. The required parameters (or aesthetics) of a given layer control its geometry and so, a layer cannot be drawn without them. For example, the `geom_line` function requires a set of `x` and `y` coordinates since no line can be drawn without these. As we shall see, in practice the required parameters are always mapped to variables in our data (in the form of an assignment within an `aes` function call). On the other hand, the optional parameters can either be mapped to variables in our data, set at constant values or left unspecified (in which case, they are set to their default constant values, such as `colour="black"` for `geom_line`, giving the line its default black color).

Function name	Required parameters	Optional parameters
geom_line	x, y	alpha, colour, linetype, size
geom_histogram	x	alpha, colour, fill, linetype, size, weight
geom_point	x, y	alpha, colour, fill, shape, size
geom_text	label, x, y	alpha, angle, colour, family, fontface, hjust, lineheight, size, vjust
geom_path	x, y	alpha, colour, linetype, size
geom_contour	x, y	alpha, colour, linetype, size, weight
geom_density2d	x, y	alpha, colour, linetype, size
geom_polygon	x, y	alpha, colour, fill, linetype, size
geom_raster	x, y	alpha, fill

There are, at the time of writing, 37 `geom` and 21 `stat` functions (visit `http://docs.ggplot2.org/` for the complete list). In this chapter, we will limit ourselves to just these nine `geom` functions, which are highly relevant with respect to spatial data.

Most of the names of the geometries are self-explanatory. For example, `geom_line` is used to draw lines, `geom_histogram` is used to draw histograms, and `geom_raster` is used to draw rasters. The `geom_contour` and `geom_density2d` functions are used to create contours based on raster values or point density, respectively, as we shall see later in this chapter. The difference between `geom_line` and `geom_path` requires clarification. While both functions are used to create a line layer, the series of (x,y) points is connected according to their order along the *x* axis in `geom_line`. On the other hand, in `geom_path`, the points are connected according to their original order in the source `data.frame` object. Therefore, the first is useful when plotting time series or mathematical functions (such as the temperature time series), while the second is useful to plot spatial line layers (such as a GPS track).

In addition to layer functions and their settings, which we briefly reviewed, three other types of components are used to control plot appearances in `ggplot2`:

- **scales**: Used to control the conversion, or mapping, between the data values and aesthetics we see on the screen (these functions' names start with `scale`, for example, `scale_x_date`)

- **faceting**: Used to produce multiple plots of different data subsets, side by side (these start with `facet`, for example, `facet_grid`)

- **themes**: Used to modify the general appearance of the plot (these start with `theme`, for example, `theme_bw`)

How are all of these components specified in practice? The first component, as we have already seen, is always a `ggplot` function call that initializes a `ggplot` object used to store all the necessary information to produce a plot. It usually takes the `ggplot(data,aes(...))` form, where `data` is the default `data.frame` object to be taken into account when plotting, and `aes(...)` is the default aesthetic mapping to be used. These are passed to all of the other layers, unless the respective layer definition specifies its own data and/or aesthetic mapping, in which case they override those within `ggplot()`. Next, the layers, scales, faceting definitions, and themes are added with each two components separated by a + symbol. In our last example, the `ggplot(dat,aes(x=time,y=tmax))` part specified that the default dataset is `dat`, and the default aesthetic mapping is to plot `time` on the *x* axis and `tmax` on the *y* axis. The `geom_line()` part then added a line layer; no arguments were specified, therefore the layer used the default dataset and the default aesthetic mapping. Scales, faceting, and theme settings were also left unspecified.

It is important to understand that in order to produce a minimal plot, we need to specify only a dataset, a single layer, and mappings for the layers' required parameters (such as x and y in geom_line). Other layer parameters (such as colour or size), scales, faceting, and themes are optional. For example, the following expression adds a colour setting and two scale definitions, but it produces exactly the same plot as shown in the preceding screenshot, since all of the components we added were already specified by default:

```
> ggplot(dat, aes(x = time, y = tmax)) +
+ geom_line(colour = "black") +
+ scale_x_date() +
+ scale_y_continuous()
```

The two scale settings used in the preceding expression (scale_x_date() and scale_y_continuous()) had no effect since a continuous variable (such as tmax) is by default plotted on a continuous scale, while a Date variable (such as time) is by default plotted on a dates scale. In addition, we have an aesthetic setting (colour="black") that had no effect either. As opposed to an aesthetic mapping (which is always encompassed in the aes function), the aesthetic setting links the layer to a constant aesthetic value, irrespective of the data in a given column. In the preceding expression, we set the line color to black in the geom_line layer, with colour="black". Again, since "black" is the default value for the line color in ggplot2, this setting does not affect the plot appearance.

The plot we produced still needs a little polishing if we would like to include it in a publication. In general, certain plot adjustments are not related to the data (for example, changing the background color), while others are indirectly related to the data (for example, changing the color scale of a raster). First of all, we would like to have proper axis titles (for example, "Time" instead of "time" for the x axis), preferably without changing the data column names themselves. In many cases a journal may require a cleaner appearance, so we may also wish to remove the gray background and grid lines. The latter two properties can be modified using the scales and themes specifications, respectively.

Through the theme functions, we can control the general appearance of the plots' nondata elements, such as plot title, axis labels style, tick marks length, background color, and so on. This can be done in two ways, which are not mutually exclusive but additive:

- The so-called complete themes can be specified to control all of the elements at once, in a predefined way. The predefined themes in ggplot2 currently include theme_grey, theme_bw, theme_linedraw, theme_light, theme_ minimal, and theme_classic. You are welcome to replace theme_bw with each of these in the following code section, to see what each theme looks like.

- Modifying individual elements can be done using the `theme` function, specifying the element names and the required arguments. For example, adding `theme(panel.grid=element_blank())` eliminates grid lines. There are currently 50 theme elements (such as `panel.grid`), which can be modified through the `theme` function (see `?theme` for the complete list). Three important things to note about themes are:

    ○ The value of each theme element can be set using the appropriate function (`element_blank`, `element_line`, `element_rect`, or `element_text`). For example, to set `axis.title`, we will use `element_text`, but to modify `panel_grid`, we will use `element_line` (unless we want to eliminate it altogether, in which case we will use `element_blank`). Consult `?theme` to see which element function is appropriate in specific cases.

    ○ Within the `element` function, we can supply a list of characteristics we want to modify for that particular element. For example, `element_line(colour="red",linetype="dotted")` for `panel.grid` will make the grid lines red and dotted. As always, all unspecified properties remain at their default values.

    ○ Some element properties inherit from others. For example, with `panel.grid=element_blank()`, there is no point modifying the `panel.grid.minor` and `panel.grid.major` (minor and major grid lines, respectively) characteristics since the properties of both are overridden by `panel.grid`.

Functions to modify the scales start with `scale`, followed by the aesthetic property and the scale type. For example, `scale_x_date` sets the *x* axis position aesthetic property to the date type. Arguments within a `scale` function control additional properties of the scale, other than scale type which is determined by the function's name. For example, the `name` parameter determines the scale name that appears along the respective axis or legend. Each aesthetic we would like to set a scale for requires an individual scale function (for example, `scale_x_date()` and `scale_y_continuous()`).

As an example, in the following code we modify several theme and scale properties of the time series plot:

```
> ggplot(dat, aes(x = time, y = tmax)) +
+ geom_line() +
+ scale_x_date(name = "Time") +
+ scale_y_continuous(
+ name =
+ expression(paste("Maximum temperature (", degree, "C)"))) +
+ theme_bw() +
+ theme(panel.grid = element_blank())
```

As you may have noticed, the *y* axis label is specified in a special way in the preceding code with `expression(paste("Maximum temperature (", degree, "C)"))`. The reason for doing this is to introduce the degree (°) symbol in the *y* axis title (see the following screenshot). The `expression` function returns an object of class `expression`, which can be used to print mathematical symbols and annotations in R. It is combined with `paste` in order to include both regular characters and mathematical symbols. In this case, the text consists of the `"Maximum temperature ("` and `"C)"` parts, while the mathematical part is `degree`, which stands for the ° symbol. The complete list of possible annotations and their syntax is available on the `?plotmath` help page.

The following screenshot shows what the new version of our plot looks like:

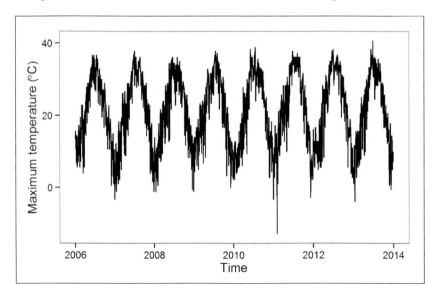

We can see that the plot is now black and white (thanks to `theme_bw`) with no grid lines (thanks to `theme(panel.grid=element_blank())`) and it has appropriate axis labels (thanks to the `scale` specifications).

> At times, a touch of interactive fine-tuning is required to introduce nonstandard elements or formatting into the graphical output from R. For instance, we may wish to put an arrow mark (such as ↓) with annotation (such as *this was an especially cold day*) on the preceding plot. Although it is possible to accomplish almost everything through the `ggplot2` syntax (including the latter example), in some situations it may be advantageous to make final adjustments by hand using a graphical editor such as Inkscape (freely available from `http://www.inkscape.org/`) or Adobe Illustrator. For this purpose, it is best to export the plot with `ggsave` to a vector graphics file (such as PDF or SVG), and then work on it in a graphical editor.

Plotting nonspatial data

Since our main focus is on plotting spatial data, in this section, we will go over just two examples of ordinary (nonspatial) plots. Most of the subsequent examples in this chapter will deal with producing spatial plots, or in other words, maps.

We will begin with a line plot, but a more elaborate one than in the previous example. As promised in *Chapter 7*, *Combining Vector and Raster Datasets*, we are going to compare, visually, the NDVI trajectory in two forests (Lahav and Kramim) according to two data sources (the Landsat and MODIS satellites). To do this, we will display the four relevant time series in a single plot. We will mark the data for each forest with a different color in order to distinguish them. In addition, we will use different `geom` functions for the data from each of the two satellites—the data from MODIS (where we have 280 data points for each forest) is best displayed with `geom_line`, while the data from Landsat (where we have only three data points for each forest) will be displayed with `geom_point`.

In terms of the `ggplot2` syntax, the data from our input table `forests_ndvi` will be divided into two parts:

- `forests_ndvi[forests_ndvi$sat == "MODIS", ]`
- `forests_ndvi[forests_ndvi$sat == "Landsat", ]`

The first subset of `forests_ndvi` will be passed as the `data` argument to `geom_line`, while the second will be passed as the `data` argument to `geom_point`. As for the aesthetic mapping (the assignment expressions within the `aes` function), x is going to be mapped to `date` and y to `ndvi`, in both layers (NDVI is plotted as the function of time). In addition, the `colour` (in `geom_line`) and `fill` (in `geom_point`) are mapped to `forest` since we want to display the time series for each forest with a different color. One instance of the aesthetic setting is used in the point layer (`shape=21`), defining the points shape as `21` (which corresponds to a filled circle; see `?points`). In addition to these two layers, six `ggplot` components are supplied to specify the various scale settings (just their names, in this case) and theme settings (no grid lines and `"top"` for the legend position). Note that the scales for `fill` and `colour` are discrete (`scale_fill_discrete` and `scale_colour_discrete`), which is appropriate for categorical variables such as the forest name.

The assigned colors are generated automatically. There is also a way to explicitly specify the color each group will take, using a manual scale. We will not go into that here; interested readers can follow the examples on `?scale_colour_manual` to see how individual colors of choice can be specified.

The entire expression to produce the plot thus takes the following form:

```
> ggplot() +
+ geom_line(
+ data = forests_ndvi[forests_ndvi$sat == "MODIS", ],
+ aes(x = date, y = ndvi, colour = forest)) +
+ geom_point(
+ data = forests_ndvi[forests_ndvi$sat == "Landsat", ],
+ aes(x = date, y = ndvi, fill = forest), shape = 21) +
+ scale_x_date("Time") +
+ scale_y_continuous("NDVI") +
+ scale_fill_discrete("Forest") +
+ scale_colour_discrete("Forest") +
+ theme_bw() +
+ theme(panel.grid = element_blank(),
+ legend.position = "top")
```

The time series plot, as shown in the following screenshot, is produced as a result:

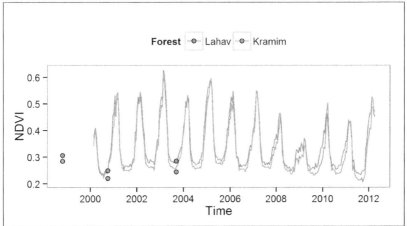

Notably, the same legend has been generated for the points `fill` aesthetic and the lines `colour` aesthetic (and so, the legend symbols are composed of both line and point geometries). The fact that the same color scale is generated by `ggplot2` for both aesthetics makes things easier.

As for the NDVI pattern the plot portrays, we can clearly see that the Kramim forest has consistently lower NDVI than Lahav and that the data from both satellites is in agreement on this. The seasonal NDVI pattern, which we have already witnessed on several occasions in previous chapters, is also apparent in the MODIS data.

In the second nonspatial example, we will plot the distribution of topographic slopes in built versus natural areas in Haifa, based on the `buildings_mask` and `natural_mask` rasters we created in *Chapter 7, Combining Vector and Raster Datasets*. This time, the data come in the form of rasters. Since `ggplot2` requires `data.frame` objects, the first thing to do is bring the data into one. We will transfer the (non-NA) values of each raster to a table with two columns: one containing the raster values and the other identifying the cover type (`"Buildings"` or `"Natural"`):

```
> build = data.frame(cover = "Buildings",
+ slope = buildings_mask[!is.na(buildings_mask)])
> nat = data.frame(cover = "Natural",
+ slope = natural_mask[!is.na(natural_mask)])
```

Then, we will bind both tables into a single one with `rbind`:

```
> slopes = rbind(nat, build)
> head(slopes)
    cover      slope
1 Natural 0.3740864
2 Natural 0.3918563
3 Natural 0.4300925
4 Natural 0.4843213
5 Natural 0.5266151
6 Natural 0.3173897
```

The data is ready to be plotted. This time, what we are interested in is visually comparing distributions. The most obvious way of doing this is to plot histograms of the two variables side by side. In `ggplot2`, a histogram layer can be created with `geom_histogram`, specifying only a single aesthetic — x. In order to produce two histograms in a single plot, we will also use faceting.

Faceting, as previously mentioned, is the generation of numerous plots of the same type for different subsets of the data, within a single graphical output. For example, in the present context we would like to create two histograms side by side: one for the `"Buildings"` cover type and another for the `"Natural"` cover type. The reason for using faceting — in addition to saving the trouble of running the same code several times — is having a similar appearance and common axes in all subplots and thereby, making the comparison easier. There are two functions to produce facets in `ggplot2`; the difference between them is in the way the subplots are geometrically arranged:

- `facet_wrap`: Used to create a continuous ribbon of panels, while (optionally) specifying the number of rows or columns (with `nrow` and `ncol`). This is most useful to create numerous subplots of the same type.
- `facet_grid`: Used to create a two-dimensional grid of panels with the rows and columns defining different levels of a given variable. This is most useful when subplots are defined by combinations of two variables.

The most important parameter of both `facet_wrap` and `facet_grid` is the formula defining the grouping factor(s) to create the facets. With `facet_wrap`, we can specify only a single factor (for example, `facet_wrap(~group)`) since the facets form a one-dimensional ribbon. With `facet_grid`, we can specify two factors: one for the rows and another one for the columns (for example, `facet_grid(group_row~group_column)`). If we wish to create facets with `facet_grid` according to a single factor, we can replace one of the variables with a dot (`.`). For example, `facet_grid(group_row~.)` will result in a vertical ribbon of facets (since there is no factor for the columns), while `facet_grid(.~group_column)` will result in a horizontal ribbon of facets (since there are no factors for the rows).

To clarify things, it is best to show an example. The following code produces two histogram facets, according to the grouping variable `cover`, using `facet_grid`. Since we have only one grouping factor, we mark the column grouping as `.` to obtain a vertical ribbon (later in this chapter, in the Spain temperature maps example, we will use `facet_grid` with two grouping factors):

```
> ggplot(slopes, aes(x = slope)) +
+ geom_histogram() +
+ facet_grid(cover ~ .) +
+ scale_x_continuous("Slope (radians)") +
+ scale_y_continuous("Count") +
+ theme_bw()
```

The resulting plot is shown on the *left* in the following screenshot. Since in this case we have a single grouping variable, the same kind of plot can also be produced with `facet_wrap`. Replacing `facet_grid(cover~.)` with `facet_wrap(~cover,ncol=1)` produces an identical plot, except for a slightly different facet labeling scheme; the latter plot is shown on the *right* in the following screenshot. Note that in both cases, the facets share a common *x* axis.

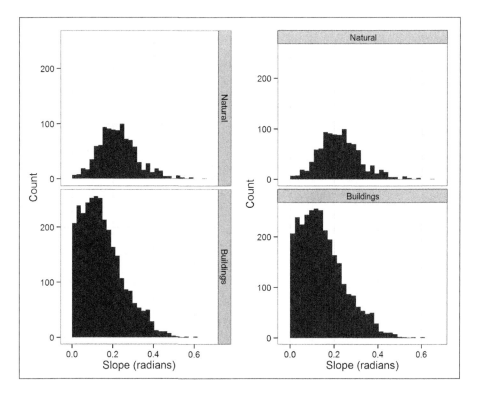

Looking at these histograms, we can see that most buildings are located on relatively flat terrain while most natural areas occupy steeper slopes, which makes sense.

> Quantitatively comparing the properties of slopes' distributions is straightforward using `tapply` and the `slopes` table. For example, `tapply(slopes$slope, slopes$cover, mean)` will show that the mean slopes for the `"Natural"` and `"Buildings"` cover types are `0.23` and `0.15`, respectively. Substituting `mean` with other functions (such as `min`, `max`, and `sd`) will yield other properties.

Saving the ggplot2 plots

In addition to the usual method of saving a graphical output in a file (see *Chapter 2*, *Working with Vectors and Time Series*), there is a specialized function called `ggsave` for saving `ggplot2` plots. For example, the first image in this chapter was incorporated into this book from a PNG file, obtained with `ggsave` as follows:

```
> ggplot(dat, aes(x = time, y = tmax)) +
+ geom_line()
> ggsave("C:\\Data\\43670S_09_01.png", width = 5.5, height = 3.5)
```

The `ggsave` function, by default, saves the last `ggplot` object that has been plotted in the graphical window. Therefore, the only mandatory parameter is the file path. The file extension provided in the path determines the file format (a PNG image in this case; see `?ggsave` for a list of possible formats). The figure dimensions are taken as those of the currently active graphical window, unless explicitly specified through the `width` and `height` parameters. For instance, in this case, the `width` is equal to `5.5` inches (inches are the default unit, cm and mm are also possible) since this is a commonly used text width in the *letter* page format.

> When saving the `ggplot2` output to PDF, it is recommended to specify `useDingbats=FALSE`. This avoids potential problems associated with plot rendering, due to the default conversion of circles to text objects, when we prefer to leave the former as geometric objects.

A `ggplot` object can also be assigned and kept in memory:

```
> tmax_line = ggplot(dat, aes(x = time, y = tmax)) +
+ geom_line()
```

It is already apparent, from the last few examples, that the `print` method applied to such an object induces drawing it in a graphical window. Assignment of a complete `ggplot2` plot, or individual layers (which we will see later), may serve at least two useful purposes:

- We can save a plot with `ggsave` providing the plot object as an argument so that we do not have to wait for the plot to be drawn in the graphical window for no good reason. This way, we also do not need to keep in mind which plot was produced last. For example, after the `tmax_line` object has been created, we can save the plot it describes as follows:

```
> ggsave(plot = tmax_line,
+ filename = "C:\\Data\\4367OS_09_01.png",
+ width = 5.5,
+ height = 3.5)
```

- We can define useful combinations of layers and/or settings, which we will repeatedly use to save us the trouble of typing the whole collection of components when producing a series of plots that have some components in common. Complete themes, such as `theme_bw`, also serve this purpose. For example, the following expression produces the same plot we saw in the first image in this chapter:

```
> tmax1 = ggplot(dat, aes(x = time, y = tmax))
> tmax2 = geom_line()
> tmax1 + tmax2
```

Plotting spatial data

So far in this chapter, we introduced the `ggplot2` package and briefly reviewed its syntax using a few simple, nonspatial examples. In the next two sections, we will move on to slightly more complicated examples, now involving spatial data. What you will see right away is that producing a map with `ggplot2` is conceptually no different from producing any other kind of plot (because spatial data, in turn, is not conceptually different from any other type of data).

A map is, in fact, simply a two-dimensional plot with points, lines, polygons and/ or rasters, with plot space corresponding to geographical space through a given CRS. Since plot space is tied to geographical space, a map has a specific aspect ratio between the x and y axes (*1:1*). In other words, we cannot stretch a map to be wider or narrower since this would distort the correct proportion between distances in the x and y directions (unlike the `tmax` time series plot we saw earlier in this chapter, for example, which can be stretched any way we like and still remain meaningful). As you may have noticed, the `plot` method, applied on spatial vector layers or rasters in previous chapters, also produces plots with a constant 1:1 aspect ratio. The difference is that in `ggplot2`, the input data comes as a `data.frame` object so the function has no way of knowing that the data is spatial. Therefore, we need to manually specify that the aspect ratio should be constant using the `coord_equal` function.

To summarize these considerations, a map produced with `ggplot2` is just like any other plot produced with this package, except for the following two characteristics:

- The plot represents geographical space through a given CRS and includes spatial data in the form of points, lines, polygons, and/or rasters

- The x and y axes scale ratio is fixed at 1:1 (using `coord_equal`)

It should be noted that `ggplot2` (along with `ggmap`, which will be introduced in the next section) is not the best choice for all spatial data visualization tasks. Maps that require, for example, substantial annotation (such as labels, scale bars, and north arrows) or special display-optimization algorithms (such as reduced overlap between street name labels and other map elements) are easier to handle in traditional GIS software. The advantage of `ggplot2`, with respect to map making, becomes decisive in fairly analogous situations to those when R itself is advantageous:

- **Automation**: When we want to automatically produce a large number of high-quality maps, for example, using facets or loops

- **Reproducibility**: When we want to make sure exactly the same map is replicated with different datasets, at different times, or among different users

- **All-in-one environment**: When we want to show certain elements computed in R on a map (such as spatial interpolation predictions) or integrate other capabilities that R has (such as downloading real-time data from the Web) without needing to transfer the data between different software

Now that the framework to use `ggplot2` with spatial data is defined in general terms, let's proceed to the practical application. So far, we witnessed that spatial vector layers and rasters are best represented in R using special classes such as `SpatialPolygonsDataFrame` or `RasterLayer`. How can we convert these data structures to `data.frame` objects to be passed to `ggplot`? Point and raster layers are readily convertible to a `data.frame` object using the `as.data.frame` function (for example, we converted the `spainT` raster to a `data.frame` object in the previous chapter). As already mentioned, however, lines and polygons are more complex than points and rasters due to the fact that each line or polygon geometry is composed of a variable number of points. The order in which the points are connected is also an integral part of the data, responsible for the correct geometry drawing. Therefore, a `data.frame` object representing a line or polygon layer must have *x* and *y* coordinate columns (as do `data.frame` objects for points and rasters), but also a grouping column (to denote which set of points forms a given line or polygon) and an ordering column (to specify the order by which the points are connected when drawing the given line or polygon). Conveniently, a function called `fortify` is already defined in `ggplot2` to convert line and polygon layers into `data.frame` objects while preserving these properties.

For example, at the end of *Chapter 5*, *Working with Points, Lines, and Polygons*, we created a `SpatialPolygonsDataFrame` object named `county` that contains the borders of US counties along with average population densities for each county in the attribute table (the `density` column). In order to bring the data in `county` to a `data.frame` form, readily available to be used by `ggplot`, we need to apply the `fortify` function. The `"regions"` parameter of `fortify` is used to specify which attribute table column corresponds to individual features. Since the `FIPS` column identifies unique counties in the attribute table, we can use it as the `region`:

```
> county_f = fortify(county, region = "FIPS")
> head(county_f)
      long       lat order  hole piece    group    id
1 1225972 -1274991     1 FALSE     1 01001.1 01001
2 1234371 -1274114     2 FALSE     1 01001.1 01001
3 1244907 -1272280     3 FALSE     1 01001.1 01001
4 1244132 -1267496     4 FALSE     1 01001.1 01001
5 1265116 -1263940     5 FALSE     1 01001.1 01001
6 1265318 -1263907     6 FALSE     1 01001.1 01001
```

This is a typical output of `fortify`. The table contains processed spatial information from the `county` layer plus the `id` column corresponding to the `region` variable (in this case, `FIPS`). The important columns, for our purposes, are as follows:

- `long` and `lat`: The spatial coordinates. Note that these are the default x and y coordinate column names, respectively, created by `fortify`, even when the layer is not in a geographical CRS.

- `group`: Individual geometries identifier.

- `id`: Individual features identifier.

Since all other attribute data columns are removed by `fortify`, we need to append the `density` column manually by joining the attribute table of `county` back to `county_f`. However, before that, we need to change the name of the `id` column to `"FIPS"`, to match the `FIPS` column in the attribute table:

```
> colnames(county_f)[which(colnames(county_f) == "id")] = "FIPS"
> county_f = join(county_f, county@data, "FIPS")
> head(county_f)
       long      lat order  hole piece   group  FIPS  NAME_1  NAME_2
1 1225972 -1274991     1 FALSE     1 01001.1 01001 Alabama Autauga
2 1234371 -1274114     2 FALSE     1 01001.1 01001 Alabama Autauga
3 1244907 -1272280     3 FALSE     1 01001.1 01001 Alabama Autauga
4 1244132 -1267496     4 FALSE     1 01001.1 01001 Alabama Autauga
5 1265116 -1263940     5 FALSE     1 01001.1 01001 Alabama Autauga
6 1265318 -1263907     6 FALSE     1 01001.1 01001 Alabama Autauga
   TYPE_2     area census2010pop  density
1 County 1562.805         54571 34.91863
2 County 1562.805         54571 34.91863
3 County 1562.805         54571 34.91863
4 County 1562.805         54571 34.91863
5 County 1562.805         54571 34.91863
6 County 1562.805         54571 34.91863
```

Using this table, we are ready to create a map showing population densities per county. However, it would be nice to add state borders as well to aid in map apprehension. To obtain states borders layer, we will download it from the GADM database (see *Chapter 5, Working with Points, Lines, and Polygons*). We will then use `fortify` on it as well:

```
> states = getData("GADM", country = "USA", level = 1)
> states = states[!(states$NAME_1 %in% c("Alaska", "Hawaii")), ]
> states = spTransform(states, CRS(proj4string(county)))
> states_f = fortify(states, region = "NAME_1")
```

```
> head(states_f)
     long     lat order  hole piece      group      id
1 1076104 -1034268     1 FALSE     1 Alabama.1 Alabama
2 1085410 -1033146     2 FALSE     1 Alabama.1 Alabama
3 1093749 -1031892     3 FALSE     1 Alabama.1 Alabama
4 1107308 -1030032     4 FALSE     1 Alabama.1 Alabama
5 1108666 -1029851     5 FALSE     1 Alabama.1 Alabama
6 1112841 -1029288     6 FALSE     1 Alabama.1 Alabama
```

To plot a spatial layer created with `fortify` (either lines, as we shall see later, or polygons), we need to map the x and y aesthetics to the `long` and `lat` columns, respectively. In addition, we need to map the `group` column to the `group` aesthetic so that each geometry will be drawn separately. For example, the California feature is composed of several geometries (the mainland plus several islands in the Pacific Ocean), and `ggplot` needs to know which points form separate polygons according to the `group` column (`"California.1"`, `"California.2"`, and so on). If we want to give certain aesthetics to each state, we can do that using the `id` column (where all California polygons share the `"California"` label).

The `group` aesthetic can also be implemented in nonspatial layers and in layers other than `geom_polygon`. It is used to identify individual geometries in order to draw them separately, when no other aesthetic (such as `colour` or `fill`) does the job. For example, in the following screenshot, we do not want each geometry (such as each island of California) to have a unique appearance, but we still want these geometries to be drawn separately rather than with a line going through all of them one by one. Try removing the `group=group` part from the following expression and you will see what a mess the result is. You can also try `group=id` to see that it messes up only those states that are composed of more than one geometry, where grouping by the `group` column is indeed essential.

Another helpful feature we will experiment with in the present example is to save a collection of the `ggplot2` components in order to integrate them in several plots and not have to type the expressions each time. We will create an object named `sp_minimal`, defining our own custom theme (based on `theme_bw`, with the axis name, labels, and tick marks removed):

```
> sp_minimal =
+ theme_bw() +
+ theme(axis.text = element_blank(),
+ axis.title = element_blank(),
+ axis.ticks = element_blank())
```

Before we plot county densities, we will start with a simpler example — drawing just the `states_f` layer — to see how spatial polygon layers are drawn in `ggplot2`:

```
> ggplot() +
+ geom_polygon(data = states_f,
+ aes(x = long, y = lat, group = group),
+ colour = "black", fill = NA) +
+ coord_equal() +
+ sp_minimal
```

A map of the states is produced as follows:

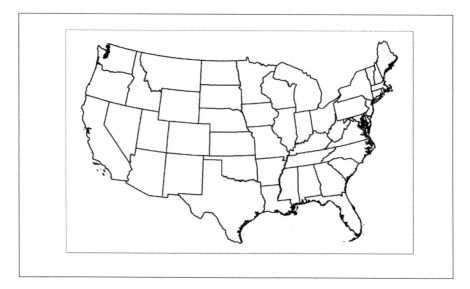

As you can see in the previous syntax, the polygons are drawn using `geom_polygon` according to the `long`, `lat`, and `group` data columns (mapped to the `x`, `y`, and `group` aesthetics, respectively), with the `colour` and `fill` polygons set to constant values (`"black"` for `colour` and `NA` for `fill`, respectively; this means empty polygons with black borders). The other two plot elements are `coord_equal` (which makes sure the 1:1 aspect ratio is maintained) and the `sp_minimal` theme we just defined.

Now, we will make things slightly more complicated by plotting both the `states_f` and `county_f` layers together. Let's first view the code and output. Afterwards, we will discuss the different components involved. Here's the code that produces a county population density map:

```
> ggplot() +
+ geom_polygon(data = county_f,
+ colour = NA,
+ aes(x = long, y = lat, group = group, fill = density)) +
+ geom_polygon(data = states_f,
+ colour = "white", size = 0.25, fill = NA,
+ aes(x = long, y = lat, group = group)) +
+ scale_fill_gradientn(
+ name = expression(paste("Density (",km^-2,")")),
+ colours = rev(rainbow(7)),
+ trans = "log10",
+ labels = as.character,
+ breaks = 10^(-1:5)) +
+ coord_equal() +
+ sp_minimal
```

The following screenshot shows how the resulting plot looks:

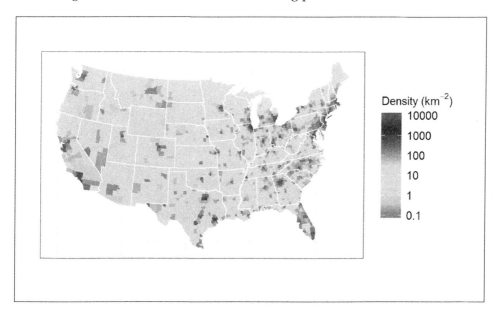

Reading the preceding code reveals, first of all, that the plot is made by combining the following five components:

- `geom_polygon` (with `county_f`)
- `geom_polygon` (with `states_f`)
- `scale_fill_gradientn`
- `coord_equal`
- `sp_minimal`

The two `geom_polygon` layers, representing `"states"` and `county` layers, are drawn differently according to our needs in this visualization. The first thing to note about these layers is their order of appearance: the `county_f` layer is added before `states_f`. This is not a coincidence; the layers are drawn on the screen in the same order in which they are provided in the code. Since state and county borders obviously overlap, and we wish to draw the states borders on top of the counties borders (otherwise the states borders will not be visible), it is important to specify the layers in the right order.

The `states_f` layer arguments are identical to those in the previous example; except that, we made the polygon borders white (with `colour="white"`) and thin (with `size=0.25`). As for the `county_f` layer, the color of the borders (rather than `fill`) was set to `NA`, resulting in borderless polygons, and `fill` was mapped to `density`. The latter is indeed the defining feature of the map we made: mapping the `county_f` polygons `fill` aesthetic to `density` is what gives different population densities different colors, and that was the whole purpose of making this plot.

We mapped `fill` to `density`, but which color gets assigned to which density level? As already mentioned, the `scale` function determines the way values in the data are matched with the aesthetic appearance. So unless we are happy with the default scale (which is frequently not the case), we have to set the scale characteristics ourselves. For example, we already used `scale_colour_discrete` in the forests NDVI time series example (applicable for discrete variables). In the present example, the `scale_fill_gradientn` function, as the name suggests, was used to set the `fill` scale type to *gradientn*. The latter is just one out of several possible `fill` scale types (applicable to the `colour` aesthetic as well; see http://docs.ggplot2.org/ for a complete list). For continuous variables, ggplot2 offers three types of color scales, which can be specified using the following functions:

- `scale_fill_gradient`: A two-color gradient, with the gradient end colors specified with `high` and `low` (see the Haifa buildings density example later in this chapter)

- `scale_fill_gradient2`: A three-color gradient, with the `low`, `med`, and `high` colors specified (see the London buildings distance to river example later in this chapter)

- `scale_fill_gradientn`: A custom n-color gradient, specified with a `colours` vector

There are several ways to create a vector of colors in R to be supplied to the `colours` parameter of `scale_colour_gradientn` as well as to other graphical functions. The simplest way, which we used in the present example, is to employ one of the predefined color palette functions that can take a numeric value as an argument and produce a series of colors (returned as RGB codes) at equal intervals. These functions can be used for many purposes:

- `rainbow`
- `heat.colors`
- `terrain.colors`
- `topo.colors`
- `cm.colors`

In the examples in this chapter, we employ `rainbow` and `terrain.colors`. You are welcomed to experiment with the other three palettes to see what they look like. The color codes these functions return are rarely useful in their own right. Instead, they are passed as color palettes to graphical functions such as `scale_colour_gradientn`.

```
> rainbow(3)
[1] "#FF0000FF" "#00FF00FF" "#0000FFFF"
```

In cases when you have a different palette in mind which is not covered by these functions, you can use the `RColorBrewer` package (which provides many more palettes) or the `colorRampPalette` function available in base R (which can be used to create custom-made color palettes; see the last example in this chapter).

A short explanation of the arguments of the `scale_fill_gradientn` function we used is in order:

- `name=expression(paste("Density (",km^-2"",")"))`: The `name` argument specifies the scale name and the way it will appear on the plot legend. We once again used the `expression` function, this time to add `-2` in superscript (see the preceding screenshot).

- `colours=rainbow(7)`: Specifies the vector of colors to create a color palette with. Here, specifying seven colors gives a good result, with the whole variability the `rainbow` palette provides represented. It may require trial and error to find out how many colors are sufficient in each case.

- `trans="log10"`: The `trans` parameter can be passed to any continuous scale function in `ggplot2`. It is used to specify a mathematical transformation for the data. In this particular example, we use a logarithmic scale (`"log10"`) to highlight the differences in the population density between different counties, which is necessary since the distribution of county densities is highly nonhomogeneous, with many low-density counties and few high-density counties. You can try deleting the `trans`, `labels`, and `breaks` arguments, and running the previous code once more to see why the default linear scale is inappropriate in this case. There are many useful built-in types of transformations, as well as methods to define custom transformations but this is beyond the scope of this book.

- `labels=as.character` and `breaks=10^(-1:5)`: The `breaks` argument specifies the breakpoints where tick marks and labels are generated, while the `labels` argument specifies the labels themselves or (as in this case) a function to format the labels with. In this case, by default, R prints the `10^(-1:5)` labels vector in mathematical notation (`1e-01`, `1e+00`, `1e+01`, and so on). This is evaded by converting the numeric values to characters (using `as.character`) to receive more comprehensive labels (`0.1`, `1`, `10`, and so on).

The last two components in the code section that produces the preceding plot—`coord_equal` and `sp_minimal`—were already used in the previous plot, so we will not repeat their meaning here.

Finally, referring to the plot itself, we can see the concentration of densely populated counties in the eastern half of the USA and along the coast of the Pacific Ocean. Further inland in the Western USA, population density is generally low.

Moving on to the second type of spatial data structure, a raster, we are going to experiment with different variations of the Haifa DEM map in the following few examples. As the data source, we will take the `dem` and `hill` rasters (see *Chapter 6, Modifying Rasters and Analyzing Raster Time Series*). Data from these two rasters will be transferred into a single `data.frame` object with four columns: cell coordinates (x and y), elevation value (`elev`), and hillshade value (`hill`). Note that in this case, we use the `data.frame` function to do this, supplying the coordinates and the vector of values from each raster separately (relying on the fact that the two rasters are geometrically identical, since `hill` was derived from `dem`). An equally good approach would have been to `stack` the two rasters and then convert the result to a `data.frame` object with `as.data.frame(...,xy=TRUE)`:

```
> dem_hill = data.frame(coordinates(dem),
+ elev = dem[],
+ hill = hill[])
> dem_hill = dem_hill[complete.cases(dem_hill), ]
> head(dem_hill)
             x        y elev      hill
2421 698971.3 3648863   19 0.3533017
2422 699061.3 3648863   20 0.3408402
2423 699151.3 3648863   19 0.3402018
2424 699241.3 3648863   19 0.3451085
2425 699331.3 3648863   20 0.3439193
2426 699421.3 3648863   21 0.3368811
```

Now that we have the dem_hill table, we can plot the data using a geom_raster layer. The geom_raster function requires the x, y, and fill aesthetics to draw a raster, as the following code and images demonstrate. In addition, since we are going to make several versions of the Haifa DEM plot, it would be best to save this basic plot as a ggplot object (hereby named haifa_relief) so that we can later update it by incorporating additional layers:

```
> haifa_relief = ggplot(dem_hill, aes(x = x, y = y)) +
+ geom_raster(aes(fill = elev)) +
+ scale_fill_gradientn("Elevation (m)",
+ colours = terrain.colors(10)) +
+ coord_equal() +
+ theme_bw() +
+ theme(axis.title = element_blank(),
+ axis.text.y = element_text(angle = 90, hjust = 0.5))
> haifa_relief
```

The syntax being used is analogous to the previous example, except that we use geom_raster instead of geom_polygon; x and y are mapped to spatial coordinates, while fill is mapped to raster values. Note that geom_raster takes aes(fill=elev) as an argument, while the missing parts (data, x, and y) are passed, by default, from the ggplot set of arguments. As we shall see right away, this mode of operation is very convenient when we would like to add another layer (in this case, the hillshade) with the same arguments so that we do not have to type them once again. The theme components this time specify that the *y* axis labels should be rotated by 90° (which is often used in maps). The resulting plot is shown on the *left* panel in the following screenshot. Note that the color scale used (terrain.colors) is particularly useful to display the topography.

Now that we have our basic relief image, we can experiment with various additional components that we may wish to show on top of it. For instance, the hillshade calculation gave us a layer of theoretical shading degree for the given topography and sun position (see *Chapter 6, Modifying Rasters and Analyzing Raster Time Series*). We can add the shading values as an all-black raster with various levels of transparency (making the shaded areas less transparent and thus darker). This will create an illusion of a three-dimensional image, which is also known as a *shaded relief* in cartography. To create shading, we need to add another raster layer with black pixels whose transparency aesthetic is mapped to the `hill` values. Transparency, in `ggplot2` as well as in other graphical functions in R, is determined by a parameter named `alpha`, ranging from `0` to `1`, with `0` being completely transparent and `1` being completely opaque. Limiting the maximum of the alpha scale to `0.5`, using the `range` parameter makes sure we do not get completely black pixels in heavily shaded areas:

```
> haifa_relief_shade = haifa_relief +
+ geom_raster(aes(alpha = hill), fill = "black") +
+ scale_alpha_continuous("Hillshade", range = c(0.5, 0))
> haifa_relief_shade
```

The resulting plot is shown on the *right* panel in the following screenshot. Viewing the two images side by side demonstrates the effect that shading has.

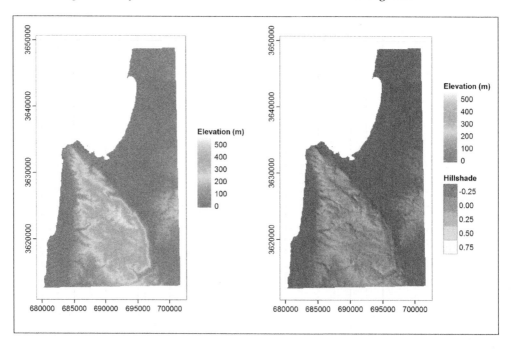

Talking about topography, another feature we may wish to add to this plot is contour lines. We already calculated contour lines from rasters both indirectly (displaying them using `levelplot`, in *Chapter 4, Working with Rasters*, for instance) and directly (creating a contour lines layer with `rasterToContour`, in *Chapter 7, Combining Vector and Raster Datasets*). Here, we are looking at yet another indirect way to calculate contour lines based on a raster using `ggplot2`. To add a contour lines layer, we can use the `geom_contour` function, mapping its `z` aesthetic to elevation so that contour lines are calculated according to it:

```
> haifa_relief_shade +
+ geom_contour(aes(z = elev), colour = "black", alpha = 0.3)
```

The following screenshot shows the graphical output that is produced, showing semi-transparent contour lines on top of the shaded relief of Haifa:

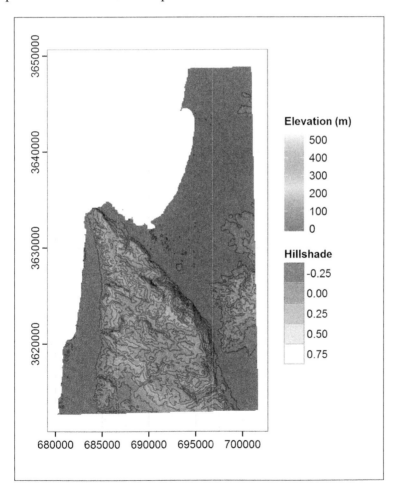

In the previous example, we generated a contour plot based on the values of an existing raster (the Haifa DEM in this case). Another common type of plot showing contours is one where contours denote the average density of events in a point pattern. Creating density contours is a common way to reduce the amount of information and make point pattern visualization more comprehensible. For example, when we have so many points that they overlap each other, it may be difficult to discern denser and sparser locations. Drawing contours is one possible solution to this problem.

A commonly used procedure to create density contours out of a point pattern is two-dimensional kernel density estimation, available through the base R function named `kde2d`. The `geom_density2d` function is a `ggplot2` adaptation of the latter function, creating contours out of a density surface calculated with `kde2d`.

As an example of `geom_density2d`, we will draw contours showing the average density of buildings in Haifa.

It should be noted that, in practice, density estimation is only meaningful for mapped point patterns, that is, point patterns where all events in the studied area have been detected. When detection is incomplete, density estimates will obviously be biased to an unknown degree in each location. In our case, for example, if the OpenStreetMap layer of Haifa buildings is incomplete, then a density estimate based on it will not be very useful as it will encompass underestimation to an unknown and variable degree.

Since density estimation requires a point pattern, we need to convert the buildings layer to a point layer by finding building centroids:

```
> haifa_buildings_ctr = gCentroid(haifa_buildings, byid = TRUE)
> haifa_buildings_ctr = as.data.frame(haifa_buildings_ctr)
> head(haifa_buildings_ctr)
         x        y
1 684013.4 3629679
2 688023.0 3629752
3 687645.0 3627410
4 685913.9 3631217
5 683144.4 3633649
6 683515.3 3628980
```

Taking the `haifa_relief_shade` plot, we will now add both the buildings point pattern (using `geom_point`) and the density contours based on that pattern (using `geom_density2d`). Using the `limits` parameter of `scale_x_continuous` and `scale_y_continuous`, we will also limit our scope to a window centered at `haifa_buildings_ctr`. In addition, the `colour` aesthetic of the contours is mapped to `..level..`, which corresponds to the contour breaks. The `level` variable is surrounded by `..`, which is a special way to signal to `ggplot2` that we are referring to a variable generated by the layer itself, rather than a variable present in `data.frame`:

```
> haifa_relief_shade +
+ geom_contour(aes(z = elev), colour = "black", alpha = 0.3) +
+ geom_point(data = haifa_buildings_ctr, size = 0.5) +
+ geom_density2d(data = haifa_buildings_ctr,
+ aes(colour = ..level..)) +
+ scale_colour_gradient("Density", low = "blue", high = "red") +
+ scale_x_continuous(
+ limits = c(min(haifa_buildings_ctr$x)-2000,
+ max(haifa_buildings_ctr$x)+2000)) +
+ scale_y_continuous(
+ limits = c(min(haifa_buildings_ctr$y)-2000,
+ max(haifa_buildings_ctr$y)+2000))
```

The following screenshot shows the graphical output:

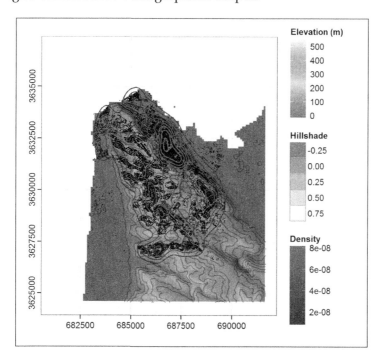

In the preceding screenshot, we see three different legends as there are three different scales: elevation, hillshade, and buildings density. According to this map (again, assuming that all buildings have been mapped), we can see that the highest density of individual buildings per unit area is found on the eastern slopes of Mount Carmel.

Our final example in this section will be to plot the time series of interpolated standardized temperature maps, which we created in the previous chapter. We already took the trouble of reshaping the data into a tidy table; therefore, we do not need to take any preliminary processing steps. Using the spainT table and the following code section, we recreate a plot similar to the rasterVis version from the previous chapter with ggplot2:

```
> ggplot(spainT, aes(x = x, y = y, fill = value)) +
+ geom_raster() +
+ scale_fill_gradient2(
+ expression(paste("Value (", degree, "C)")),
+ low = "blue", high = "red", limits = c(-4,4)) +
+ geom_contour(
+ aes(z = value),
+ colour = "black", size = 0.1, breaks = c(-4:-1,1:4)) +
+ coord_equal() +
+ facet_grid(variable ~ year) +
+ sp_minimal
```

The following screenshot shows the graphical output:

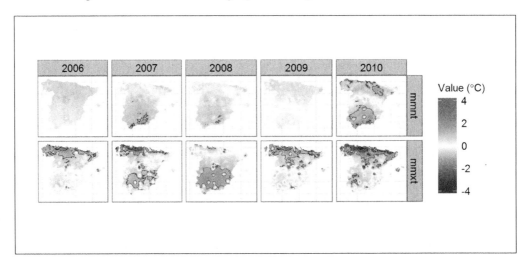

Note that we have once again utilized our `sp_minimal` custom-made theme to eliminate the axis annotation. The `geom_contour` function has been used to generate contour lines, similar to the Haifa DEM elevation contours, only that now we specified the exact vector of breaks, specifying where contour lines will be generated. Using `facet_grid(variable~year)`, we arranged the facets in rows according to `variable` and in columns according to `year`.

Adding static maps from the Web

Nowadays, cartographers and spatial analysts are lucky to have a variety of online resources for map creation. We already used freely available satellite imagery, DEMs, and administrative border datasets, for example. However, to recover and process such datasets is not always a quick and straightforward task. We may need to figure out the spatial location in question, search for available resources, import them into R, and so on. On the other hand, several applications, such as Google Maps and OpenStreetMap, provide readily available maps of the entire earth with a variety of features that can be unreasonable to collect ourselves each time we want to create a background for a quick visualization (satellite and aerial imagery, roads, borders, town names, and so on).

The `ggmap` package is an extension to `ggplot2`, providing a simple interface to download static maps from such online resources and easily incorporate them as the background when creating maps within the `ggplot2` framework. We already used the `ggmap` package for geocoding (see *Chapter 5, Working with Points, Lines, and Polygons*), and mentioned the introductory paper on this package by Kahle and Wickham (2013).

By static maps, we refer to maps that cannot be manipulated by scrolling, zooming in and zooming out, and so on, as opposed to dynamic maps that respond to such user feedback. The whole `ggplot2` framework, in that sense, may be referred to as static plotting. It should be noted that dynamic plots and maps (and even entire web applications; see the `shiny` package) can also be produced in R. As for dynamic maps, for instance, we have already seen a short example of using the Google Earth software as a platform for dynamic spatial data display from R using the `plotKML` package (see *Chapter 4, Working with Rasters*). Another example is the `plotGoogleMaps` package, which can be used to display spatial data from R on top of interactive Google Maps in a web browser.

The static maps incorporation with ggmap is quite simple in practice. Using the get_map function of the ggmap package, we first need to download the required background image. Then, we can use that image as a background layer with the ggmap function of the same package. Any additional layers and components can be added to the plot initiated with ggmap the same way as to a plot initiated with ggplot.

Our first example featuring ggmap will be to display the City of London buildings and their distances to the River Thames, as promised in *Chapter 5, Working with Points, Lines, and Polygons*. Since layers obtained with ggmap are always defined in a geographical CRS, we must first reproject the two relevant layers that we will plot to such a CRS as well. The layers we are going to plot, in this case, are as follows:

- buildings: City of London buildings
- city: City of London boundary polygon

The following expressions reproject these layers and save them as new objects buildings_geo and city_geo, respectively:

```
> buildings_geo = spTransform(buildings,
+ CRS("+proj=longlat +datum=WGS84"))
> city_geo = spTransform(city,
+ CRS("+proj=longlat +datum=WGS84"))
```

To specify the location for which we would like to download a map with get_map, we can use the coordinates of the buildings layer centroid, obtained in the following manner:

```
> buildings_ctr = coordinates(gCentroid(buildings_geo))
> buildings_ctr
           x         y
1 -0.09222641 51.51499
```

Next, we will fortify the buildings_geo layer, to make the data available in the form of a data.frame object. The region in this case is the osm_id attribute table column, which holds unique building identifiers:

```
> buildings_f = fortify(buildings_geo, region = "osm_id")
> head(buildings_f)
        long      lat order  hole piece       group        id
1 -0.09962729 51.51428     1 FALSE     1 100684524.1 100684524
2 -0.09952849 51.51429     2 FALSE     1 100684524.1 100684524
3 -0.09942449 51.51429     3 FALSE     1 100684524.1 100684524
4 -0.09941299 51.51424     4 FALSE     1 100684524.1 100684524
5 -0.09951839 51.51423     5 FALSE     1 100684524.1 100684524
6 -0.09961579 51.51422     6 FALSE     1 100684524.1 100684524
```

Similar to what we saw in the `county` example, `fortify` removes the attribute table; therefore, we need to attach it back manually:

```
> colnames(buildings_f)[which(colnames(buildings_f) == "id")] =
+ "osm_id"
> buildings_f = join(buildings_f, buildings@data, "osm_id")
> head(buildings_f)
          long      lat order  hole piece          group      osm_id
1 -0.09962729 51.51428     1 FALSE     1 100684524.1 100684524
2 -0.09952849 51.51429     2 FALSE     1 100684524.1 100684524
3 -0.09942449 51.51429     3 FALSE     1 100684524.1 100684524
4 -0.09941299 51.51424     4 FALSE     1 100684524.1 100684524
5 -0.09951839 51.51423     5 FALSE     1 100684524.1 100684524
6 -0.09961579 51.51422     6 FALSE     1 100684524.1 100684524
         name type dist_river
1 Temple Bar <NA>   378.7606
2 Temple Bar <NA>   378.7606
3 Temple Bar <NA>   378.7606
4 Temple Bar <NA>   378.7606
5 Temple Bar <NA>   378.7606
6 Temple Bar <NA>   378.7606
```

As the output shows, each building is now, once again, associated with a `dist_river` value.

Finally, we will `fortify` the `city_geo` polygon as well. Since there is no attribute data of interest along with it, we do not have to join anything to the resulting `data.frame` object in this case:

```
> city_f = fortify(city_geo, region = "CTYUA13NM")
> head(city_f)
          long      lat order  hole piece                group
1 -0.09671385 51.52319     1 FALSE     1 City of London.1
2 -0.09669776 51.52316     2 FALSE     1 City of London.1
3 -0.09668468 51.52317     3 FALSE     1 City of London.1
4 -0.09662369 51.52318     4 FALSE     1 City of London.1
5 -0.09646984 51.52282     5 FALSE     1 City of London.1
6 -0.09601742 51.52295     6 FALSE     1 City of London.1
               id
1 City of London
2 City of London
3 City of London
4 City of London
5 City of London
6 City of London
```

Examining the `group` column in this particular case will reveal that it has the same value (`"City of London.1"`) in all rows since the `city` layer is composed of a single polygon.

The layers are ready. What is left to be done is download the background and produce the map. To download the background, we will employ the `get_map` function. In order to efficiently work with this function, we need to provide arguments for just these three parameters:

- `location`: The center of the map to be downloaded, which can be a longitude/latitude pair.

- `maptype`: The type of map to be downloaded. This is source-specific, but for Google Maps (the default data source), `"terrain"`, `"satellite"`, `"roadmap"`, and `"hybrid"` are applicable. See the following screenshot for an example of a `"hybrid"` map; for a `"satellite"` example, see the screenshot after the following screenshot.

> The default data source, and the one we use here, is Google Maps. Note that the Google Static Maps API is used by `get_map` to download the images in such cases, and that by using this function, you are agreeing to the Google Maps API Terms of Service (https://developers.google. com/maps/terms). Other data sources can be selected by modifying the source parameter of `get_map`, with possible sources being Google Maps (`"google"`), OpenStreetMap (`"osm"`), Stamen Maps (`"stamen"`), or CloudMade maps (`"cloudmade"`). See `?get_map` for details.

- `zoom`: The zoom level; an integer between 3 and 21 (the default value is 10). The best zoom value for a given map is determined by trying higher or lower magnifications and examining the result.

In our case, to get a static map of the City of London composed of a photographic map with roads and other features marked on top (a `"hybrid"` map), we can use the following expression:

```
> city_map = get_map(location = buildings_ctr,
+ maptype = "hybrid",
+ zoom = 14)
```

Now, plotting this map on its own (to inspect the `zoom` argument's effect, for instance) can be done by simply typing `ggmap(city_map)`, that returns a `ggplot` object by default, plotted in the graphical window—as we have already seen earlier. However, to add our supplementary layers based on the `buildings_f` and `city_f` objects, we need to incorporate them using two `geom_polygon` function calls. A few minor settings are also introduced in this particular example, which are as follows:

- To use muted colors, for a prettier color scale, the `muted` function of the `scales` package is being used

- Forcing the legend heading `"Distance to river (m)"` to be split over two lines is achieved using the new line symbol `\n`

- The `labs` function is used to easily modify axis titles, instead of modifying the scale itself with the `scale` functions

The code to produce the City of London buildings map appears as follows:

```
> library(scales)
> ggmap(city_map) +
+ geom_polygon(data = buildings_f,
+ aes(x = long, y = lat, group = group,
+ fill = dist_river),
+ size = 0.1, colour = "black") +
+ geom_polygon(data = city_f,
+ aes(x = long, y = lat, group = group),
+ colour = "yellow", fill = NA) +
+ scale_fill_gradient2("Distance\nto river (m)",
+ low = muted("blue"), high = muted("red"),
+ midpoint = 500) +
+ labs(x = "Longitude", y = "Latitude")
```

The resulting map looks like the following screenshot:

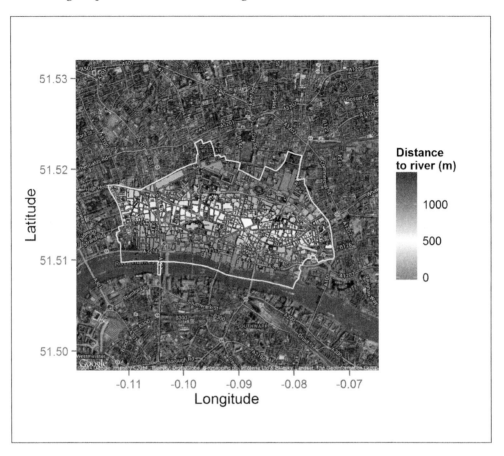

The map shows an up-to-date `"hybrid"` map of London downloaded from Google Maps, with the City of London boundary (in yellow) and buildings (in blue to red colors, according to their distance to the River Thames) on top of it.

To practice using `ggmap` some more, we will create another map with the following components encompassing all three vector layer types—points, lines, and polygons—along with a static map downloaded from the Web:

- A `"satellite"` static map background
- `towns`: A point layer of two towns' locations (see *Chapter 7, Combining Vector and Raster Datasets*)

- `track`: A line layer of a GPS track (see *Chapter 5, Working with Points, Lines, and Polygons*)

- `forests`: A polygonal layer of two planted forests (see *Chapter 7, Combining Vector and Raster Datasets*)

As in the previous example, we first need to bring all of these layers to a geographic CRS:

```
> towns_geo = spTransform(towns,
+ CRS("+proj=longlat +datum=WGS84"))
> track_geo = spTransform(track,
+ CRS("+proj=longlat +datum=WGS84"))
> forests_geo = spTransform(forests,
+ CRS("+proj=longlat +datum=WGS84"))
```

Next, we need to use `fortify` on the line and polygonal layers (`track_geo` and `forests_geo`) in order to bring them to a `data.frame` form. Point layers, as previously mentioned, have a much simpler structure than lines and polygons, so no `fortify` method exists for them. Instead, we can always manually construct a `data.frame` object to represent a point layer. In the present case, for example, `towns_geo` is a `SpatialPoints` object and `towns_names` is a character vector. Using the `coordinates` functions and `data.frame`, we can combine them into a `data.frame` object:

```
> towns_f = data.frame(coordinates(towns_geo), name = towns_names)
> towns_f
        lon      lat          name
1 34.87131 31.37936 Lahav Kibbutz
2 34.81695 31.37383       Lehavim
> track_f = fortify(track_geo)
> head(track_f)
      long      lat order piece group id
1 34.85472 31.36520     1     1   0.1  0
2 34.85464 31.36540     2     1   0.1  0
3 34.85458 31.36559     3     1   0.1  0
4 34.85454 31.36519     4     1   0.1  0
5 34.85443 31.36639     5     1   0.1  0
6 34.85445 31.36733     6     1   0.1  0
> forests_f = fortify(forests_geo, region = "name")
> head(forests_f)
      long      lat order  hole piece    group      id
1 34.87591 31.33830     1 FALSE     1 Kramim.1 Kramim
2 34.87559 31.33831     2 FALSE     1 Kramim.1 Kramim
3 34.87560 31.33858     3 FALSE     1 Kramim.1 Kramim
```

```
4 34.87528 31.33858     4 FALSE      1 Kramim.1 Kramim
5 34.87529 31.33885     5 FALSE      1 Kramim.1 Kramim
6 34.87529 31.33912     6 FALSE      1 Kramim.1 Kramim
```

The three `data.frame` objects (`towns_f`, `track_f`, and `forests_f`) are now in memory. The missing component is just the background static map, which can be downloaded with `get_map` as follows:

```
> forests_ctr = coordinates(gCentroid(forests_geo))
> forests_map = get_map(location = forests_ctr,
+ maptype = "satellite",
+ zoom = 12)
```

The following code is used to combine all of these components into a single plot. Note that `track_f` is introduced through a `geom_path` layer (which is the appropriate geometry for spatial lines) and `forests_f` is introduced using `geom_polygon`. The point layer `towns_f` is added as a `geom_text` layer, rather than `geom_point`, in order to display the towns' locations as name labels instead of points. The `label` aesthetic of `geom_text` controls the text that each point is associated with, which in our case is the `name` column that holds town names.

```
> ggmap(forests_map) +
+ geom_polygon(data = forests_f,
+ aes(x = long, y = lat, group = group, colour = id),
+ fill = NA) +
+ geom_path(data = track_f,
+ aes(x = long, y = lat),
+ colour = "yellow") +
+ geom_text(data = towns_f,
+ aes(x = lon, y = lat, label = name),
+ colour = "white", size = 2.5, fontface = "bold") +
+ scale_colour_discrete("Forest") +
+ labs(x = "Longitude", y = "Latitude")
```

The resulting map is shown in the following screenshot:

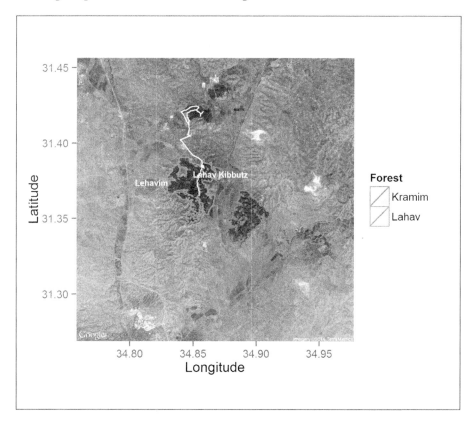

This map shows the towns' locations (as white text labels), the GPS track (as a yellow line), and the forest borders (as polygons, with border colors according to the forest identity).

Making 3D plots with lattice

Three-dimensional visualization, although undesirable for certain purposes (where precise interpretation is important, such as in the scientific literature), can nevertheless be particularly impressive and aesthetically appealing. In this section, we are going to use `lattice` to create three-dimensional plots of spatial and nonspatial data, which is not possible to do with `ggplot2` since it only allows two-dimensional plotting. The `lattice` graphics framework and syntax are no less complex than those of `ggplot2`, and a single section is far too short to comprehensibly review the subject. Our purpose here is much more modest: to show some of the things that can be achieved and inspire interested readers to investigate further. For more information on `lattice`, readers are referred to the authoritative overview in the book by package author Deepayan Sarkar, *Lattice: Multivariate Data Visualization with R*, *Springer*, which was published in 2008.

As already mentioned in *Chapter 2*, *Working with Vectors and Time Series*, `lattice` is an R package defining a graphics system in R (in addition to base R and `ggplot2`). We have already been using `lattice` indirectly, in fact, since the `levelplot` function from the `rasterVis` package is an adaptation of a function with the same name from `lattice`.

> It is worth noting that `lattice` is not the only package that can be used for three-dimensional visualization in R. The most notable alternatives are the base R function called `persp`, which can be used to create plots analogous to the ones we are going to create with `lattice`, and the `rgl` package, which allows you to create dynamic, rotatable 3D plots.

There are, generally speaking, two main types of three-dimensional plots. We can plot points (also known as point clouds or 3D scatterplots) or grids/surfaces. In both cases, the input data comes in the form of (x,y,z) coordinate sets, but to create a grid, these points need to be equally spaced along the *x* and *y* axes, while in point clouds there is no such restriction. For example, in statistics, we may have a dataset with two independent variables and one dependent one, and we may wish to plot the observed data points (as points in 3D space), the predicted surface generated by a regression model (as a 3D grid), or both. In `lattice`, the `cloud` function can be used to create a three-dimensional scatterplot, while the `wireframe` function can be used to plot three-dimensional grids. In the following two examples, we will concentrate on `wireframe`, but keep in mind that points can be plotted essentially the same way with `cloud`.

Our first example will involve the already familiar Haifa DEM, and this time we are going to create a three-dimensional representation of this raster. The best way to pass data on to `lattice` is through a `data.frame` object (although, unlike with `ggplot2`, other options are also possible). To create a three-dimensional plot, the `data.frame` needs to contain three columns, holding the *x*, *y*, and *z* coordinates. The following code section creates a `data.frame`, named `dem_df`, after the DEM is five-fold aggregated (to make the grid sparser and visually simpler):

```
> dem_df = as.data.frame(aggregate(dem, 5), xy = TRUE)
> dem_df = dem_df[complete.cases(dem_df), ]
> colnames(dem_df)[3] = "z"
> head(dem_df)
            x         y          z
123 693841.3 3648773   4.000000
124 694291.3 3648773   5.647059
125 694741.3 3648773   7.250000
126 695191.3 3648773   6.500000
127 695641.3 3648773   9.550000
128 696091.3 3648773  11.300000
```

Before applying `wireframe`, we need to figure out the right aspect ratio for our 3D plot. The default aspect ratio for the dimensions of the 3D box encompassing the plot is *1:1:1*, referring to the *x*, *y*, and *z* axis lengths, so that the box forms a cube. This ratio is specified with the `aspect` parameter of `wireframe`, which accepts a two-element vector specifying the y/x and z/x ratios (with the default being `c(1,1)`). In the case of `dem_df`, the data represents geographical distances on all three axes. Unless our DEM, by any chance, represents a cubical geographic extent, these aspect ratios are inappropriate. For example, similar to 2D plots produced with `ggplot2`, we are usually interested in equal cell dimensions on the *x* and *y* axes. To accomplish this, we need the y/x ratio to correspond to the ratio of the coordinates' range of *y* and *x*. For example, if our DEM represents a rectangle of 100 meters on the *x* axis and 200 meters on the *y* axis, to correctly represent it with `wireframe`, we would have to specify a y/x aspect ratio of 2 (200/100). In our case, the ranges of values on each axis are as follows:

```
> x_range = diff(range(dem_df$x, na.rm = TRUE))
> x_range
[1] 21600
> y_range = diff(range(dem_df$y, na.rm = TRUE))
> y_range
[1] 36000
> z_range = diff(range(dem_df$z, na.rm = TRUE))
> z_range
[1] 527.0933
```

The correct y/x ratio is thus equal to y_range/x_range or 1.666667. As for the z/x ratio, since the *z* axis range of 527.0933 (the difference, in meters, between the lowest and highest points of the DEM) is much smaller than either the *x* or *y* axes ranges, drawing the 3D plot with realistic proportions between elevation and x-y distances (z_range/x_range or 0.02440247) would result in a very flat image, with the relief hardly protruding. Unless we make an image of a small area with very steep topography, it is very common to use an exaggerated z to x-y distance ratio in 3D topographic plots, thus making the topography more tangible. Choosing a z/x aspect ratio is really a matter of taste. For this particular plot, a seven-fold exaggeration was chosen, but lower or higher values are also appropriate. It is obviously important to declare the fact that exaggeration has been used when such an image is used in a publication.

Now that we have decided which aspect ratios we are going to use, we are ready to apply wireframe on dem_df. Let's first see the code and the image produced and then review its components:

```
> library(lattice)
> wireframe(z ~ x * y,
+ data = dem_df,
+ drape = TRUE,
+ colorkey = TRUE,
+ col.regions = terrain.colors(100),
+ screen = list(z = 165, x = -60, y = 0),
+ aspect = c(y_range/x_range, 7*(z_range/x_range)),
+ zoom = 1.1)
```

The following screenshot shows the graphical output:

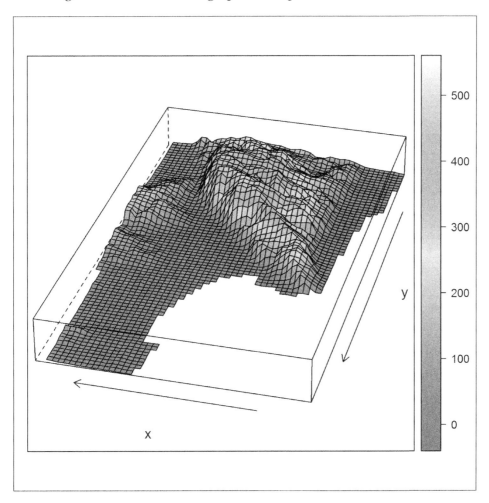

The first thing to note is that the `lattice` syntax is analogous to the base R plotting, in the sense that we have distinct plotting functions for each type of plot (such as `plot` or `wireframe`), and each function has a set of parameters covering all modifiable elements of the respective plot type. This is very different from the `ggplot2` approach, where a plot is constructed layer by layer using numerous function calls rather than just one.

As for the set of parameters we used in this case (which is only a small fraction of all parameters that wireframe has), here is a short explanation for each one:

- x: In case the data is a data.frame object, this argument should be a formula specifying the columns to use, as a formula object with the dependent variable to the left of the ~ operator and the independent variables to the right, separated by * (for example, z~x*y means we plot z as a function of x and y).

- data: The data.frame where the values come from.

- drape: Determines whether the surface will be covered with color (TRUE) or remain a simple skeleton of intersecting lines (FALSE).

- colorkey: Determines whether a legend is drawn (TRUE) or not (FALSE) alongside the plot.

- col.regions: The vector of colors used to draw the surface, analogous to the colours parameter in ggplot2.

- screen: A set of parameters defining the viewing direction by specifying the x, y, and z rotation with respect to the origin (it is really a matter of trial and error to come up with a list of arguments giving the desired perspective).

- aspect: The aspect ratios of the three-dimensional box encompassing the plot. The effect of this parameter was discussed earlier. In this case, a seven-fold exaggeration of the z axis is specified by multiplying the true z/x ratio by 7 in 7*(z_range/x_range).

- zoom: A scale factor to magnify or shrink the plot.

It is important to keep in mind that three-dimensional plots are useful to display any kind of three-dimensional dataset and not just topographic surfaces. For example, returning to the spatio-temporal dataset s that we created from the MODIS images time series (see *Chapter 6, Modifying Rasters and Analyzing Raster Time Series*), we can produce a three-dimensional image with:

- Time on the *x* axis

- Space (*y* coordinate, in this case) on the *y* axis

- NDVI on the *z* axis

Similarly to the previous example, we first have to create a `data.frame` object, which we will name `s_df`, out of the raster `s`. Using the combination of `as.matrix` and `as.data.frame`, we can convert `s` to a `data.frame` with columns corresponding to `s` columns and rows corresponding to `s` rows (remember that using `as.data.frame` directly on a raster results in `data.frame` with rows representing raster cells, which is not what we want in this case):

```
> s_df = as.data.frame(as.matrix(s))
```

Since we know that the columns of `s` represent dates of image acquisition, we can assign dates as the column names:

```
> colnames(s_df) = dates$date
> s_df[1:5, 1:5]
  2000-02-18 2000-03-05 2000-03-21 2000-04-06 2000-04-22
1   0.341684   0.397015   0.408640   0.416793   0.359633
2   0.341664   0.396391   0.428758   0.427817   0.352741
3   0.349044   0.405022   0.426911   0.429224   0.352297
4   0.351129   0.413696   0.434334   0.417303   0.344761
5   0.358012   0.408954   0.439244   0.411540   0.344320
```

Since we also know that the rows of `s` correspond to *y* axis spatial coordinates, we can assign these coordinates to an additional column (named `coord`). To obtain the vector of *y* coordinates of a raster, we can use the `yFromRow` function of the `raster` package. All that is left to do after that is to `melt` the `data.frame` in order to move the dates from separate columns into a single one:

```
> s_df$coord = yFromRow(r)
> s_df = melt(s_df,
+ id.vars = "coord",
+ variable.name = "date",
+ value.name = "ndvi")
> head(s_df)
    coord       date      ndvi
1 3494750 2000-02-18 0.341684
2 3494250 2000-02-18 0.341664
3 3493750 2000-02-18 0.349044
4 3493250 2000-02-18 0.351129
5 3492750 2000-02-18 0.358012
6 3492250 2000-02-18 0.342920
```

What we have here is a `data.frame` representing a regular (in the x-y direction) three-dimensional grid, so in principle everything is ready to apply `wireframe`. Unfortunately, however, `lattice` does not have an automatic method to format date values and draw an appropriate set of tick marks and labels (such as what we have seen in `ggplot2` with `scale_x_date` earlier). Therefore, we are compelled to give up the `Date` formatting of the `date` column in `s_df`. Since what we have is an annual-scale series, a simple way to make proper labels is to convert the dates to numeric values representing year fractions. For example, 2000-1-1 can become `2000`, 2000-1-2 can become 2000+1/365=`2000.003`, and so on. Although it would not be difficult to write our own function to make such a calculation, there already is a function in the `lubridate` package that does exactly that, called `decimal_date`:

```
> library(lubridate)
> s_df$date = decimal_date(as.Date(s_df$date))
> head(s_df)
     coord     date     ndvi
1 3494750 2000.131 0.341684
2 3494250 2000.131 0.341664
3 3493750 2000.131 0.349044
4 3493250 2000.131 0.351129
5 3492750 2000.131 0.358012
6 3492250 2000.131 0.342920
```

The `lubridate` package contains a very helpful set of convenience functions to work with dates and times more easily than through base R packages. For more information on this package, see the introductory paper by Grolemund and Wickham (2011).

The resulting `data.frame` can now be passed to `wireframe`:

```
> wireframe(ndvi ~ date * coord,
+ data = s_df,
+ drape = TRUE,
+ arrows = FALSE,
+ col.regions =
+ colorRampPalette(c("darkred","white","darkblue"))(100),
+ screen = list(z = 15, x = -55, y = 10),
+ aspect = c(0.3, 0.2),
+ panel.aspect = c(0.45),
+ lty = 0,
+ scales = list(arrows = FALSE, cex = 0.6),
+ xlab = list("Time"),
+ ylab = list("Y", cex = 0),
+ zlab = list("NDVI", cex = 0),
+ zoom = 0.95)
```

The graphical output is shown in the following screenshot:

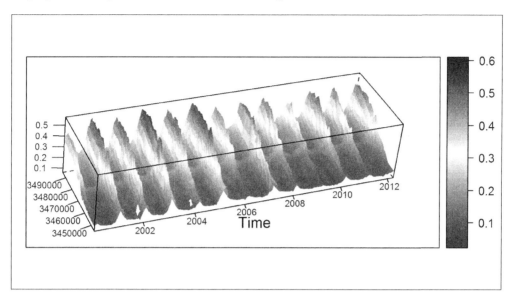

This time, the `colorRampPalette` function was used within the `wireframe` function call to create a custom color scale (going from dark red, through white, and to dark blue). An interesting point to note in this respect is that the function call `colorRamp Palette(c("darkred","white","darkblue"))` in fact returns a `function`. Indeed, there is no reason why the returned object of a function cannot be another function. The returned function is then used to create a vector of color codes (analogous to the way we did so with built-in functions such as `terrain.colors`). The other parameters used in the latter `wireframe` function call (`arrows`, `panel.aspect`, `lty`, `scales`, `xlab`, `ylab`, and `zlab`) refer to minor details regarding plot appearance and we will not discuss them here (see `?wireframe` for more information).

The plot itself shows the periodic behavior of NDVI, which we already visualized in *Chapter 6, Modifying Rasters and Analyzing Raster Time Series*, where NDVI was mapped to color alone (rather than to both colors and the *z* axis position, as in the present visualization), and so the plot was two-dimensional. We will leave it up to the reader to decide which version is prettier or easier to interpret. The important point here is that spatio-temporal data is inherently three-dimensional and therefore it is only natural to consider three-dimensional visualization of such data.

Summary

In this chapter, you learned some of the most useful methods for advanced visualization of spatial data in R, using the packages `ggplot2`, `ggmap`, and `lattice`. It was shown how these tools can be used to conclude a spatial analysis procedure and create publishable maps and plots of the results, all within the R environment. In this context, it has been noted that not everything can be accomplished in R, and at times we need to migrate to traditional GIS software or graphic editors for interactive customization of the graphic output. Nevertheless, visualization in R is extremely flexible, while at the same time bringing all of the benefits of programming. Once you become more familiar with the techniques presented in this chapter, it is almost inevitable that R will become the primary tool of choice for data visualization. I sincerely hope that after completing this book you feel the same way about geospatial data analysis in R.

A
External Datasets Used in Examples

Most of the code examples in this book use data from external files. To reproduce the examples, you are encouraged to download these files from the book's website and then copy them to a single directory on the hard drive. In the example code, the files are assumed to reside in `C:\Data`. To use a different directory, the examples code should be modified accordingly.

The external files in this book's examples, in an alphabetical order of first filenames, are listed in the following table:

Dataset	Associated files	Description

Daily meteorological data for Albuquerque International Airport	`338284.csv`
	
	`GHCND_documentation.pdf`
		Daily climatic records from the Albuquerque International Airport, New Mexico, United States meteorological station. Downloaded from the NOAA Climate Data Online website at `http://www.ncdc.noaa.gov/cdo-web`. Accessed May 2014.

Dataset	Associated files	Description

Monthly meteorological data for Spain	`343452.csv`
	
	`GHCNDMS_documentation.pdf`
		Monthly climatic records from meteorological stations in Spain. Downloaded from the NOAA Climate Data Online website at `http://www.ncdc.noaa.gov/cdo-web`. Accessed May 2014.

US Census data	`CO-EST2012-Alldata.csv`
	
	`CO-EST2012-alldata.pdf`
		US Census County Population Change 2012 data. Downloaded from the United States Census Bureau at `https://www.census.gov/popest/data/counties/totals/2012/CO-EST2012-alldata.html`. Accessed May 2014.

Administrative areas of England and Wales	`CTYUA_2013_EW_BFE.docx`
	
	`CTYUA_DEC_2013_EW_BFE.dbf`
	
	`CTYUA_DEC_2013_EW_BFE.prj`
	
	`CTYUA_DEC_2013_EW_BFE.sbn`
	
	`CTYUA_DEC_2013_EW_BFE.sbx`
	
	`CTYUA_DEC_2013_EW_BFE.shp`
	
	`CTYUA_DEC_2013_EW_BFE.shp.xml`
	
	`CTYUA_DEC_2013_EW_BFE.shx`
		Shapefile of administrative area boundaries in England and Wales. Downloaded from the Office for National Statistics at `https://geoportal.statistics.gov.uk`. Accessed May 2014.

GPS log	`GPS_log.gpx`	GPS track record from a trip in Lahav and Dvira forests. Downloaded from a GPS device.

Dataset	Associated files	Description

OpenStreetMap Shapefile of buildings in Haifa	`haifa_buildings.cpg`
	`haifa_buildings.dbf`
	`haifa_buildings.prj`
	`haifa_buildings.qpj`
	`haifa_buildings.shp`
	`haifa_buildings.shx`
		A polygonal Shapefile of buildings based on OpenStreetMap data (`http://www.openstreetmap.org`). Accessed May 2014.

OpenStreetMap Shapefile of natural areas in Haifa	`haifa_natural.cpg`
	`haifa_natural.dbf`
	`haifa_natural.prj`
	`haifa_natural.qpj`
	`haifa_natural.shp`
	`haifa_natural.shx`
		A polygonal Shapefile of natural areas, based on OpenStreetMap data (`http://www.openstreetmap.org`). Accessed May 2014.

Portion of Landsat satellite image of central Israel obtained on October 15, 1998	`landsat_15_10_1998.tif`	A six-band raster, corresponding to Landsat bands 1-5 and 7. Image taken on October 15, 1998. Downloaded from `http://earthexplorer.usgs.gov/` and preprocessed to obtain reflectance values.
Portion of Landsat satellite image of central Israel obtained on October 4, 2000	`landsat_04_10_2000.tif`	A six-band raster, corresponding to Landsat bands 1-5 and 7. Image taken on October 4, 2000. Downloaded from `http://earthexplorer.usgs.gov/` and preprocessed to obtain reflectance values.

Dataset	Associated files	Description
Portion of Landsat satellite image of central Israel obtained on September 11, 2003	`landsat_11_09_2003.tif`	A six-band raster, corresponding to Landsat bands 1-5 and 7. Image taken on September 11, 2003. Downloaded from `http://earthexplorer.usgs.gov/` and preprocessed to obtain reflectance values.
OpenStreetMap Shapefile of buildings in London	`london_buildings.CPG` `london_buildings.dbf` `london_buildings.prj` `london_buildings.shp` `london_buildings.shx`	A polygonal Shapefile of buildings based on OpenStreetMap data (`http://www.openstreetmap.org`). Accessed May 2014.
OpenStreetMap Shapefile of natural areas in London	`london_natural.CPG` `london_natural.dbf` `london_natural.prj` `london_natural.shp` `london_natural.shx`	A polygonal Shapefile of natural areas based on OpenStreetMap data (`http://www.openstreetmap.org`). Accessed May 2014.
A portion of NDVI images of central Israel from MODIS satellite data from February 18, 2000 to April 6, 2012	`modis.tif`	A 280-band raster, with NDVI images for the period February 18, 2000 to April 6, 2012. Data obtained from the MODIS product MOD13A1. Downloaded from `http://earthexplorer.usgs.gov/`.
Dates of acquisition of images in each layer in `modis.tif`	`modis_dates.csv`	Table with supplementary information (dates) regarding each layer in `modis.tif`.

Dataset	Associated files	Description
A sample raster file for demonstration in *Chapter 1, The R Environment*	`rainfall.tif`	Annual rainfall amount in northern and central Israel, interpolated from meteorological stations data.
Digital Elevation Model (DEM) layer of Spain	`spain_elev.tif`	DEM data from the SRTM dataset (see `http://srtm.csi.cgiar.org/`). Downloaded through R and preprocessed by reprojection, masking, and aggregation to 900 meters resolution.

GADM Shapefile of the USA counties with FIPS codes	`USA_2_GADM_fips.cpg`
	
	`USA_2_GADM_fips.dbf`
	
	`USA_2_GADM_fips.prj`
	
	`USA_2_GADM_fips.qpj`
	
	`USA_2_GADM_fips.shp`
	
	`USA_2_GADM_fips.shx`
		Polygons corresponding to the second level administrative division (counties) of the USA with several attributes such as county names and **Federal Information Processing Standards (FIPS)** code.

B
Cited References

Now that we have covered everything, let's take a look at some external references for further reading:

- Bivand, R. S., Pebesma, E. J., and Gómez-Rubio, V. *Applied Spatial Data Analysis with R Second Edition*. Springer. 2013.

- Chang, W. *R Graphics Cookbook*. O'Reilly Media. 2012.

- Cowpertwait, P. S. P. and Metcalfe, A. V. *Introductory Time Series with R*. Springer. 2009.

- Diggle, P. and Ribeiro, P. J. *Model-based Geostatistics*. Springer. 2007.

- Grolemund, G. and Wickham, H. "Dates and Times Made Easy with lubridate". Journal of Statistical Software. 2011. `http://www.jstatsoft.org/v40/i03/paper`.

- Hengl, T. "A practical guide to geostatistical mapping of environmental variables". JRC Scientific and Technical Reports. 2007. `http://spatial-analyst.net/book/`.

- Hengl, T., Roudier, P., Beaudette, D., and Pebesma, E. "plotKML: Scientific Visualization of Spatio-Temporal Data". Journal of Statistical Software. 2014. `http://cran.r-project.org/web/packages/plotKML/vignettes/jss1079.pdf`.

- Kahle, D. and Wickham, H. "ggmap: Spatial Visualization with ggplot2". The R Journal. 2013. `http://journal.r-project.org/archive/2013-1/kahle-wickham.pdf`.

- Lamigueiro, O. P. *Displaying Time Series, Spatial, and Space-Time Data with R*. CRC Press. 2014.

- Murrell, P. *Introduction to Data Technologies*. CRC Press. 2009. `https://www.stat.auckland.ac.nz/~paul/ItDT/`.

- Pebesma, E. "spacetime: Spatio-Temporal Data in R". Journal of Statistical Software. 2012. `http://www.jstatsoft.org/v51/i07/paper`.

- Sarkar, D. *Lattice: Multivariate Data Visualization with R*. Springer. 2008.

- Van der Loo, M. P. J. and de Jonge, E. *Learning RStudio for R Statistical Computing. Packt Publishing*. 2012.

- Wickham, H. "Reshaping Data with the reshape Package". Journal of Statistical Software. 2007. `http://www.jstatsoft.org/v21/i12/paper`.

- Wickham, H. *ggplot2: Elegant Graphics for Data Analysis*. Springer. 2009.

- Wickham, H. "The Split-Apply-Combine Strategy for Data Analysis". Journal of Statistical Software. 2011. `http://www.jstatsoft.org/v40/i01/paper`.

- Wickham, H. "Tidy Data". Journal of Statistical Software. 2014. `http://www.jstatsoft.org/v59/i10/paper`.

- Wickham, H. *Advanced R*. CRC Press. 2014. `http://adv-r.had.co.nz/`.

Index

melt function
  used, for shifting between long and wide
    formats 86-90
merge function 181
missing values
  dealing with 43
  detecting, in vectors 44
  effect, on data 43
  used, for performing calculations
    on vectors 45
multiband rasters
  creating 110, 111

N

nearest-neighbor interpolation
  using 246-249
Near Infrared (NIR) 109
nonspatial data
  plotting 291-296
Normalized Difference Vegetation Index
  (NDVI) 117
Not A Number (NaN) 20
numeric vectors of indices
  used, for vector subsetting 40, 41

O

object
  removing, from memory 32
  saving, with assignment operator 30, 31
object types, R
  about 21, 22
  data, storing in data structures 23
  functions 23
  sample session 23-25
Ordinary Kriging (OK) interpolation
  about 249
  using 258-262
overlay operations, raster 123-128

P

paste function 35
plotRGB function 149

point data
  spatial interpolation 242-245
points
  about 135-138
  used, for raster value extraction 230-234
polygons
  about 140
  used, for raster value extraction 235-238
predefined symbols, R
  FALSE 20
  Inf 20
  NA 20
  NULL 20
projectRaster function 192

R

R
  downloading 8
  installing 7, 8
  object types 21
  URL 8
  using, as calculator 9, 10
R symbols
  %b 52
  %B 52
  %d 52
  %m 52
  %y 52
  %Y 52
raster
  about 102
  aggregating 184, 185
  algebra 123
  creating, from vector layers 212
  cropping 183, 184
  data structures 107
  disaggregating 184, 186
  files, writing 112
  merging 182
  multiband rasters, creating 110
  multiple layer subsets 120, 121

Thank you for buying
Learning R for Geospatial Analysis

About Packt Publishing

Packt, pronounced 'packed', published its first book, *Mastering phpMyAdmin for Effective MySQL Management*, in April 2004, and subsequently continued to specialize in publishing highly focused books on specific technologies and solutions.

Our books and publications share the experiences of your fellow IT professionals in adapting and customizing today's systems, applications, and frameworks. Our solution-based books give you the knowledge and power to customize the software and technologies you're using to get the job done. Packt books are more specific and less general than the IT books you have seen in the past. Our unique business model allows us to bring you more focused information, giving you more of what you need to know, and less of what you don't.

Packt is a modern yet unique publishing company that focuses on producing quality, cutting-edge books for communities of developers, administrators, and newbies alike. For more information, please visit our website at www.packtpub.com.

About Packt Open Source

In 2010, Packt launched two new brands, Packt Open Source and Packt Enterprise, in order to continue its focus on specialization. This book is part of the Packt Open Source brand, home to books published on software built around open source licenses, and offering information to anybody from advanced developers to budding web designers. The Open Source brand also runs Packt's Open Source Royalty Scheme, by which Packt gives a royalty to each open source project about whose software a book is sold.

Writing for Packt

We welcome all inquiries from people who are interested in authoring. Book proposals should be sent to author@packtpub.com. If your book idea is still at an early stage and you would like to discuss it first before writing a formal book proposal, then please contact us; one of our commissioning editors will get in touch with you.

We're not just looking for published authors; if you have strong technical skills but no writing experience, our experienced editors can help you develop a writing career, or simply get some additional reward for your expertise.

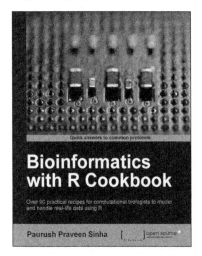

Machine Learning with R

ISBN: 978-1-78216-214-8   Paperback: 396 pages

Learn how to use R to apply powerful machine learning methods and gain an insight into real-world applications

1. Harness the power of R for statistical computing and data science.

2. Use R to apply common machine learning algorithms with real-world applications.

3. Prepare, examine, and visualize data for analysis.

4. Understand how to choose between machine learning models.

Statistical Analysis with R

ISBN: 978-1-84951-208-4   Paperback: 300 pages

Take control of your data and produce superior statistical analyses with R

1. An easy introduction for people who are new to R, with plenty of strong examples for you to work through.

2. This book will take you on a journey to learn R as the strategist for an ancient Chinese kingdom!

3. A step-by-step guide to understand R, its benefits, and how to use it to maximize the impact of your data analysis.

Please check **www.PacktPub.com** for information on our titles